Barclay Boy

Season in the Sun

Kick it off, throw it in,
Have a little scrimmage
Keep it low, a splendid rush,
Bravo, win or die
On the ball city
Never mind the danger
Steady on, now's your chance
Hurrah we've scored
City, city

To my family, my friends and my fellow fans

Barclay Boy

Boy James Scoltock

Season in the Sun

First published in Great Britain in 2012 by The Derby Books Publishing Company Limited, 3 The Parker Centre, Derby, DE21 4SZ.

ISBN 978-1-78091-018-5

Contents

Foreword

It was a clear memory in my mind – and a question clearly not appropriate at the time. But as a sports journalist covering the fortunes of the club I supported as a boy, it was the first one on my mind.

A chilly Bank Holiday Monday evening. May 2, 2011 at Fratton Park. Let's say 9.45pm. It was wet. By the time I'd gathered my thoughts after a jubilant final whistle and wandered through Portsmouth's archaic stand to the pitch, I was staring at the muddy playing surface. Unusually, I didn't mind ruining my suede shoes.

Soon heading for us was a wave of Norwich City pitch invaders – a frightening sight, even when everyone has a smile on their face.

Next was the media scrum; waiting for Delia Smith, David McNally and the rest of City's powerbrokers to break from their tears and embraces. It's an always rude but necessary interruption so those fans rushing on the pitch, those watching and listening beyond the four stands, get the reaction they all want to enjoy in the morning – probably alongside a sore head.

And that question? How on earth could Norwich City – a side barely two years earlier seemingly destined to be beached in the third tier of English football for seasons rather than months – possibly make a success of taking on the most brutal domestic league in the world?

Not the most positive of reactions, I grant you. I was happy – in truth I was delirious. 'Working' on such an occasion is a dream. As a fan, City's previous promotion to the Premier League in 2004 saw me sitting in Indian internet cafés trying to follow events through emails from my dad. And all despite being a season ticket holder in the Lower Barclay (row U, seat 113). Needless to say, the prospect of Darren Huckerby playing in yellow and green was a little far fetched when I booked those flights.

No, even as a fan this was the pinnacle. Back-to-back promotions under arguably the Canaries' finest of managers in Paul Lambert. Heady days.

But still... really... how on earth would City cope? The answer comes through James' book of course – but to rattle off a cliché, none of this is about the destination. It's all about the journey.

When you become a journalist following your club the rules change. You fret over whether a ground will have wifi good enough to get through 90 minutes of the Pinkun's live match coverage. Or whether to stop for grub on the way to the likes of The Emirates in case proper food isn't served on arrival (the answer is a comprehensive no – Arsenal's tucker was second only to The Etihad). They all feel like legitimate questions. Honest.

And alas, you always find yourself looking ahead. Sometimes, looking back feels like a waste of time.

But for fans, the idea should be quite the opposite. Even after all the words I've written this season, James has given me my first chance to look back properly and enjoy a truly captivating campaign in both football and specifically at Carrow Road.

For every supporter these things are about more than just football. It is about the passion required to follow your club.

There are the old issues shared through generations. Sharing time and love between a football club – your football club – and everything else that's near, dear and just as important. Albeit, in a slightly different way. James has all of these: health, wife and son, family commitments and a bunch of mates dishing out their own brand of vicious lad-mag mischief and dressing room banter.

And then there are the new issues with following a team like Norwich, while living somewhere else, with the Premier League's global spotlight and all the distractions that come with it. The internet age, bringing with it unprecedented coverage and a social networking platform that continues to bring out the best and worst in football and its fans. Praise, rumour, ridicule and abuse. Twitter trending and messageboard invasions, revolutions and revulsions. James deals with these a treat too.

I have my own favourite moment from the 2011-12 season. A low key one. Grant Holt winning a free-kick from Laurent Koscielny in the centre-circle at Arsenal. The red majority of 60,000 supporters were up in arms, pouring their vitriol all over the City skipper who stood there, arms outstretched in a nonchalant gesture of innocence. It was the same gesture, the same vitriol City fans had seen from 4,000 supporters at Yeovil and 4,500 fans at Scunthorpe. And now it was happening at Arsenal.

Clearly it takes a lot of time and effort to put together your thoughts on an entire campaign – never mind searching for one of my correct pre-match predictions – and James has done a grand job with his project.

Whether City could cope? That was the question we all asked as soon as the final whistle blew at Fratton Park, and the 12 months waiting for the answer was the fun part.

This is very much James' story. His personality. A man following his club with a sturdy yellow and green hat sitting proudly on his head. Or maybe that should be yellow and green trainers upon his feet.

Either way, it was good of the Canaries to provide the perfect backdrop.

Michael Bailey

Introduction

I am unashamedly one dimensional. Outside work, outside being a husband, outside being a father, my passion is football. Football is the only hobby I have, it's what takes up the majority of my free time and what remains is allocated to sleeping. My passion for football would probably be diagnosed by a psychologist as a shield from being unhappy at work or an escape from a fruitless home-life. But along with the hundreds of millions of fans around the world, neither of those reasons are true.

But it is all consuming. My wife often wonders how successful my career could be if I channelled as much enthusiasm into work as I did into football.

She has labelled me a quitter. I once started kick-boxing at a gym down the road, but stopped going pretty sharpish – dragging myself out of bed on a Saturday morning was just not going to happen. I've also bought numerous pieces of fitness equipment only for them to fall into disuse after a couple of weeks, and spend the rest of their lives gathering dust under the bed or on top of the wardrobe. I bought just about every Japanese language book, CD and tape going only to lose interest moments later. But football is a different matter altogether.

I'll wake up at the crack of dawn to drive hundreds of miles to watch a game. Spend ludicrous amounts of money on tickets, train fares even extravagantly hiring cars to make it to games, all without a second thought. Lunch breaks at work are spent perusing the internet for the latest news, even morning trips to the toilet are a chance to check the discussion boards on my smartphone. It's all encompassing and there's nothing I can do about it.

I haven't always been like this; in fact for much of my life football was nothing more than an occasional hobby fulfilled by watching a game or two on the television. Yes I'd shout and swear at the box in the corner of the room, but once it was over I'd switch it off and start thinking about something else (that's what I thought anyway, family members and ex-girlfriends would probably beg to differ).

I played football at school. I was a goalkeeper in my primary school team. At high school every second of every break time was spent kicking a ball around, the clichéd jumpers for goalposts, double digit scores and teams of 20-a-side.

Born in the 1980s Liverpool were the team to support, and Christmas brought a replica Liverpool kit. In fact, much to my shame I followed Liverpool's travails until they won the Champions League in 2004 against AC Milan. But at the back of my mind Norwich was always lurking, the Canaries' result always a must-see, even when Liverpool were at their prime. And that affection for my local team grew even in the most exotic of places.

I worked in Japan for three years as an English teacher where, in an increasingly small world, a number of Ipswich fans had decided to reside. That made me more proud to be from Norfolk and shout more loudly about Norwich.

The year I returned to the UK Norwich were in the Premier League, but it was such a fleeting stay and I was, at that point, so ill having been diagnosed with ulcerative colitis, the whole experience passed me by.

But moving to London to start a new career as a journalist only made me more passionate about my local team.

Some say that if you're tired of London, you're tired of life, but I don't think there are many people that truly believe that twaddle.

Living in London makes you more aware of what is outside the capital and what it has to offer. And being so large, diverse and hectic it forces you to latch onto a group so you don't disappear into the crowd. So at work I came to be known simply as 'Norwich', a tag I wore with pride.

And the more you talk about something, the more you find out, the more the seed grows and the more it becomes part of your life. And as a fully paid up part of society and the workforce I had some disposable income. I didn't just have to pay the bills, but I could also enjoy my free time. And what better way than to buy a ticket for the football when Norwich came to the big smog. Stand in a crowd at Crystal Palace or Charlton knowing that everyone stood around you could also be known as 'Norwich'. You were part of something.

But then the tipping point came. When you get a taste for the beautiful game it's difficult to refuse it if someone offers more.

Which is why in 2008 when the club advertised half season tickets it was impossible to refuse, especially as there was a free seat next to a mate I'd known since high school. Every fortnight I'd not only get to watch Norwich in the flesh at Carrow Road but also meet old friends regularly – friends it seems, in the sprawl of London are a difficult commodity to come by, not helped by my unsocial nature.

Looking back my wife probably regrets saying yes, as a half season turned into a whole season, which turned into an unquenchable thirst for more, more, and more.

A four hour, 200 mile drive to watch Norwich lose at Cardiff, I'll be there. A 150 mile slog to Bristol to watch a 3-0 win, I'm in. Coventry on the opening day of the season, by coach, Norwich lose, I've nothing better to do.

Travelling to away games isn't a great stretch when you have a 240 mile round trip to watch home games.

But how different is a desire to watch the football team, that is my second heart beat, to anyone else's passion: gigs, sailing, motorsport, concerts, festivals all make people do silly things. I'm an automotive journalist and the extent that some petrolheads go to to visit motoring events, motor shows, and races puts me and my little foible to shame.

And it could be worse, I don't drink (regularly), I don't smoke, I don't do drugs and I'm not harming anyone (bar the eardrums of the people sat close to me as I shout profanities and sing out of tune).

It's also therapeutic. Football is a vent, it de-stresses and is the sports fans equivalent of colonic irrigation. After a week of work I need to shout and scream, swear and jump, sing and groan.

I realise it isn't everyone's cup of tea, I can't imagine going to watch the football as a family, although I would love to take my son with me one day, and would be over the moon if he was to willingly attend.

But I realise this is my disease. Football has come a long way, rightly or wrongly, since the days of working class men piling out of their factories and into the local football ground. Money has corrupted, sanitised and made prima donna's of the modern day footballer. But it doesn't make me love it any less.

My name's James Scoltock, I'm a football fan and so very happily one dimensional.

Championship

17 January 2009, Norwich 4–0 Barnsley

The hairs on the back of my neck stood up on end. I'd always bought casual tickets, sitting on random seats around the ground, surrounded by thousands of people, but alone all the same. Not today. Today was the first game, going with friends, sitting in a seat that will be mine for every game. Upper tier of the Barclay stand, the home end, and what a game to start with.

When *On the ball city* rang out it was incredible, over 20,000 people all as one. People say football is tribal, but I don't care.

Jonny and Ben, who love the green and yellow army, may have been dubious about my attending to begin with – was I going to be a lucky a charm or a ball and chain – but we won convincingly. We willed the ball into the net: Wes Hoolahan in the 55th minute, Jamie Cureton in 75th, Sammy Clingan in the 88th and even Darel Russell scored in injury time. It might be doom and gloom at the moment, but after a game like that we're 19th in the League and surely can't get relegated.

League One

8th August 2009, Norwich 1–7 Colchester

Bollocks! Bollocks!

27 March 2010, Norwich 1–0 Leeds

Firstly, what a bunch of animals. We won get over it. Why come out of a ground and try and start on the locals. I don't mind banter, no one does. Chants from the terraces, it's what it's all about. But to walk out of a stadium and to pick on kids, the elderly and anyone who even mentions the scoreline, why?

But let's mention that scoreline. Chris Martin, 89th minute, 21 goals this season, nine points clear at the top of League One.

First the Barclay was biting its nails, then, when Stephen Hughes picked out Martin, it went mental. Who are ya? Who are ya? Who are ya? Rang out from all around the ground. Madness, madness, madness. 25,445 fans in the stadium, 2,000 of who have their head in their hands, the rest delirious with pleasure. Going up, up, up.

Championship

2 May 2011, Portsmouth 0–1 Norwich

There's an irrational fear among football fans, that our actions, however removed from the game, have an effect on the outcome of any given match. We think for some bizarre reason that if we wear a certain pair of pants, socks, trousers or shoes the team stands a better chance of winning. It's all a load of rubbish, and everyone will agree, but try getting them to stop their weekly pre-match ritual or routine and you're more than likely to end up with a thick lip or a beaten sense of reality.

I'm no different. Norwich never win if I watch them on television. They never win if I forget to wear my green and yellow socks, and if I go to the game, they never win if I go through the right-hand turnstile. It's also touch and go if they'll get a result if I buy a match day programme.

But today was different. With all Cardiff's Premier League players, extortionate wage structure and 26,000 supporters hoping they could reach the holy land of the Premier League they choked. When I woke up they were a point behind Norwich, a win would have allowed them to leap-frog us. They were only playing Middlesbrough, who'd long decided mid-table obscurity was the place for them, their players were likely already on their summer holidays. But then out of the blue Leroy Lita got between two Cardiff defenders in the third minute and headed the ball into the back of the net. Ten minutes later, Barry Robson put them two up and by the 21st minute Richie Smallwood had killed the match. Cardiff 0–3 Middlesbrough.

By the mother of all things holy, what the flipping heck happened there, Norwich win, and we're promoted. The only stumbling block, the game was live on satellite television where everyone knows we don't win.

But you know the twisted part of the brain. The part so far at the back it's rarely used. The part that when you drive past a road accident or an ambulance on the street, it forces you to turn your head and take the briefest of glances. Not knowing what you're going to see, but so curious that you simply can't resist. And no matter how much you tell yourself you aren't going to and don't need to you do.

Morbid fascination is part and parcel of being a football fan, whether you're in the top tier or dragging yourself to a regional league game on a blustery, wet Saturday afternoon.

The thing is, if I didn't watch the game, knowing that I could have, I wouldn't have been able to concentrate. I'd have been pacing up and down, become snappy, and more than likely I'd have looked up the score on the internet. But then that's an almost identical process to watching the game. Shifting my rear end in the seat like my pants are full of creepy crawlies. The nervousness in the pit of my stomach stealing my appetite. I can't even drink beer – I mean what's all that about?

But this game could now define Norwich's season. Win and we're up. How could anyone, no matter how nervous, morose or pessimistic not watch?

Jonny sent me a text halfway through asking how much of my fingernails I had left. What did he think, I couldn't eat, I didn't want to watch but I couldn't look away.

Not long after he sent another text telling me he had only bloody stumps left where his hands had been. But then, wonder of wonders, David Fox, a midfielder long travelled from Manchester United via Colchester flicked the ball high into the air towards the Portsmouth penalty area. In slow motion it span around in the air, until it dropped. It wasn't a hit and hope, it was a pin point pass. It fell right onto the head of Simeon Jackson. GOAL!

I couldn't shout, I couldn't scream because my one-year-old son was in bed. So all I did was sit there, at the dining table, computer screen alive jumping green and yellow bodies, with my hands in the air, with the longest, most exaggerated 'yes' muttered under my breath. The wife thought I was crazy. Little does she know what effect the Premier League is going to have on me!

Saturday 7 May, Norwich 2-2 Coventry City

By rights I should be battered and bruised, but I've got away unscathed. It's been a mental day, and not even the trains ballsing up has managed to dampen my mood. Normally at 7am I would be dreading having to wake up, jump on the train and drag myself into the office, but today I was out of bed before the alarm.

With the mother-in-law taking over the spare bedroom for three weeks, I ran in and stole my clothes the night before: yellow and green socks, yellow and green shirt and yellow and green scarf, and to keep my dignity a pair of jeans too.

The train from London Liverpool Street left at 9am and got into Norwich at 10.48, from there it was the Coach and Horses and a pint or two of the locally brewed CHB to loosen the vocal chords ready for the final game of the season.

Unfortunately after a couple of drinks I was in such a good mood that I spent £8 on a flag that even a sweatshop worker wouldn't want to put their name to. But It was worth it, the buzz around the city was fantastic, on the slow walk to the ground each bar we stopped at was full to bursting point with punters. The club shop was alive, cash registers ringing merrily. Inside the stadium, every seat had a cardboard fan stuffed in it, ready to make a wall of noise as Norwich were clapped by 25,000 people.

Expectations for the game? Who cared, it was the final fling of the 2010–11 season, we were promoted and the sun was shining.

Coventry had a few ex-City players. David Bell, a midfielder with a modicum of talent, but by all accounts hadn't got on with our previous manager, was homesick for his family back in Northamptonshire and showed his ambition. Norwich to Kettering, his hometown is 106 miles. Coventry to Kettering is a tad closer at 36 miles. Come on, grow a pair. He got an obligatory and deserved boo or two. But the terrace really put its mind to it when Sammy Clingan got hold of the ball.

He was the only player who showed any sort of fight when Norwich were relegated to the third tier, but left pretty sharpish afterwards. So the fans obliged with a tuneful: 'It could have been you, it could have been you, oh Sammy Clingan, it could have been you!'

In fairness many believe he was pushed out because the club needed to reduce player wages, but as terrace chants go, that was banter at its best.

The celebrations went on for an eternity after the final whistle. A lap of honour by the team, children by their sides. Waving to the crowd, some throwing their t-shirts and boots to the jubilant fans. Building the atmosphere up, before all the players dived

We are Premier League – It could have been you Sammy Clingan.

towards the Barclay. Perhaps most enjoyable of all was watching green and yellow shirts, scarfs and flags appear from the away supporters end. Those who couldn't get tickets with their brethren running the gauntlet of sitting with the Coventry supporters. Even a mum with her very young daughter took a chance.

More hasty thinking by the terraces and as each waved to the home supporters they were met with a gleeful: 'We're here, we're there, we're every fucking where, Norwich fans, Norwich fans'.

A three o'clock finish meant seven hours to meet friends and have another celebratory drink or two. Jonny always comes out for a drink after a game, and we tend to meet friends, who, for better for worse we've known since the beginning or high school.

We've all long decided that our bodies aren't designed for nightclubs, so instead there's a pub we go to with live music, The Blueberry. It isn't a family pub. The bands play rock music, the punters wear leather, and their idea of high art is tattoo design. Where we fit into that mix who knows, but it vents some steam.

Jonny's an exuberant drunk, bouncing off walls, I reckon he has an acute version of drunken OCD. He bounced off me during one outing. His forehead, my nose, lots of blood, and even more drunken man hugging apologies. He is infectious though, on one occasion I've been bouncing around the dance floor so much I was a little bit sick in my mouth. My triumph was that I managed to hold it in, get to the toilet, spit it out and get back to the task of mindless jumping around. Other events have included three of us standing around drunkenly – always drunkenly – deciding who had the hardest punch via practical demonstration on one another. Foolhardy.

Bottled it – Post-Coventry take on an odd turn.

Tonight's entertainment was more civilised: bar mat catching. I managed four, Jonny, five, Button, 15, and Twon 18. Jonny then used the mats as ninja stars, he's also somewhat of a provocateur. We shoved an inflatable canary into an empty bottle, harassed the band and its manager. Now that's entertainment.

12 May 2011

I'm having palpitations, butterflies in my stomach, every time I hear Norwich mentioned, see a sliver of green and yellow or a Premier League logo all I can think of is August, Manchester United, Liverpool, Chelsea and all the players we're going to be pitting our wits against. I logged on to the internet last night and listened to the season review on local radio. I might be in London and an exile, but when you need to get your fix of football, the internet is a wondrous thing. There are certain commentator's phrases that are stuck in my mind. From the Old Farm Derby against Ipswich when we won 4–1: 'This could get a lot worse for Ipswich, it has got a lot worse, it's Wes Hoolahan', to the local radio for the game against Derby County, when Simeon Jackson scored in the 96th minute to keep our noses ahead of Cardiff in the promotion race: 'Lansbury's corner. It's gone all the way through! CHAAAANCE! Blocked on the line! AND ITS GONNA GO IN, IT'S GONNA GO IN! SIMEON JACKSON COMPLETES HIS HAT-TRICK IN STOPPAGE TIME! AND IT'S UTTER CHAOS AT CARROW ROAD! NORWICH THREE, DERBY TWO'

My shins took three weeks to recover after the victory over Derby. The lunatic jumping in celebration meant countless batterings, as my lower leg grated up and down on the back of the seat in front of me.

15 May 2011

West Ham United are relegated. They lost 3–2 at Wigan. One more team we won't be playing next season. The Premier League really has turned into squeaky bum time at the foot of the table. One game left and it could be any two from Wigan, Blackpool, Birmingham, Wolverhampton or Blackburn joining them.

The internet rumours have started too. Apparently we're buying Danny Graham, the leading striker in the Championship this season with 24 goals from Watford for £3.5 million. And Sulleyman Muntari, a half decent, but nomadic Ghanaian midfielder, from Inter Milan – though his purported £100,000 a week salary may be a stumbling block. It's amazing what murmurs start when your chairman announces that all of the £40 million for being promoted will go into the manager's transfer kitty. I wonder who'll be next?

It's going to be a long three months of whispers, tabloid headlines and sightings of 'the next big thing' in a local petrol station as he fills up his blinged out SUV, after a meeting at the Colney training ground.

17 May 2011

After a hard day's work what better thing to come home to than the local paper's season review, via your footballing mate Jonny – though the 'tosser' garb on the envelope was a bit uncalled for.

WE ARE PREMIER LEAGUE scrawled across the front cover. Page after page of Norwich loveliness: Demolition Derbies, Holt's Golden Goals, Lambert's Loyalty, Just Fan-tastic and Late, Late Shows. The wife isn't happy, even on the off season, there's no escape from the utter engrossing nature of the game.

So engrossing that watching the Play-off semi-final highlights of Swansea City's 3–1 win over Nottingham Forest filled me with a warm, yet slightly unnerving, unable to believe we're up, fuzzy feeling. And as I write in the other Playt-off game, Cardiff are losing 0–2 to Reading.

All is good with the world, and Russell Martin, the Norfolk Cafu got a call up to the Scotland squad. Not sure how that works really, he's got a London accent, but then Zak Whitbred our American central-defender is suspiciously scouse. Is this the monster that is mass immigration?

The image of Martin in black briefs celebrating promotion in Fratton Park's away changing rooms is burned into the deepest, darkest, depths of my brain and now the tartan army can sing 'Russell Martin in his pants, in his pants, in his pants. Russell Martin in his pants, he loves City.'

26 May 2011

I've been neglecting my thoughts, mainly because work has been getting in the way. I think it's a problem many football fans face. All the time you could spend thinking, contemplating and talking about the beautiful game is taken up with the monotony of everyday life.

But in the time it's taken me to get back to noting down Norwich's tribulations, our manager has been linked with the vacant job at West Ham. Why any manager would move from a team in the top flight to a team that has just dropped down to the second tier with debts, pornstar empire owners and less direction than a rudderless yacht is beyond me. But in the next breath Paul Lambert has now signed a new deal to stay with us and in the words of the great man himself: 'We want to try and make this club the best it can possibly be.'

The most marvellous words to my ears.

Although making Norwich the best it can possibly be won't include signing the former England striker and boy wonder Michael Owen or Germany's international goal poacher Miroslav Klose. I'm praying it also doesn't include the clueless Heurelho Gomes, Tottenham Hotspur's flapping Brazilian goalkeeper, or Matthew Upson, the Norfolk-born, but over-the-hill central-defender. But the list of possibles is growing all the time: Keiron Westwood from Celtic, David Nugent from Portsmouth, David Bentley from Tottenham Hotspur, Jack Hobbs from Leicester City, Craig Gardener and Scott Dann from Birmingham City and Craig Bellamy from Manchester City via Cardiff City. My head hurts.

Maybe we can swipe some of Blackpool's players. Poor buggers were relegated at the weekend. After taking the lead at Old Trafford, they ended up losing 4–2. It would've been nice to have a bit more colour in the League. Norwich's green and yellow and Blackpool's tangerine kit. What a mixture, it would've looked great on the TV.

28 May 2011

We have signed our first player! James Vaughan. From Everton. A striker. 22 years old. £2.5 million. Am I excited? Hell yeah. One down six more to go, because according to Paul Lambert we need seven players in to 'help the lads out'. The new kit is just around the corner, and the Premier League fixture list is only 2–3 weeks away. The down side is that there are still over 2½ months until the season starts. The wife has already had enough of me whining about it, and I'm at a loose end. I stood washing the dishes, wondering how I'm going to fill my time.

My boy, George should be a good distraction. One-year-olds are fascinating little blighters, all dribbles, clapping and crawling into places they shouldn't. Good for dad's, bad for mum's – they worry more. The current concern being he hasn't flushed his system for two days.

I saw that Norwich is advertising for a new media journalist. So who knows maybe I'll apply, surely they can use someone with my quality turn of phrase. All will be revealed.

30 May 2011

Received a text from Jonny last night – we're off to the Goodwood Festival of Speed, and the poor boy's beside himself with excitement – saying we're signing a Millwall player. The rumours are continuing. Checked a very dodgy website to verify Jonny's musings, which said there'll be two signing this week: Steve Morison from Millwall for £2 million rising to £3 million, and our £20,000 striker Cody MacDonald will go the other way, and then Peter Whittingham, name doesn't mean anything to me, but apparently we're going to pay an initial £1.5 million rising to £2 million. As for people being shown the door, as well as Cody to Millwall: Chris Martin, our much troubled home-grown striker to Cardiff or Nottingham Forest, Oli Johnson, Stephen Hughes, Owain Tudor Jones, Matt Gill and Anthony McNamee all going to clubs unknown. Steven Smith, who was homesick, (for that I always read no guile and a bit of a mummy's boy is staying at Aberdeen) and finally Declan Rudd, another home-grown youngster between the sticks is off on loan to a club yet to be named.

It's the Championship Play-off today, Swansea City verses Reading. I was listening to the radio the other day, and because Swansea are a Welsh team the national anthem won't be played before the game. Odd. It's played before every other play-off game. Is this a sign that perhaps Welsh teams should play in the Welsh Leagues? I don't know, there were some irate phone calls to sports radio talk shows.

Honestly, I couldn't care less. We're not in the lottery of the play-offs, because we are Premier League (already) baby.

Speaking of babies, the wife is happy, three poos yesterday. And apparently I don't worry enough, but I think that's just a reflection of a man's more laid-back attitude to life. Anyway I have more pressing issues when it comes to childcare. I started the City indoctrination long ago, but have taken to wearing an old home shirt to bed, so when I wake up green and yellow are the first colours the boy sees. And although his brain isn't necessarily wired for football yet, I hope it's having a subconscious effect. He does seem attracted to the badge.

31 May 2011

Interesting day for everyone connected with Norwich and who uses social media. And the catalyst was something the beautiful game has tried so hard to exterminate –

racism. Some arse decided it was OK to use a most hideous word against our new striker, James Vaughan. No sooner had he signed his name in the signature box, then it all blew up on the internet.

A cretin who should know better thought it wise to mention the virtues of having a team made up of white British players, and labelled Vaughan using a word used only by gangsters in Hollywood movies. And did so on Twitter for all the world to see.

No sooner had he typed his shambolic views, Mark Bright, a former striker who started at Leek Town and ended up at Charlton Athletic via Sheffield Wednesday and Crystal Palace, and is now a BBC pundit picked up on it.

Needless to say all hell broke loose. Bright didn't hide his disgust, and decided he wanted nothing more to do with Norwich fans, banning them, and generally being as facetious as he possibly could be – 'A Norwich shirt and Premier League badges don't go together.'

Bright's intentions were honourable. He wanted to teach the racist idiot a lesson, which he did. The club gave the moron a life time ban. But he also insulted every Norwich fan, and through his comments near as damn it labelled us all bigots.

I did try to reason with the two individuals. Simply stating that they'd embarrassed themselves. The racist Norwich fan agreed, Bright smugly replied 'Thanks for your invaluable input.' How very erudite. I would never condone racism, it's an ugly boil on society, but how you tackle it should be done with consideration. Nice to feel ashamed and labelled a racist with no way of rectifying it.

I have felt like this one other time. It was at the Ipswich away game in 2009. We lost 3–2, and as usual were being kept in to allow the home supporters to disperse. One Ipswich fan in particular had stayed behind – I don't know if my ears deceived me, but as much grief as he gave the Norwich fans, I could have sworn I heard a few monkey chants directed towards him. I can't say I definitely did, but that's what I thought, and I was disappointed to the core.

1 June 2011

Local radio, nearly five minutes (well two minutes but where's the harm in a little exaggeration), and my opinion has been given on the whole dreadful racism saga. There were some nutty people phoning into BBC Radio Norfolk, but I hope 'James, in London' sounded a little less disjointed and removed from reality.

Odd isn't it that people still think in terms of us and them, the world is either black or white, not wonderfully multi-coloured.

Still much discussion about the new kit. Will it be announced this week, will we still be waiting long into the summer. Why did our chief executive say we would all be donning the new green and yellow in April? We have to hold onto any tit-bit of news during the long summer months.

In's and out's are picking up pace. Local lad, Fakenham's very own Matty Gill has been shown the door. The midfielder is a boyhood fan of Norwich, but his dream move didn't really workout. Shame, but that's the way the cookie crumbles. It's a dog-eat-dog world out there.

Mr Lambert – whom we trust more than our own mother – seems to be opting for strikers. First Vaughan signs, then bid after bid for Morrison at Millwall is rejected, and not forgetting Craig Mackail-Smith from Peterborough United. The lad has scored 80 goals in 185 appearances for the Posh, not bad statistics, but how are we going to fit all these players in. Play five up front? I guess goals win games, but surely there's a limit.

2 June 2011

It's all starting to sink in. Pre-season and we've got a home game against Real Zaragoza. Real Zaragoza, not bad for a little club on the edge of nowhere. OK, it's slightly tempered by the fact we're also playing Gorleston, Wroxham, Histon and Billericay, but at least it's a team most people in the football fraternity have heard of. Whadda ya think, a famous city win?

3 June 2011

So we're in for Robert Snodgrass, the Leeds United winger. At Least we're looking at players to fit somewhere other than up front. But it's not gone down well with the Yorkshire fans on their We Are Champions, Champions of Europe discussion board, they're bursting blood vessels as they type:

*'I really **** hate Norwich. That drunken hag they have in the board room and her husband who looks like Roz from Monsters Inc, the ugly fat mole-looking ****, their six fingered fans, playing music after they score a goal like the tinpot no-mark bastards they are, and the fact that everything they have done, and I mean everything since they were relegated has been that little bit **** better than what we've done. That they signed a fat bricklayer who was **** for Halifax Town and got him scoring 20 goals a season at whatever level. Their manager who looks like he doesn't care that you just beat him at chess because he spent the night before shagging your mum. THEY PLAY MUSIC WHEN THEY **** SCORE THE ****, and sell more season tickets than us. We could get promoted unbeaten and find out that the **** have solved World hunger and found a two-state solution in the Middle East. BASTARDS!!!"*

How delightful, if wonderfully true.

4 June 2011

After yesterday's musings from our friends up north, those down south also have a view about Norwich. Taking Brighton's players probably won't fill them with joy, but they seem to think we're preparing for the Premier League season the right way:

'I wouldn't blame Bennett for trying his hand in the Premier League. It just seems unfair that we've got promoted and our two best players have left us. This is a tough one to swallow.

Lambert is clever though, he's not signing average Premiership players who would command big wages and not give everything for Norwich, he's getting young, hungry footballers. Just a shame he got Crofts last year and (probably) Bennett this year.'

And it's not the only sentiment on the Brighton discussion boards:

'Agree entirely, Norwich have adopted the perfect strategy for success without 'doing a Wigan'.

It's all sustainable growth and they are not only keeping the wages real by targeting who they are, but getting the benefit of that extra edge that a batch of hungry players provides individually AND as a team.

I believe we intend to follow a similar path, though it's immensely frustrating that Norwich didn't have to deal with another Norwich with their shrewd policy while we have i.e. we lose some of our best where they didn't. So a harder task I will be for us to try to achieve what they did as we have more rebuilding forced on us than they did.'

Finally got around to writing my assessment of the canaries' prospects for the 2011–12 season in the Barclay's Premier League as part of the application for the role of new media journalist at the club.

'Assessing the Canaries' prospects in the 2011–12 Barclay's Premier League campaign.

Norwich City either has a mountain to climb, or may have already achieved greatness. Whatever your view, their first season back in the Premier League in six years will be a roller coaster.

A meteoric rise through English football's leagues brings new challenges. Manchester United, Arsenal, Liverpool and a host of other teams, both respected and admired will be facing the Canaries both home and away.

But the challenge of the 2011–12 Premier League season doesn't have to fill the players, management and fans with dread – excitement, enthusiasm and togetherness count for so much.

Blackpool are the instant port of call for any new team hoping to play the right way, win games and give the club the best chance of staying at the top table in English football.

They drew plaudits for their never say die attitude and attacking flair – qualities that Norwich has in abundance – which helped them to victories against Liverpool, Tottenham and Stoke among many others.

The final game of the season, and the Tangerines only needed a win at Old Trafford to keep their status as a Premier League team. They came close. At one point, in the 57th minute, they were 2–1 up after a Taylor-Fletcher strike.

Blackpool, like the current Norwich team was made up of, not superstars, but players hungry to succeed. Nine of the team that walked out onto the pitch at Manchester on the 22nd May, played for the team in the second tier, helping them gain promotion. And the club's players will define whether next season is a success or failure for Norwich.

Teams of individuals struggle, each player looking only as far as their next club, their next big move. Players that make the journey from the lower leagues, are forever ready and willing to prove themselves on the biggest stage. And players that make that journey together as part of a close nit team work hard for one another.

A core of players have taken Norwich from League One, through the Championship and into the Premier League.

Some have international caps for their respective countries, some started off as tyre-fitters, but all work hard for each other. And on a blustery night in Bolton or Wigan that relationship will be key to nicking a late winning goal or keeping a clean sheet.

Because it's at these grounds that Norwich's season will be defined.

It shouldn't be difficult for any player, no matter what their background to raise their game when stepping out at the Emirates, Anfield or Standford Bridge. But where Blackpool lost to Blackburn, Birmingham and Wolverhampton, Norwich will need to bring points home from the less glamorous ties to survive.

Jumping, noisy, revelling fans home and away will help players complete one more lung-busting run forward in the dying seconds of a game, as will a few additions to bolster the squad. So, come May 2012 hopefully Norwich will be applauded just as Blackpool were, but take it one step further and stay in the league.'

Wonderful prose even if I do say so myself. I wonder if head of media Joe Ferrari will think the same?

5 June 2011

It's not just players and managers who get poached. Scouts do too. According to the *The National,* a government run newspaper in Abu Dhabi our chief scout is being eyed by Chelsea.

The amount of money swilling around for the most average of players even the big guns need some help to find a reasonable priced gem, and it seems, according to this paper, that Ewan Chester fits the bill. Arse is all I can say. We only nabbed the bloke from Rangers last year. Double standards and hypocrisy on my part, but it's not nice having people stolen from underneath your nose.

8 June 2011

Errea has brought a little bit of Italy to Norwich, the new kit's out, but no medium sized shirts in stock. At least that gives me time to think about what I want written on the back. It's £1 a letter so Scoltock makes it a bit pricey. Maybe my old nickname, Junk, is the better option. I did think about having the number nine and Holt, but I wasn't sure if that was just a bit weird for a 31-year-old. There does seem to be a divide as to whether you should even wear replica shirts at games.

It's a good thing that the kit has been revealed, us fans had been waiting for long enough – and they actually put together a humorous promotional video to go with it. And it's nice to have something slightly different to hover your attention over. In other news my digestive system is playing up, ulcerative colitis may be a problem with the bowels and therefore sneered at and made fun of, but running to the toilet and passing substances other than faeces isn't pleasant, especially when you're doing it five or six times a day – minimum.

The Norfolk Cafu also suffers, which makes us mere mortals feel better. And once the drugs kick in, the body and mind will be back fighting fit. Bring on the anti-inflammatory steroids.

9th June 2011

New kit, new furore. Apparently we're xenophobic now. Well according to a little website known as *The Spoiler*. I hadn't heard of it myself until it popped up in the internet search, but according to the headline 'Norwich use xenophobia to sell their new football kit.'

All because of a sales video. Just goes to show, if you give a soapbox to the man on the street you'll end up having to put up with the utter tosh they spout. Luckily balance was found in *The Telegraph*:

'To a soundtrack of classical opera squad members spare no lazy national stereotype bar pinching the posterior of a local waitress and eating mama's homemade pizza.

Instead Norwich players in both home and away kits foul each other, complain to opponents and the referee before a cheeky free kick is curled past a goalkeeper more interested in sipping a cappuccino than muddying his knees trying to stop the shot.

Paul Lambert, watching on while trying to read his copy of *Gazzetta dello Sport*, has had enough by the end and storms off tossing his paper in to the air behind him.

The scene ends with a mandatory scooter departure and Grant Holt getting over excited by hitting the rider on the back with a ball for 10 meters.'

I don't know why, but no one decided to take the honour of a byline, shame really, I quite liked the tongue-in-cheek style. Although many a fan would have been quite justified in correcting the young whipper-snapper of a journalist, it wasn't the away kit, it was the training gear, and it wasn't cappuccino, but an espresso.

10 June 2011

Drugs working, bowels getting back to some kind of order. Though ulcerative colitis is a bit of a drag – going to the toilet half a dozen times a day is enough to take it out of anyone – it's easy to make yourself feel better. New green and yellow trainers on order, new replica shirt being delivered on the 23rd – haven't told the wife.

Had a quick scooby at the official Premier League website because there's an interesting poll – which of the promoted teams will finish highest – QPR, Swansea or Norwich. Of the 34,416 respondents 61.2 per cent think it'll be QPR, why?

And according to one of the betting shops we're 8/13 to be relegated and 5/2 to finish bottom. Ouch. Oh and 5000/1 to win the League, but only 500/1 to finish in the top four.

13 June 2011

Arse. Got ahead of myself, no fixtures until Friday. Time to twiddle my thumbs until then.

14 June 2011

New winger, new winger, we finally got Elliot Bennett from Brighton on a three-year deal for an undisclosed fee. Their fans don't seem to be as up in arms about it, there is some grace left in the game:

'All the best Benno and thanks for playing your part in getting us here!

If he'd gone to Southampton or another Championship club I'd have issues, but to play in the Prem is a chance he can't turn down!

Keep Calm and Carry On!'

And I'm not the only one slowly losing the plot during the off season, a quick check of the Norwich discussion board this evening shows people all around the country are a few kicks away from a padded room. I take no credit for this, the club shop is being refurbished so:

'Can't reveal my sources but I have heard we are going into administration and shop has been shut as a cost cutting measure. Premier League money has already been spent on servicing the debt and that McNasty has run off to Barbados to live with Chrissy Martin and Chrissy Jackson off Radio Broadland.

Paul Lambert has been poached by Birmingham to replace McGleish and Grant Holt has been allowed to speak to Dereham as a potential replacement for the Linnets bound Danny Beaumont.

Rumour has it that our only chance of survival is a consortium lead by Danny Mills and Mark Fotheringham. His contract at Formagusta having been a damn sight more lucrative than we previously thought.

The new kit will remain unavailable as Errea have stopped production due to unpaid bills and that the Italian highly leftwing and heavily unionised workforce have taken massive umbrage with our racist promo video.

The club's a shambles. Sack the board. It's all Stephen Fry's fault and you can't even be racist anymore.'

Oh, and I've not heard anything from the club about my application for the position of new media journalist. Could it be that forgetting to give my postal address has had me struck from the 'to interview' pile?

15 June 2011

Norwich City is even used to advertise other clubs. On the walk to the station after dropping the boy at nursery, whose face should I see but Simeon Jackson's. Before my eyes was a billboard for Crystal Palace, but with none other than our number 10 in all his yellow and green glory helping sell tickets to the Eagles. We.Are.Massive.

16 June 2011

So my illustrious return to Nelson's County has been postponed. Saturday's, from August onwards, remain a celebration of pub, food and football. My application to be Norwich City's next new media journalist was unsuccessful. Mr Joe Ferrari, head of

We.Are.Massive – Norwich advertise lesser clubs.

media works late even when the season isn't in full swing, he sent me an email at 19.30, which though polite was a little disappointing to read:

> *Dear James,*
>
> *Thank you for taking the time to complete your application for the position of New Media Journalist here at Norwich City Football Club.*
>
> *I regret to inform you that on this occasion your application has not been successful. Competition for this post was the fiercest I have witnessed for any job we have advertised in the media team since I joined the Club in 2001, with no less than 184 applicants.*
>
> *More than half of those who applied were or are about to become media graduates with work experience in the field, so whittling down to a manageable number to invite for interviews has been a very tough process.*
>
> *Thank you again for your interest in Norwich City and I wish you all the very best with your future career.*
>
> *Yours sincerely, Joe Ferrari Head of Media*

What can you do apart from suck it up and move on, though I reserve the right to feel slightly sorry for myself.

On a plus note my new yellow and green trainers have arrived from Finland. I think they're cool, my better half thinks I'm slightly sad.

17 June 2011

Fixtures are out. Wigan away first game of the season, that's a long old poke even from London. Four hours in the car or two hours on the train. Not sure I can get away with it, especially as Stoke is the first home game of the season the week after, which I of

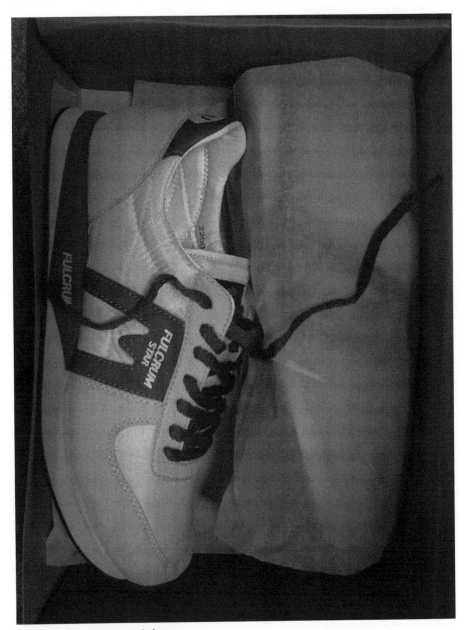

Stand out – New season, new trainers.

course will be heading to, and then it's Chelsea away, which I'd be stupid not to go to as I live in the big smog.

The back end of the fixture list looks a bit tasty – difficult even – which will do nothing for the heart rate: Everton, Spurs, Man City, Blackburn, Liverpool, Arsenal and Aston Villa.

But with the fixtures out it means the BBC has updated its football website and Norwich are now officially in the Premier League section, sitting pretty in 12th.

Alphabetical League tables are good to look at. Still giving me butterflies in the stomach thinking we're there.

I wore my yellow and green trainers today, and was strangely annoyed that no one noticed, especially as I felt a little self conscious. Yellow doesn't half stand out. When you're part of a few thousand fellow fans you don't think about it, when you're on your own, you do wonder if you look a twat. Better than wearing blue though.

Our rivals down the road seem to be scraping the bottom of the barrel, stuck in the Championship and filling the off-season with the following, very popular article in their local rag:

Canaries crushed: We launch countdown to Norwich City relegation

Friday, June 17, 2011

Let's be avenya! Tonight the Evening Star launches a valuable new service to all our readers.

'Off the Boil City' is a countdown clock recording the days until the Canaries regain their rightful place in the football hierarchy – The Championship.

And we're sure that Town fans will be Delia-lighted to pass the old enemy coming up if our new manager takes his Jewells up to the Premiership next season.

The clock starts now and gets going in earnest in August. You can see it on the homepage of our sports section.

The only question is, of course, when the sands of time will run out for Norwich City.

Will they be relegated by Easter . . . or will they carry on in limbo like this year's relegated teams until the last match of the season. Time will tell.

Oh dear. Poor blighters.

21 June 2011

Sometimes the world gets in the way, be it work or family, the time you spend thinking about football can become interspersed with other activities. It could be a deadline that your boss gives you, a shopping trip that your wife forces upon you or a dirty nappy that your little nipper happily, and aromatically produces. But there are times, usually just before you drift into unconsciousness last thing at night, that your mind lets you drift over the hallowed turf of your club, hear the crowd cheer, sing a terrace anthem, and bask in the glory of supporting you team. The butterflies fill your stomach, the thrill resonates through your thoughts, and all is good in the world.

So no matter how busy I've been with other things, always at the back of my mind has been one thing – the yellow and green army.

And come Thursday, it's going to become plainly obvious that it's been playing on my mind, because the new replica shirt should arrive, emblazoned with the number nine, and my old school nickname, Junk.

I've also got to try and talk the missus into letting me go to a couple of pre-season friendlies.

One shouldn't be too difficult as it's only a couple of miles down the road at Crystal Palace. Selhurst Park is a dive of a ground in the middle of a dump in south east London – I know I used to live in Penge, a stone's throw from Norwood. It's full of half rotten wooden seating, rusty corrugated iron roofing and toilets over flowing with just about every body fluid going. They moved the away fans to a corner away from the most boisterous home support for safety reasons – so now the sight impaired Palace fans listening to the game on their headphones get to sit with the away mob.

The second is more difficult. It's a home game two weeks before the season proper starts, but it's against Parma. Exotic, no? When was the last time we could say we're playing Italian opposition? Probably when we had our last foray into European club football and the UEFA Cup, against Inter Milan. That was getting on for 20 years ago, so you have to make the most of these opportunities. Time to start thinking of some good excuses.

22 June 2011

Again, apparently Norwich's stop in the top flight won't last long, and again it's Ipswich fans bleeting on. This time it was wrapped into a BBC feature on town's up and down the UK vying for city status – after failing on numerous occasions, Ipswich aren't applying this time.

But in among the discussion pipped Tim Edwards, an Ipswich town fan with these sagacious words: 'Ipswich City sounds stupid, ICFC is horrible. It sounds like a DIY store. I wouldn't want city status, even if it meant catching up with Norwich. Norwich has four things they can lord over us – a cathedral, an airport, it's a city and they are in the Premier League. We are only bothered about the Premier League and we are confident that won't last for long.

23 June 2011

No replica shirt-shaped package was on my doormat when I got home from work. Postman should be shot, the Royal Mail should be disbanded and IT SHOULD BE HERE!!!

24 June 2011

I may have just landed myself in hot water with the missus. After missing out on Olympics tickets I was convinced by the power of an email from the FA that I should buy tickets for the England verses Wales European Championship qualifier on 6 September. Now how do I broach the subject and what excuse do I use? I may have to start earning some brownie points between now and then, although that could be difficult considering it isn't long until the pre-season friendlies start, and then in the blink of an eye it's the beginning of the season proper.

This is the problem when the person you marry, co-habit or simply go out with doesn't hold the same passions as you. Quite honestly I think the wife thinks I am not only mad, but also extremely sad and perhaps a little bit selfish. But then what football fan isn't?

It's not like I plaster the walls with memorabilia, wear replica shirts every day and drink from a Norwich City mug (although this is soon to change the more I think about it. A shiny new green and yellow mug is only £6.95). Yes, I have a Norwich alarm clock, a Norwich piggy bank and one or two Norwich related polo shirts, ties and perhaps one or two other things, but they were gifts. I'm easy to buy Christmas and birthday presents for, it's a good thing.

Anyway Kana hasn't got a leg to stand on; she paid for half of my season ticket, along with her mum, who also thinks I'm mad.

STILL NO SHIRT!!!

28 June 2011

Ten minutes on the phone trying to find out where my shirt is. I had called earlier and left a message with the stuttery lady on the answering machine, but no one called back. They take your money but don't supply the goods, I don't know what the world is coming to.

3 July 2011

You've made it when you're in a glossy magazine, not me obviously, the chances of me being in a glossy magazine are slim to nothing, but Paul Lambert, our glorious manager is in *FourFourTwo*.

The football magazine that used to sit there, on the newsagent's shelf, staring down at you, so pretty and shiny, with all its wonderfulness, its in-depth interviews with players from around the world; you knew it would be wonderful to read but you also knew there'd be nothing about your team, so paying £4.50 just wasn't worth it.

Not anymore. After four pages, (p90 – p93), of Norwich City and Paul Lambert, Norwich fans now know that:

When Lambert arrived, usurping Bryan Gunn, the players weren't fit enough, 'It's fair to say they weren't fit enough and a lot of hard work was needed.'

As much as Lambert enjoyed his time at Colchester United, when Norwich came in for him 'I saw the fanbase, I knew it was a proper club.'

Man-management is key, 'I keep my distance with the players but I still have a laugh and a joke.'

He's buying hungry players he knows he can rely on, 'I've signed players I know because I can trust them. I know what I'm going to get from them because I've already seen them at close quarters.'

Which is probably why Bradley Johnson has just joined the team on a free transfer from Leeds United, the 'tenacious' midfielder has signed a three-year deal. Not too shabby, that's the fifth player to join, so another couple and we're just about ready for the season to begin. One rumour is that number six could be our old loan goalkeeper from the League One stint, Fraser Forster. But at £2 million it seems unlikely, and why sign another goalkeeper when we have Ruddy and two youngsters in as backup?

As a side note, still no shirt and no amount of phone calls to the club or trips to the local Royal Mail delivery office seem to find me an answer as to where it is. Either the nation's mail company or my home town team are telling me fibs. Haven't decided which yet, but I am quite miffed.

6 July 2011

Apparently, and I can't quite believe it, but it can take anything from two all the way up to 12 working days for a Royal Mail special delivery to arrive. Which means two things, firstly is it any wonder that the Royal Mail, the nations logistics company is finding it tough to keep its customers, and secondly, that my new shirt, with carefully chosen wording and number combination isn't likely to arrive until next Monday – if at all.

Without wanting to sound like a moaning old git, why, why, why, why, why, why, why, why, why, why, why, why, why, why, why, why, why, why, why, why, why, WHY?

It would have been bloody quicker to drive all the way to the club shop, buy the sodding thing and drive all the way back to south east London. My lesson has been well and truly learned.

7 July 2011

It's not really Norwich related, it's not even football related, but it's huge news nonetheless: the *News of the World*, Britain's biggest Sunday newspaper by some considerable distance will be no more after this weekend's edition.

After a week of unbridled attacks from politicians, celebrities, and the general public over the newspaper's use of phone hacking, of not only television and film personalities and politicians, but also murder victims and those in the armed services who have died in name of the country, its owners, News International – the Murdoch's – have pulled the plug. So a newspaper has gone to the wall, not because the medium is dead, but ironically because of a scandal, the very thing the paper uncovered for many years.

Never read the thing, not even as a employee of News International working for *The Sunday Times* as a wet-behind-the-ears underling on the business section, and now never will, but it's quite a thing.

On a more football related footing, Norwich has signed an out-and-out winger from Huddersfield – Anthony Pilkington. 'Pilks' can play on either the left or right and is a young whipper-snapper at only 23 years of age, but it's exciting to know that we have six fresh faces in the squad in time for pre-season. Excited? You'd better believe it.

I had a quick flick onto the Pink'un website this morning as I was dropping the kids off at the swimming pool, (if you don't know what that actually means then you should look it up), and there seems to be a movement among supporters to adorn the Barclay stand with a new banner in honour of our commander-in-chief. So come 20 August, when we play Stoke in our first Premier League fixture at Carrow Road since the 2004–05 season, the television camera's could be panning round the ground showing the world: 'Welcome to St Paul's Cathedral'. Marvellous.

I've been away from home for a day or so, Poland, Krakow to be precise, and I'm hoping that when I get home there'll be a parcel, or at least a 'we tried to call' card from Royal Mail – I'm not holding my breath…

…there was no package waiting for me.

12 July 2011

I'm behind the curve, Sky television has released its first batch of televised matches for the new season, and bugger me if it doesn't mean I am already having to cross off games that I just won't be able to see. Monday 26 September, at 8pm Norwich verses Sunderland, which means unless I invent some sort of transporter then I won't be making the trip from London to Carrow Road to watch the match. I know that Sky can't show 3 o'clock kick-offs because they supposedly don't want to kill off the act of actually going to the games, but damn and tarnation, every time games are moved it makes life difficult – but the wife will probably be happy.

And it isn't the only game moved, but thankfully the other games have just been moved around the weekend: West Brom moves to 1.30pm on Sunday, Norwich verses Arsenal is now on Saturday 19 November at 12.45. Shouldn't complain too hard as the away Liverpool game is now on TV too, meaning I can either go to the pub or find a completely legitimate website to watch it on.

Will probably have to get used to missing games as I'll be toddling off on holiday at Christmas – two weeks in Japan – the busiest part of the footballing calendar. I wonder if Japanese cable or satellite will have the games?

13 July 2011

Another conundrum, applications for Chelsea away are now being accepted. How do I get that one passed Kana? And at £50 a pop it might be a little difficult to justify the trip down the road to west London on economic grounds. But it's too close to miss, and it's the first chance to go to one of the 'big four's' grounds, (apologies Manchester City but you aren't one of the big teams yet, no matter how much you've spent. Many might say the same about Chelsea, but you can't hide from the fact that they have won a few trophies over the last five years of so).

What I need is an excuse, something that I can dangle in front of my good lady and she'll accept without question.

The first option is to simply not tell her. I could try bribery. Either force her out with her friends, encourage her to stay out as late as she wants, come home slightly the worse for wear, and then play the 'Well you go out, I had to stay home and look after the boy.'

I could bargain with her. Go to Chelsea and forgo a random home game – Wigan or Bolton perhaps – that's balance isn't it?

The other option is honesty, as much of a long shot as that might be. Just front up, stare her straight in the eyes, take a deep breath and blurt out that I'm going to watch Norwich play Chelsea, and there's nothing she can do about it.

Yeah, let's be honest, I'm not that brave, and there are some advantages to being married.

It seems my new replica shirt is now officially classed as 'lost' by Royal Mail, so now I, in theory, can get Norwich City's shop to claim a refund and they can send me a replacement. The only thing is that Diane from the club is on holiday until next week and the lady who called me back – no one seems to answer the phone when you call – isn't authorised to send one out. I couldn't help but think she also thought I was telling fibs and was trying to swindle the club.

16 July 2011, Gorleston 0–7 Norwich

Football is back!!! They may only be Ridgeons League but they were an opposing football team, and that is something that we have all been missing since the season ended. I would love to describe it, but I wasn't there. A trip up to Norfolk was never going to be an option – I've still got to get Chelsea passed the missus, and I've only just managed to get the Crystal Palace friendly signed off. All sounds like it went like clockwork, according to the official match report on the club's website:

'CITY got their preparations for Barclays Premier League football off to a winning start with a 7-0 win over Ridgeons Premier League side Gorleston this afternoon.

A brace from skipper Grant Holt and further strikes from Zak Whitbread, Korey Smith, Simeon Jackson, Bradley Johnson and Aaron Wilbraham secured the seven goal margin.

On the result, Manager Paul Lambert said: "It's important to get a touch of the ball again and see how it goes.

"Pre-season is all about getting the lads fit and ready for that first game and today was a good run out. I'm pleased with how it went today and have been pleased with how it's gone since we've been back.

"Gorleston have a terrific set up here and did really well last season, but for us it's preparation for what is ahead."

Boss Paul Lambert gave the travelling Canary fans a first glimpse of five of his six summer signings at Emerald Park – although defender Ritchie De Laet was the only one to start the match. The defender, on loan from Manchester United, lining up alongside Zak Whitbread at the heart of the City defence for the first time.

On a rain-soaked afternoon it took City just six minutes to open the scoring with skipper Grant Holt taking the mantle of firing home the Canaries' first goal of the

2011–12 campaign. A quick free-kick taken by Chris Martin put Holt through on goal and the ace marksman guided the ball past Elliot Pride in the Greens' goal.

Martin then looked to get a goal of his own, hitting a powerful shot into the side netting before Zak Whitbread headed home the Canaries' second goal on 12 minutes.

City were in the mood for goals, and Holt soon scored his second and City's third goal when he converted a 27th minute penalty after Martin was upended by defender Adam Thurtle.

The half-hour mark saw Lambert make his first changes of the afternoon with Steve Morrison and Simeon Jackson replacing Holt and Martin.

Soon after, the Canaries were hitting the net again, scoring a fourth goal of the game after 33 minutes as Korey Smith hit a powerful shot from 20 yards out that went through a ruck of players before beating Gorleston 'keeper Pride.

On the stroke of half-time City made it 5–0, Morison's cushioned header finding Jackson who in turn headed home easily to give the Canaries a hefty lead going into the break.

Half-time: Gorleston 0 Norwich City 5

The half-time interval saw wholesale changes with only Morison and Jackson featuring in both halves. It saw the introduction of Elliott Bennett and Bradley Johnson who got their first tastes of life in the yellow shirt.

And it took Johnson little time to make a positive impression as he rounded a series of Gorleston defenders before powerfully firing home City's sixth goal of the game just four minutes into the second period.

Fellow newcomer James Vaughan was later introduced alongside Aaron Wilbraham replacing Steve Morison and Jackson in attack after 61 minutes.

Both were soon threatening a seventh. Vaughan went close with a spectacular overhead kick and looked very lively in his brief debut for the Canaries, but it was Wilbraham who scored City's seventh and final goal after 75 minutes as he fired home a left footed shot into the bottom corner.'

So that's that, the first win is under the belt, now the squad fly over to Germany for some team building. I wonder if it'll include the same lame, team building exercises they make office workers do. Climbing across a scrub of land with only a plank of wood and a bucket, and not being allowed to touch a single blade of grass. Or maybe orienteering. Everyone, even Holt and Lambert dressed in kagools with a compass and map in hand, dropped on a windswept mountainside, with the rain pelting down. Doubtful but it's a thought.

17 July 2011

Jonny, the delightful friend that he is sent me a text today: 'This will make you sick. Just been on the hallowed pitch.' Git. Yes that does make me sick. Not only has he walked on the grass at Carrow Road but he also didn't bother to elaborate, not even after my frightfully witty reply: 'How, why, streaking again?'

It's every football fan's dream to walk on the turf of the team they support. Who can put their hand on their heart, and honestly say they haven't wistfully thought about pulling on the jersey, running out of the tunnel into the sun, and the thrum of a packed stadium. And Jonny's done it. Well kind of. Well I'm not sure, until he starts being a little more elaborate with his messages.

18 July 2011

No, no, no! I don't want to wait for another two weeks to see 'what happens' I want my replica shirt! I paid for the thing over a month ago and have nothing to show for it. I don't care that the club will be out of pocket, I'm out of pocket. Bloody hell!!!

19 July 2011

Called the club at 23.30, thought it was the best way, wouldn't have to speak to anyone and could just leave a forthright message for them to pick up in the morning. It also allowed me to cover up my grave error when I spoke to them the first time. I forgot to mention that Royal Mail had said that because the package hadn't been delivered for 15 working days it was now classed as lost in the system, and THE SENDER WOULD HAVE TO SUBMIT A CLAIM FOR COMPENSATION. Perhaps if I had said that in the first place I could have got Diane at the mail order warehouse to come around to my way of thinking more quickly. One thought does occur to me though, is calling at that time of day a sign of weakness, cowardice or just plain weirdness?

20 July 2011

I'm a lucky beggar according to Jonny, Twon, Button and Cruso – in fact everyone come to think of it – I'm an automotive journalist. I spend a bit of time attending new car launches in various countries around Europe. But I should have died today at the launch of the Audi A6 Avant in Frankfurt.

I picked up the keys to a test car at the airport and was driving down the autobahn on the way to the lunch stop when a VW Passat in front of me started veering around the fast lane, he veered so much his tyres clipped the central reservation – needless-to-say he started shaking and veering a hell of a lot more, and for a split second I thought this could get bloody. Luckily he held it and got himself back on track. But that wasn't the worst episode.

I pulled out into a dual carriage way without looking, with traffic coming in both directions! I know I'd been up since 5am, but I don't think I was even aware of driving, let alone where I was in relation to the rest of the world. How I missed every car I don't know, and I can only thank the man in the VW Golf who swerved out of the way in time for stopping something quite dreadful happening. Not only could I have done myself a mischief, but worse, I could have done a lot of innocent people some serious damage too.

It's time to take a day or two off and recharge the batteries, and more importantly the sensors.

Diane called, my replacement shirt is being posted out today, weakness, cowardice or just plain weirdness works!!!

21 July 2011

Fame and fortune await, all thanks to Twitter, who'd have thought social media would actually work and help opportunities arise. ESPN has come a calling, they've seen my talent. I've been asked to do an 'ident'.

Dom Crofts tweeted that he needed a London-based Norwich fan, and the PR man from BDA Creative, responded to my response. Not long after I had an email sitting in my inbox:

'We are filming 20 idents for ESPN's coverage of the new Premier League season. The idea is to capture fans either in their workplace or pursuing one of their favourite hobbies. So far we've had milkmen, builders, martial arts experts and photographers getting in touch, and we're open to all sorts of possibilities.'

Wasn't entirely sure what an ident was but checked on the internet and it turns out its a shortened form of 'station identification', and according to Wikipedia means: 'Station idents are normally used in between shows, and by some are considered the most important portion of a network's presentation.'

I'm going to be the most important portion of ESPN's Premier League football coverage come the 2011–12 season. As an automotive journalist all I have to do is don my Norwich shirt, (hopefully it arrives soon, and Diane and the Royal Mail don't fail me again), and stand in front of an exotic car.

So now I have to find a car. Hopefully Lotus can help, I've dropped them a line, so keeping my fingers crossed, Gary Haddon and Alastair Florence of the company's PR department don't fail me! But why wouldn't they do it, it's free air time on TV? What should I go for, an Elise, an Evora, or how about a classic Esprit? Decisions, decisions.

But not to count my chickens I've thought of some back-ups should Lotus not come to the table: Audi (R8 GT), Nissan, (GT-R) or perhaps Jaguar (XKR-S).

I might be eager to grab my 15 seconds of fame with ESPN a fairly large and weighty broadcaster, but after a daily internet search of Norwich City I came a cross an interesting blog written by Luke Smith, ESPN's Norwich correspondent. I'm not sure the chap's opening paragraph is going to warm him or ESPN to the average City fan:

'There are very few good reasons to ever leave Norwich City center. However, if you find yourself in England's eastern capital city and you're feeling adventurous, (i.e. if there's nothing good on T.V. on a Sunday afternoon) consider taking the A47 road out of Norwich City centre and drive east for about 40 miles. If you're paying close attention, eventually you'll stumble upon the miniscule seaside town of Gorleston. As you're probably well aware, this fine seaside town, with a population of less than 7,000 fine Norfolk coastline lovers, played host to Paul Lambert's newly promoted Canaries on Saturday afternoon for their first pre-season fixture. Naturally, it drew a massive bidding war from sports broadcasting companies worldwide...'

Not the best start, and not certain to ingratiate yourself to the locals, but at least it went on to give a bit of analysis on our team and its chances in the new season.

'Apparently, Paul Lambert and his backroom of miracle workers had missed the mass email that almost every other Premier League team received. The subject line read, 'Anyone Fancy Preseason in the States?' No fewer than six top flight teams are spending at least a portion of their preparation time in North America. Both Manchester City and United have crossed the pond, but it's not just the league's cash cows making an appearance. Everton, Newcastle and Bolton have made U.S. appearances this summer, while West Bromwich were welcomed to California by the San Jose Earthquakes. (If you're thinking to yourself, 'San Jose Earthquakes? That name sounds familiar and unnecessarily dramatic,' you'd be right to do so. They are the Major League Soccer team who famously signed Norwich City legend Darren Huckerby for the final 28 games and nine goals of his career, when he arguably should have still been on City's roster.)

Nevertheless, you'll not hear a single complaint out of the Norwich camp, despite being subject to a damp and dreary 3 p.m. kick-off in the cultural Mecca of 'downtown' Gorleston. The Premier League awaits them for the first time in six years and the team seemed raring to go as they demolished Gorleston 7–0. Despite a seemingly casual second half performance, the squad seems to be progressing and gelling. There was a pair of goals from City's captain, Grant Holt, as well as goals for Zak Whitbred, Korey Smith, Simeon Jackson, Bradley Johnson and finally Aaron Wilbraham completed the win. New import Bradley Johnson showed the kind of quality that will have brought a wry grin to the shrewd shopping Paul Lambert as he finished with a sweet strike from twenty yards out.

Norwich have been among the busiest Premier League teams during the transfer window, with six new faces coming in. Five of the six new faces made their first City appearance along with 21 more familiar City players. Anthony Pilkington was the only new signing to miss out. He will now race against the clock and hope to reach match fitness in time for Aug. 13 and the opening match, away at Wigan.

The transfer rumors seemed to have reached a quiet lull, at least for the time being. Norwich fans will be hoping that at least one of the whispers featured in the ever-sensational Sun newspaper turns out to be true. The perfect number of summer signings was seven according to Lambert and with Newcastle's third choice goalkeeper, Fraser Forster, still a topic of conversation, many are hoping for that piece of business to be announced soon. My personal wish list, however, is topped by Henri Lansbury. Despite reportedly turning down a 1.5 million bid from Norwich, Arsene Wenger appears to have no need for him. If he can conjure up the creativity and quality he showed last season while on loan with Norwich, he will undoubtedly prove to be a vital weapon in Paul Lambert's own arsenal.

The signings Lambert has made and the preseason warm-up he scheduled have sent a clear message about the game plan for the next 10 months; City will not be buying their Premier League survival. The management will be banking on the six new players fusing with the rest to emulate the graft, determination and team spirit we've seen in the last 20 months since Lambert began his wizardry.

It's a brave philosophy.

With very little Premier League experience (in most cases, no experience whatsoever) in the squad, the Canaries will look to players who have recently risen *through the lower leagues to demonstrate the character and leadership required against the best players in the world. It was a principle that was justified in League One, two seasons ago and reaffirmed last season in the Championship. The question is will it translate to the most competitive league in the world?*

A trip to Germany, three domestic lower league opponents followed by intriguing home clashes with Real Zaragoza and Parma will conclude the remaining preseason. By the time the fulltime whistle is blown at the end of the final fixture against the Italian Serie A team, we'll hope to know a great deal more than we currently know; which 25 players will form the squad, how the team has gelled and perhaps most significantly, if the new signings and old philosophy will be enough to land the Canaries in seventeenth position or higher by the end of the season.

I wonder if Luke Smith is from Norwich, Norfolk or even the UK.

23 July 2011

The proud owner of a new home shirt, I sent a picture to Jonny, announcing its arrival, and what message do I get in reply. Not 'looks good', not 'how did you chose what to have written' but:

'First sign of gay is your own name on your shirt'.

Charming.

25 July 2011

Some lady who is apparently 'tackling football in heels' wrote: 'Efan Ekoku of Norwich City was the first player to score four goals in one Premier League match. #welcomebacknorwich' on her Twitter feed.

Now I don't know who Hayley McQueen is but she seems like a salt of the earth type of lady who knows quality when she sees it. Perhaps I should

Decisions – The effort it takes to decide what wording should go on the back of my new shirt.

search for her on the internet. The only problem that produces is, that if my wife was ever to check the browser history of our computer she might be lead to believe I was some sort of pervert – I do have a habit of looking people up if I've never heard of them before, and there always seems to be more females I've never heard of than males. But I digress.

Ms McQueen's acknowledgement of Norwich was also borne out in more coverage of the team on Sky Sports News, although the interviews with Lambert, Morrison and Holt perhaps didn't shed them in the best light. Lambert mumbled a bit, Morrison just said something about the facilities being top notch and Holt repeated 'team' a lot in the single sentence. But as long as they show their magic on the pitch who cares.

And the real challenge starts tomorrow at Crystal Palace.

Until now friendly matches against, Gorleston and Sparta Gottingen, RSV Gottingen and a Nordhausen/Regional Select XI in Germany have racked up 26 goals without conceding any, but as much as I'd love for that to continue things are going to start getting a lot more difficult. Starting tomorrow.

Let's be honest, Selhurst Park is a dump of a ground, half the stadium needs to be demolished and rebuilt. The wooden seats are half rotten, the tin roof leaks and the toilet facilities might as well be a hole in the ground. Mind you it's a reflection of the general area: South Norwood.

Hardly the most affluent part of London, most of the surrounding area is made up of past-their-best terraced housing, and having lived a stones throw from the ground for over a year, the typical resident isn't all that fussed about building the place up, (I lived in a converted house which contained three flats, our neighbours were burgled twice, once the burglars were armed with a knife and baseball bat).

But as rough as the area is, I've never had any trouble, the worst that has ever happened is a bit of lip. I've walked through South Norwood in my green and yellow, once a drunk bloke swung round the pub door and shouted, 'Where's your combine harvester?' at me. And later the same evening three good for nothing young teenagers muttered, 'Good luck tonight mate, you're going to need it'. Wasn't sure if that was meant to be a threat, but I just shrugged my shoulders and carried on to the turnstiles, a piss-soaked floor and my knackered wooden seat. And I'll do it all again tomorrow, just like I do every bloody year. It doesn't seem to matter what League we're in, if we don't play the Eagles then the Gods aren't happy.

26 July 2011, Crystal Palace 1–0 Norwich City

I didn't want to be at work today. The idea of sitting in a stuffy office for eight hours filled me with dread from the moment I woke up. Not only was there an overwhelming feeling of monotony, but there were also far better things to do with my time. I spent most of the daylight hours yesterday searching the internet for compilation videos that fans had put together of the best bits from last season.

It's a simple pleasure, but skipping from goal to goal, with an awe inspiring soundtrack playing really does get you in the mood for some boisterous terrace singing and screaming. Which makes the blandness of the office even more soul destroying.

Déjà vu – It doesn't matter which division we are in Norwich play Palace every year.

To try and ease the pain, and take my mind off where I actually wanted to be, the admittedly dank surroundings of Selhurst Park, I wandered down to the local bookshop and thumbed through a copy of *Fever Pitch*.

I've never read it – it's about Arsenal – but I wanted to get an idea of what writing about football was all about, and as this particular novel is a million selling chart topper it's probably a good starting point. Snobbery and more importantly, jealousy aren't nice characteristics but I really don't care: it's a rubbish read.

Backward looking, memory-driven writing means you miss things out, skewer facts and view everything through rose-tinted spectacles. And I know that *Fever Pitch* is guilty of all of these things because in the 10 minutes I read it for (the backcover synopsis, inside cover comments by reviewers and the author's introduction), I was only ever wondering how on earth you can remember your first game from 30 years ago, when I can barely remember what I did at the weekend. Perhaps when I've sold over a million copies I'll be less critical.

While football literary acclaim is still sometime away one glimmer of hope was movement on the ESPN ident. The idea of me being filmed with a Lotus has been put to the executives and by all accounts they like the concept and are just contemplating a decent location. There might be a little bit of a lull between them giving it the nod and filming as they need to sign off the priority teams – the one's being shown on ESPN in the opening two weeks of the season first, (Norwich aren't on the channel until they play Liverpool away on 22 October). But once that is done fame beckons.

With no boss in the office today, there has been more scope than usual to be a little slack. It's also the fact that it's the summer and there always needs to be a little downtime in the schedule, especially when the previous night you spent being kicked and pushed out of bed by a 15-month-old baby with a cough. But having downtime and using it to make a cup of tea isn't always a safe thing to do, don't get me wrong I enjoy the usual football chatter while the kettle boils as much as the next person, but when the person you're speaking with supposedly supports Chelsea and Brighton, I don't know how to react. Two teams is an impossibility. How do you put 100 per cent of your passion and enthusiasm into two teams?

You have to play the game though, which means calling on every scrap of information you know about the clubs to keep the conversation going and not appear rude or disinterested.

Luckily I know Brighton have a new stadium (the result of a £90 million interest free loan from the chairman apparently), they have a decent manager in Gus Poyet, have bought a striker from Peterborough, (Craig MacKail-Smith who we lost interest in, in March according to our chief executive) and we bought their star winger, Elliott Bennett. Crisis averted.

I would like to know what 'mustard' means in cockney rhyming slang, it came up in the conversation and I just had to nod along in agreement. Although it brought up an interesting challenge, can I use bishybarnabee in conversation, and will the person I'm speaking to ask what it is or just nod and try and smile over it.

The Palace game itself was a little mooted, though I was treated to a plastic seat which was a bonus for the backside. Along with me, 400 hundred other fans dragged themselves to south London, some in suits had come straight from work.

Many of the younger fans need to slow down on the sugar intake, shouting out 'you look gay' and 'how camp are you' isn't really the done thing, especially at a friendly when no one really cares about the result. They'll learn that effing and blinding is best saved for the blood boiling frustration of League matches. Having said that there were some mutterings from the bloke in front of me about Holt's positioning.

Russell Martin was so relaxed about the evening that as the referee was about to blow his whistle for the beginning of the second half he was still down with the fans having his photo taken.

But it felt good to be at a football ground, belt out a couple of chants, sing on the ball city and savour the atmosphere. The half-time hotdog was absolutely disgusting, nothing like eating a Delia pie.

And I could get used to the chants from opposition fans of, 'Premier League, you're having a laugh,' it just means they're jealous. Probably get the same from Chelsea when we play them at Stamford Bridge, entries for the ticket ballot close tomorrow, so fingers crossed I'll be one of the lucky buggers who gets a ticket.

It'll be nice when they start singing, 'going down, going down, going down,' to retort with 'on your mum, on your mum, on your mum.'

27 July 2011

Dear god the mentalists have left the asylum, a few nutters have gone on the internet discussion boards:

'Happy with a defeat to a poor Championship team? Lambert needs to wake up and smell the coffee. It's all very well wasting most of preseason playing park teams, does

he even know we are playing in the Premier League next season??!! *You wouldn't think so looking at the signings made so far, we need some Prem experience and we need it fast!! – Ged Steroo'*

Whoever this Ged Steroo chap is I think he needs to start taking his medication again, otherwise he'll be hyperventilating come the season proper.

28 July 2011

The wheels may have started coming off the QPR machine long ago, Bernie Ecclestone and Flavio Briatorie aren't the type of owners who instil confidence for all their wealth. But even in the face of adversity at least the fans can still hold their heads high with a sarcastic smile.

Step forward Mr Roberttheblogger on www.blogandwhitehoops.wordpress.com:

'We the Q.P.R fans wish to respond to the recent allegations in the press that our club is being run by two mercenary crooks and their yapping Italian lapdog by agreeing with you and distancing ourselves from these plonkers.

The recent revelation that it will cost £50 to sit in the away end at Loftus Road has led to a twitter campaign #boycottQPR, we strongly endorse this boycott. We have seen the upper tier of the School End, we know it's a shithole, we know the view is terrible and we know that watching Patrick Agyemang is not worth £50 (unless you are interested in a comedy evening). We feel that whilst we are stupid enough to be fleeced by our tight fisted owners when it comes to paying through the nose for tickets, you don't have too. The joys of Sky and streaming mean you can watch the game anyway without a questionable substance dripping on your head from the leaky roof above you.

We the fans are as shocked as you the press at the lack of transfer funds given to our manager. We cannot understand why over the last 3 years our Small and Orange owners have felt the need to part with their money in order to secure the signings of Liam Miller, Gary Borrowdale, Nigel Quashie, Damiano Tommasi and Allesadro Pellicori yet are now stalling once we have reached the promised land of The Premier League and will only allow for free transfers. We also wonder if the owners regret spending millions of pounds on chandeliers to hang in the club offices for no particular reason.

To the compilers of season preview packages, we also can't understand why we are yet to see a new kit for the season. Surely releasing a new home shirt and charging £40 for it a few months ago would have generated income due to the wave of optimism garnered from our promotion? We agree with you that it's sodding annoying that the only team in The Premier League that don't have a new kit yet is Q.P.R.

Fans of other clubs that were excited to see a founding member of the Premier League back in England's top flight. We were excited too. It's a shame that we are unrecognizable from the family club that went down in 1996. If it helps, we still hate Chelsea just as much. In fact we hated Chelsea before hating Chelsea was even *cool. We can't promise you that we will be a credit to the Premier League, we can't promise that our owners won't make you pay handsomely to sit in the smallest ground in the league, we can't even promise you that Leon Clarke won't sully the fine traditions of your club by daring to appear against you. But we can promise you that we the fans will strive to keep the name of Q.P.R clean and out of the press for the wrong reasons.*

Finally to the owners that saved our club. I saved a cat once, I don't walk around kicking it, pissing on it and blowing in it's ears before reminding it that it wouldn't be alive if it weren't for me. I leave the cat alone with owners who care about it.'

In other news Norwich drew nil-nil with Southend United this evening, I haven't looked at the imbeciles who will have come out of the woodwork to pen their thoughts on the discussion boards.

29 July 2011

FourFourTwo magazine says we'll finish 14th, that'll do.

1 August 2011

It's back, ulcerative colitis has once again swept into my life with all its frequent, and slightly painful, trips to the toilet. The first course of steroids hasn't seemed to have nipped it in the bud, so I'm now waiting for the local chemist to take delivery of my prednisalone retention enemas – life really is a roller coaster of fun and excitement sometimes.

A fun trip to the doctors, who was very understanding and a fellow football fan which made small talk

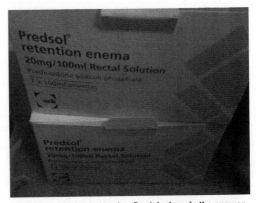

When the going gets tough – Prednisolone is the answer.

easier, followed by an hour wait for a blood test has been and gone. I've no problem having a blood test, it doesn't make me feel squeamish, with colitis you have so many of them it's like brushing your teeth, but usually the nurses are at least polite. Not in my local surgery. The entire conversation consisted of two words: 'Scoltock' and 'clench' followed by a grunt in recognition that I said thank you after it was all over.

The wait to see the happy chap was at least filled with some useful reading: *FourFourTwo*. The new issue of the magazine travels with me everywhere, it's an extension of the wallet and keys that every man has in his pocket.

Somewhere within its pages were some prophetic words: you don't judge an actor on their rehearsal. That sums up Norwich's pre-season, and its fans.

The doubters have jumped on the fact we haven't been able to beat Crystal Palace or Southend, smashing our hopes in the coming season before it's even started.

But fickleness is a trait that every sports fan seems to suffer from. Jonny is a prime example. Every game he finds a player to have a moan at, they're the worst, the laziest, the most useless, they can't dribble for toffee, can't hit a barn door. But do something right, a moment of magic and they become the best thing since sliced bread in the blink of an eye. So at the weekend what should happen but Norwich beat Coventry City 3–0 (Wilbraham, Morison and Bennett all on the score sheet). The doubters have gone and everything is wonderful again. Fans being fans, and fickleness being fickleness, this new found optimism may only last until Wednesday when Real Zaragoza turn up.

Me? I'm staying positive, my glass is half full. I have a ticket for the first game against one of the big four teams, Chelsea, and I've been given permission to travel the 12.9 miles to Stamford Bridge.

I'm using that enthusiasm to keep my thoughts and feelings high until my medication comes in and the drugs rather than the positive mental attitude start to make the body feel more human again. (One other thing that is helping in the meantime is that I can see the first runner beans growing on my little balcony garden. I call it a garden, it's actually six pots.)

Not everything is positive. I found out that someone else has written a diary of a Norwich season, 18 years before I started this: *Norfolk 'n' Good: A supporter's view of Norwich City's best-ever season*. Not only that but it was well received. Arse. I'd better hope that 2011–12 is better than the one Kevin Baldwin wrote about.

2 August 2011

Over my poached eggs on toast the BBC had a story on the cost of going to a football match, which deduced that it's expensive. Insightful. The cheapest ticket to watch Liverpool play is £39 and Arsenal £35. The depressing thing is that the cheapest ticket to watch Norwich is £28, the same price as Manchester United, and a game at Man City could cost as little as £25 (we won't mention how cheap places like Blackburn and Wigan are because their grounds are half empty every Saturday). But what's really interesting is that of all the clubs in the Premier League Fulham and Man City don't sell pies.*

*According to BBC statistics.

3 August 2011

Nothing quite like 20mg of prednisolone sodium phosphate suspended in 100ml of a clear colourless liquid to make you feel human again. The downside is that the clear colourless liquid isn't digested via the mouth. No, when you have a problem like ulcerative colitis that affects the large intestine, the clear colourless liquid has to be taken rectally. Lying in the foetal position every night, covering the tube in vaseline to shove up your jacksey isn't the best way to spend an evening but it does give you time to consider current world events. Read the latest news online, debt crisis, famine, revolution and the fact the BBC lied about Fulham and Man City not having pies – both of them do! It's enough to make you want to stop paying your TV licence fee.

All this being ill, and currently off work, isn't much fun. Today was the Real Zaragoza friendly (1–1, De Laet scored with a header), had I been firing on all cylinders I could have gone and witnessed the power cut during the thunderstorm which knocked out the floodlights for 10 minutes and the intermission entertainment, our left-back, Marc Tierney doing cartwheels in the middle of the pitch – there are no prima donnas on the team.

4 August 2011

ESPN seems like it could be hanging in the balance. I had a call from Zoe A'Court today, production manager for BDA Creative. The management at ESPN still seem to like the idea of me with a sports car wearing my Norwich shirt, but how the contextualise that so people understand that I'm an automotive journalist and not just some random nob standing next to a flash car they haven't figured out yet. That's not my problem, I'm just there to grab my 15 seconds of fame. And Zoe's email suggested that she was going to have a chat with the 'creatives' at the company to 'work out what environment we could place you in' to let people know what I do.

This would be so much easier if I was a fireman or worked on a fishing boat, they're obvious jobs that you see and know exactly what the chap is doing everyday of his working life. Journalists, even automotive ones, tend to sit in front of a computer most of the time – hardly exciting – and not much room to park a car, no matter how flash. I hope I don't miss out, if nothing else I'd like to rub Jonny's nose in it!

Now it's time for some more of that clear colourless liquid.

8 August 2011

The chance to star in an ESPN ident is barrelling along rather than hanging in the balance. The lovely Zoe A'Court from BDA Creative emailed me today in reply to the pictures of the Lotus Elise, Exige and Evora I sent over, to say that any would be perfect. ESPN would like a yellow variant for obvious Norwich kit-coloured reasons.

Alastair at Lotus is doing his best to be accommodating and has said an Evora will be available if necessary, but has also pro-offered the assembly line at Lotus's Hethel plant to do the filming – the creative types think that an engineering environment is the best place for me to stand as it relates to what I do in the day job. I can't help but think people will assume I'm a mechanic but hey-ho.

I've given Zoe Alastair's contact details so they can work it all out, I am after all just the lump of meat sitting in his green and yellow replica kit, leaning on the car in front of the camera.

As long as it all comes together it'll be one in the eye for Jonny, after all of his rantings and ravings about meeting players in Norwich and getting signed shirts.

9 August 2011

Two good things happened today. Firstly Zoe called and said ESPN loved the pictures of the assembly line and we are a go for shooting, either next Wednesday or Thursday. Might have to tell a little white lie to the boss though, maybe I'll have a doctor's appointment at the Norfolk and Norwich University Hospital.

And secondly, the money has been deducted for my Chelsea ticket so it should be winding its way to me in the post.

10 August 2011

Why is nothing simple, ESPN filming has now been pencilled in for 4pm next Thursday rather than 11am. Oh to be an A-list Hollywood actor who can chose the filming schedule and sit in a trailer sipping on the most fashionable alcoholic beverage of the time. Definitely getting a feeling I may be usurped by someone more flexible and possibly more local to Hethel. Would that be such a bad thing, I don't even have ESPN and don't know anyone that does, so what's the point of being in an ident when no one you know will see it?

A few more preview pieces are appearing in the nation's media, and for that matter the international media. Some good, some bad, and some truly horrific. Whoever invented the word 'soccer' should be shot, and whoever decided that America should become interested in the sport of 'soccer' should also be shot. And while I'm on the matter of who should be shot, so should the 'folk' at Fox who pay someone called Jamie Trecker to cover 'soccer' for them.

Mr Trecker apparently grew up watching 'soccer' in Scotland though there seems to be no basis for thinking he has any knowledge of anyone but the big teams in his rantings about Norwich City in the forthcoming 'BPL' season, (what the hell is the BPL anyway?). Latino.foxnews.com should be ashamed:

'On the first of February, the Canaries beat Millwall 2–1 thanks to a stoppage-time goal from Henri Lansbury, a victory that proved to be a pivotal result. With that win, Norwich cemented second place behind Queens Park Rangers. They would lose only a single game for the rest of the season – and that to fellow BPL new boys Swansea - to cruise home into the Premier League, and accomplishment punctuated by the Canaries' disemboweling of sorry Scunthorpe in early April. Then, a rare double hat-trick courtesy of Grant Holt and Simeon Jackson pushed Paul Lambert's side to 6–0 win.

Now comes their long awaited return to the top flight, a place the Canaries have flown before. Norwich City were a founding member of the Premier League, a fact that is easy to forget because, um, Norwich crashed and burned into the third division not so long ago. Two promotion campaigns later, and Norwich City's goals can shift from climbing to surviving.

Paul Lambert has a tall order here, though. The Paisley-born manager has never helmed a team in the top-flight and doesn't have a lot to work with. That allowed, Lambert has the experience from his playing days. He was one of the few Scots to labour in the Bundesliga, playing in the nascent Champions League with Borussia Dortmund. He was also a stalwart midfielder with Celtic, so he knows something about pressure. Given Norwich's quick trigger finger with gaffers – they've run through seven in 11 years – he's going to need a cool head.

That would be easier if Lambert could add a couple of thoroughbreds, but although Norwich city have picked up a few guys that can help, this is still a First Division squad trying to punch above their weight. They have some swagger and some movement thanks to Grant Holt and Simeon Jackson up top – but very little else. Now, Steve Morison is an interesting pickup as is James Vaughn: Lambert is clearly looking for some reinforcements up top. That still leaves some softness in the gut.

But don't expect much change on opening day. John Ruddy, a much-travelled keeper (and only 24!) has played almost every game for the Canaries, and unless he falls into a ditch, that will not change. Norwich plays with a sweeper in a 5–3–2 formation with David Fox handling the clean-up in front of Russell Martin, Elliot Ward, Leon Barnett and Adam Drury. Andy Crofts and the one-time Scots youth international compress the center of the field with Wesley Hoolihan up top.

As for goals, Grant Holt has been the team's MVP for the past two seasons. Now paired with Canadian international Simeon Jackson, the two have been lighting it up. Holt had 21 goals last season in league play; Jackson had 13. Jackson seems to have nailed down the starting role over Chris Martin but also is used as a late sub off the bench to provide speed and width.

By the way, American Zak Whitbread is on this team and when he's been healthy, he's been really solid. Unfortunately, he breaks down more often than a Yugo.

But no matter how you look at this squad, the Canaries enter as an immediate candidate to go down. They have some talent – Holt is a baller, no doubt – but these guys are really pretty thin in some key areas and a good Premiership team is going to expose them as slow and tactically naïve. If Norwich can get to December without just being blitzed, they have a chance to stay up. If not, well, it could be a long year.'

What exactly is a baller, and how is Ruddy much travelled – he's had three permanent clubs since turning professional at 17 – and how on earth did he manage to compare Zak Whitbred to a Yugo?

Things get a little more sensible over at Talksport radio who predict us to finish 14th, a place above Newcastle, and then we descend into humour with the Daily Telegraph and Jonathan Liew's 'not-so-serious' club-by-club guide to the new season.

According to Mr Liew Norwich are made of 42 per cent crazy, never-say-die fans, 40 per cent unassuming Scottish pragmatism, 10 per cent spirit of Jeremy Goss and 8 per cent Delia's pasties.

Pasties, bloody pasties, since when has Norfolk been in Cornwall, she makes pies mate. It's Delia's pies, pie of the day, match-day pie and beer. The only thing we have in common with Cornwall is that there are no motorways in either county.

And as for his Norwich related headline of the season: 'If Steve Morison scores a League goal will the last person to leave Britain turn out the lights'.

Blah, blah, blah, blah, blah…

12 August 2011

I had dreamed of being in front of the camera, the lighting and make-up transforming me into a handsome god of the small screen, unfortunately Zoe A'Court and Alastair Florance seem to have other ideas.

The shoot for the ESPN ident has been pencilled in for Thursday 18 August, between 16.00 and 18.00. Not only does it mean a rushed two hour drive up to Nelson's county but also an irate wife who has to collect George from nursery without the benefit of a car. And without a car it means catching not one, but two London buses, and no one in their right mind wants to catch a London bus on their own, but with a buggy and a sprog in tow?

The problem is I haven't told my wife what the short notice trip is for, other than I have to visit Lotus, her assumption is that it's for work, but she still isn't happy even with that idea. Telling her it's a jolly to do some filming for ESPN will probably end in divorce. (The white lie I'd have to tell work is something I can live with and is unlikely to weigh down my conscience.)

But if I do the decent thing and don't go some other bugger will get my slot and I'll forever be the person who was nearly on TV, forever the nearly man – not that such selfish thoughts are going to concern her who must be obeyed. Regret and guilt are two terrible feelings. Not that everyone suffers from guilt in the same way.

Jonny has booked a short summer break for his family. Nothing fancy just a quick trip up to Butlins so his wife and daughter can escape for a few days and recharge the batteries.

Unbeknown to his wife he's booked it to start on 29 August, two days AFTER Norwich play Chelsea in London, some might call him sneaky, some might call him underhand, I want to call him up and ask for advice.

On the plus side his cunningness means I get to go for a beer before the game in the big smog with a mate rather than meandering down to the ground on my tod.

13 August 2011, Wigan 1–1 Norwich

The 214 miles to the DW Stadium was a little off-putting. Four hours in a car even to watch the first football of the season just wasn't bearable, nor realistic considering how much time I spend on the road during the season to go to the home games. But where there is a will there is a way, and given the power of the internet even UEFA's rules banning UK broadcasters from airing 3 o'clock kick-offs (supposedly done to maintain ticket sales and attendances at smaller clubs), can't stop most from watching their teams.

Click on certain websites and every game from every corner of the country is there. Admittedly the Spanish commentary takes a little getting used to, as does the pixelated screen and the juddery picture, but it's all their for you to find.

Even as the morning dawned I was having palpitations. Norwich in the Premiership isn't something that's real yet, and it still won't sink in for some time to come. Although the way some of our defenders reacted to receiving the ball during the game, how easily they lost it through sheer faffing around shows the quality of the opposition has definitely improved – even if it's only Wigan. DeLaet lost the ball and gave away a penalty for the Latic's goal. (Arse).

But a respectable draw means we have a point on the board and sit fifth in the table – carry on like that and we'll be in Europe next season.

But no matter what the pundits say – we're cannon fodder for all the teams bar QPR, (who were hammered four-nil by Bolton in their first game), and Swansea – we're in this League and have scored our first goal thanks to a mistake by Wigan's 'keeper and a fox-like poachers strike by Wes Hoolahan. Eat that Paul Merson, (former Arsenal defender and now television commentator who thinks we won't keep a clean sheet all season), next up Stoke.

Kana included there are going to be a lot of football widows. I like to think I balance my time in the stands with some domestic help for Kana and the boy, and offering to give Kana time to herself to break free and relax. Others are perhaps less fortunate.

Kana's friend was heavily pregnant – a week away from her due date – when her husband flew over to mainland Europe to watch Fulham in the Europa Cup Final. And while perhaps not on the same level, an acquaintance through social networking, Alice Bhandhakravi, BBC London journalist has given up her living room to football and is now considering a fairly long reading list to get through the season.

Social networking is a strange invention, like most of the internet it brings people together from disparate areas. Why would I have a conversation with a BBC journalist unless I'd been collared on a street corner as they were looking for vox-pops.

But no, in this augmented reality, I can talk to that BBC journalist about cooking squid, or becoming a football widow.

Although if Alice wants sympathy she may have come to the wrong place, the 'it's.just.so.boring' reply while causing a wry smile only made me feel a stronger bond with her unknown other half.

I would like to point out at this point that Alice as an arm of the BBC, a national organisation has only 1,575 followers, while I, working for a much less grand organisation muster a very passable 1,220.

The other strange concept in the world of the internet: my voice is (almost) as loud as employees of the BBC who's face is on television most days.

Though my voice may shrink a little as I'm still racked by guilt about this ESPN malarky. I think I have convinced myself to go. I'd be stupid not to, it's an opportunity that won't arise again. My fears remain that my wife will divorce me and my boss will sack me as they both unravel my crude white lies and deceit through omission. But I'll be on the telly.

15 August 2011

Well that's that then. My conscience got the better of me and I cancelled my Thursday trip to Lotus, so I'm no longer going to be the face of Norwich City on ESPN. Disappointed doesn't begin to explain the emotional range I am feeling at this point in time.

Guilt is a completely useless feeling and one that does nothing more then hold you back. Now some random fan from Lotus is going to take my place, and every time I see ESPN I am going to relive the moment I declined Zoe from BDA Creative. Torture would be a kinder fate.

I think in these difficult circumstances I should be reimbursed by Lotus, this opportunity wouldn't have arisen had I not been in contact with BDA, though thinking about it, that logic probably puts me in the same mould as the worthless cretins that sue after breaking a fingernail – always after something for nothing.

I'm going to make myself a cup of tea and shove 100ml of prednisolone up my rectum, maybe it'll make me feel better.

16 August 2011

There is a foreboding that has started to rise from the pit of my stomach. I made the mistake of watching Man City wipe the floor with Swansea last night and it has done nothing for my season nerves. Swansea, to give them credit played some nice football, playing the ball around sweetly, but still let in four goals. Yaya Toure ran through their defence as if it wasn't there, DeSilva made a mockery of their whole team, dancing and dashing all over the place – he may as well have been playing in the park by himself, doing the odd trick to keep himself amused.

It's another hammer in the coffin of the promoted teams after QPR had their breaches pulled down by Bolton on Saturday and their bottoms smacked.

It's Stoke on Sunday and my nerves are in tatters just thinking about it. Not a team filled with superstars, but a team that have managed to stay in the League and bought strong, talented players. It could prove to be our own first tonking of the season.

But for all the fear of being hammered like Ipswich, they lost 9–0 to Man Utd in 1995, I'm excited too. Rooney, Gerrard, Lampard, Torres et al. at Carrow Road plying their trade this season. Many moan about the cost, quality and morals of the modern day game but everyone wants to see the best players, just like you want to see the best actors on the stage or the leading musicians in concert.

Still seething about ESPN. Bastards.

17 August 2011

Manchester United here I come, possibly, maybe, well if the application for tickets is successful. Bankruptcy and divorce may be the key results from this season as Jonny has my membership number and is applying for tickets for Old Trafford for the match at the beginning of October.

It's pricey, £52, hence the bankruptcy, and I haven't told Kana yet, hence the divorce. Going to hold off on the honesty thing until it's a definite. Jonny was of little use, only telling me that it'd be worth it.

It's an aside, but the shower gel I bought is like washing with sand. It's meant to be a mineral massage with Dead Sea salt and aloe vera extract, which will help me discover the ancient secrets of the Dead Sea in my shower. And while it's also meant to provide a gentle scrubbing action to make my skin feel velvety smooth and my body relaxed all it succeeds in doing is make me feel like some git has sold me a dodgy knock-off, and I'm actually lathering up with cement. Bring back the mint and aloe vera variety that makes your gentlemen's bits all tingly.

18 August 2011

It should have been me. I should have been at Lotus today, chatting with the film crew from BDA Creative, beautified by make-up and ready to take my bow as an ESPN star. Instead I'm sat in the office, writing a feature on open source software and the benefits of using it in automotive applications: the joys of being a car journalist.

I'm bitter and won't deny it. Now some grease monkey from Lotus who would have known nothing about ESPN's project will be standing under the lights and looking into the camera. He'll be telling his friends and family how excited he is, how cool it's going to be and for them all to keep an eye on the TV come match day. What an arse. What an underhand, downright rotten git. I'm bloody seething, I'm bloody jealous, I'm bloody... ...bloody.

I'll get my day in the sun though, Zoe A'Court emailed me to apologise and that it was a shame I couldn't make it – damn you conscience, damn you to hell – but she will keep my details for next year's idents. Norwich had better stay up, my fame depends on it.

19 August 2011

I could have a seat booked for the Arsenal game at the Emirates stadium on 5 May. My work colleague and friend Christian is married to a lovely lady called Emma, who works for a PR firm which represents an automotive company with a box at the ground. Needless to say they wondered if anyone supported Norwich.

20 August 2011

It's almost here, one more sleep and it's back to Carrow Road. No more fuzzy internet streams, no more hasty searching of scores on the mobile phone, no more dreaming. And to celebrate I've stolen the work of one CanariesSoccer, a talented chap who uses the not606 discussion board, and has previewed the game verses Stoke in an American style:

Hey Sports Fans! Welcome to The Official CanariesSoccer Match Centre for the ballgame featuring: Potterz @ Canaries
Sunday sees Potterz visit Canaries in *The Barclays® FA™ Prem-eer™ League,* **live from The DeliaDome™.**

Canaries will be going into this matchup following a successful series-opener @ Latics. In that ballgame even overtime couldn't separate the two franchises, with the scores ending at One versus One. Canaries score-attempt was converted by midfield-linesman W. Hoolahan, which was his first Prem-eer-League-senior-squad-conversion.

Coach Lambert: "I was delighted with a lot of things in the game, sometimes we were a bit open [In the de-fense] and we might need to tighten up abit, but the majority of it I'm happy with.

During the off-week, Coach Lambert has boosted his depth-charts with the draft-pick of RedSox defensive-linebacker D. Ayala, who spent some of last series at NPC®Franchise Humberside Tigerz. The draft pick has been well reviewed by CEO D. McNally and the Canaries Fans.

Potterz will be using this matchup to build on their impressive tiegame versus West-London Bluez @ The Britannia™ Building Society Sports SemiBowl®. Since that series-opening-ballgame, Potterz have competed in The Europa International Matchup Series, defeating Swiss Franchise FC Thunder.

Coach Pulis: 'To get a result like that, and a clean sheet as well, is a fantastic achievement, as good, if not better, than the victory in Split a fortnight ago.'

Potterz are well known for their use of a direct style, which see's them move the football large distances from a single play. This approach will give Coach Lambert a chance to set up a strong de-fense and use the short-pass-playbook on the counter-offense, however the Canaries more-lightweight players may struggle to compete against the size of the Potterz linesmen.

This sure is going to be a great Soccer matchup, so fill up your *Coca-Cola*™ tankards, get your hot-dog's and grab a seat for this smash-and-grab matchup, brought to you exclusively on *Not606*!

CanariesSoccer I salute you. I also salute Lee Tomlin, Paul Taylor, Grant McCann and Peterborough United who beat Ipswich Town seven-one today. Yes, **SEVEN-ONE**!

21 August 2011, Norwich 1–1 Stoke

Home at last: the Barclay, upper tier, area EU, row I, seat 120. It's been far, far too long, but it's been worth the wait.

Up bright and early to gain as many brownie points as possible by watching the boy and letting the wife have a lie in. Then it's kisses goodbye and jump in the car.

I like the drive to Norwich. Compared to the hectic rudeness of London the M11 is an oasis. A flick of the radio and there it is, long-wave radio, sports news and debate. A press of the cruise control button and it's a steady 65mph filled with discussions on the latest transfers, match previews and interviews. And just me in the car. Heaven. Peace and quite for two hours.

And as the miles clock up the scenery changes from grey to green, from tall concrete buildings to the vast lines of trees of Thetford. You're almost there when you see the Norfolk sign standing proud, this is Nelson's County. I switch to Radio Norfolk.

I often dream about living in one of the expensive houses on Newmarket Road in Norwich. It's a marked contrast after rolling into the city off the A11 with their manicured lawns, enormous trees and long driveways with luxury cars parked up ready to be given their weekend wash. How easy it'd be to walk to Carrow Road.

But the drive is good, therapeutic.

It's a short walk from the car park at Rose Lane to the pre-match pub. I don't actually know how the Coach and Horses became the pre-match pub, but it is and will remain so until Jonny either keels over or becomes a teetotal, and I know which my money is on.

Jonny likes beer, not lager but beer, real ale to be precise, and none of that mass produced John Smith's malarky. No Jonny seems to have a taste for the micro-brewery. Luckily the Coach and Horses does a good number in CHB – or GBH if you've had one too many and try and order a refill – and business is booming on match days.

It's good for the soul and the in-match vocals, loosens you up, but it does nothing for the bladder. I swear one game I will see the entire 90-plus minutes, but it isn't going to happen while we continue to down CHB.

There was one disappointment in the pre-match build up, no pies. How can Delia not have pies. A beer (at this point you're in the ground which seems to have an adverse affect on Jonny and he drinks lager), and pie for £5 is a must. It's like strawberries and cream at Wimbledon, popcorn at the cinema or jelly at a kids birthday party.

As for the game, we received a taste of our own medicine after all those late goals in the Championship to help us get promoted. Kenwyne Jones in the 94th minute steals a draw for a Stoke team that could have been main characters in Roald Dahl's BFG.

Jonny, Ben and I were bags of nerves, this was the first home game, the first taste of playing in the Premier League. And we passed the test with flying colours, bar one arse of a refereeing decision that saw us down to 10 men and a git load of added time.

But the noise at Carrow Road was immense, every kick, every pass, every whistle was met with a wall of noise from the crowd. I thought the Stoke fans were meant to be loud, but they hardly muttered a word throughout the 90 minutes.

What was surreal was the Stoke fans singing 'I wanna go home, I wanna go home, this place is a shit hole, I wanna go home' at the end of the game. They're from Stoke for godsake, they should be trying to stay in Norwich for as long as possible!

24 August 2011

Someone has got their nickers in a twist, the BBC has been banned from the club. And the club want an apology. Who'd have thought that a local news programme could cause such a stir. But this is Norwich 2011, not the meek and feeble club from years gone by that put its tail between its legs and ran away whining at the first sign of danger.

No, today we have David McNally – or McNasty if your prefer – at the helm, and he doesn't take any crap from anyone or anything.

The *Daily Mirror* tried to pull a fast one with a story about something that wound him up – it must have been trivial as I can't remember for the life of me what all the fuss was about – and he sued.

Before that we tapped up Lambert and received a six-figure fine for our trouble and lest we forget the micro brewery that had the audacity to name a beer after the club, which happened to sell reasonably well. That was swiftly shut down. This time the BBC is feeling our wrath.

Not the BBC as whole, just BBC East, and one programme in particular – *Late Kick Off*. Poor old Dion Dublin, one time city player and now football pundit, he should have kept his mouth shut rather than start talking about Peterborough striker Craig MacKail-Smith and whether we were or weren't interested in signing him.

NcNasty has even gone so far as to issue a club statement:

'*Following recent comments broadcast by BBC East regarding editorial access granted to them by the Club, Norwich City wishes to clarify the matter for the benefit of our supporters.*

Although BBC East have broadcast references to this issue in the last few weeks, they have actually been restricted in their access to the Club since March 14, 2011.

On that evening the BBC regional football programme Late Kick Off broadcast a factually inaccurate story regarding an alleged multi-million pound transfer we were, according to them, about to complete with Peterborough United for their then striker Craig Mackail-Smith.

Not only was the story unhelpful to Norwich City and inaccurate, but at no stage were the Club contacted to seek either verification of the story or to be given the basic courtesy of an opportunity to comment.

The Club has a number of very important relationships with key regional media partners, organisations such as BBC East who have worked with us for decades. We would hope for and expect a positive and constructive relationship with these long-term media partners based on mutual respect and trust – and the fact that we need to work together day-in, day-out.

The handling of this factually incorrect story led to the decision being made to withhold non-contractual access to BBC East and Late Kick Off, until we could discuss the matter with them and obtain from them a satisfactory understanding as to how the story came to be broadcast.

We have held meetings and had conversations with senior representatives of BBC East and Late Kick Off since March to try and resolve this issue so that they can once again enjoy normal editorial access.

They know exactly what they need to do to regain that access. One simple phone call is all that it would take and we very much hope they will make that call as we would prefer for this issue to be resolved.

We wish to stress we continue to have an excellent working relationship with BBC Radio Norfolk as well as national BBC broadcasters such as BBC Radio 5Live, Match of the Day, Football Focus and others.

We would respectfully urge BBC East to take the simple step required to resolve this matter and we sincerely hope they will do so.

In the meantime of course coverage of interviews with Paul Lambert and the City players are available to supporters through Canaries Player and also various independent television broadcasters including SKY and ITV Anglia.'

25 August 2011

England verses Wales, Wembley here we come. Entrance D, block 515, row 21, seats 30 and 31. Now I just have to figure out some very tricky logistics.

For some bizarre reason the wife has booked a medical check-up for the same day as the big match, which means I could well have to rush back from my business trip to pick the boy up from nursery before turning tail and getting back on the train to get to the ground in time for the kick-off – surely Transport for London won't fail me. I could just tell the missus to stop being so selfish, cancel her appointment and let me go to the football straight from the airport. Not sure how long I'd keep my balls attached to the rest of my body if I tried that though. I hope Steve – a friend who's returning to the motherland after two years in Saudi Arabia – has a cunning plan I can steal and call my own, after all one of the tickets is his.

It is strange that on Saturday at Chelsea I'll be shouting and swearing at Frank Lampard, John Terry and Ashley Cole, but on 6 September I'll be cheering them on against the Welsh, conversely Steve Morison and Andrew Crofts will be jeered. Fickle hey?

26 August 2011

The night before the big game. Bring it on.

27 August 2011, Chelsea 3–1 Norwich

F@!&*?s!!!

Silence is golden – Stamford Bridge may as well stay empty during games its equally quiet when full.

28 August 2011

I've had time to ponder yesterday's game, my musings include:

- I won't be spending another £47 to visit Chelsea again.
- Stamford Bridge is like a morgue with fans who don't sing, dance or act like lunatics when the club they supposedly live and breathe score.
- The chap who started the chant 'Just a ground full of tourists' was spot on.
- The chap who randomly shouted out 'Torres, you're a c**t' was quite funny.
- When Holt hooked the ball into the back of the net in the 63rd minute, although I'd travelled to the game by myself, sat on my own in silence waiting for kick-off, at that moment I was among 3,000 friends. I'd only said excuse me to the chap next to me, but when the ball crossed the line, I turned to that same man, we both gurned wildly, eyes wide and though complete strangers we shared a special moment together of utter exhilaration.
- I was strangely happy Didier Drogba was knocked out cold by John Ruddy (I did, however, respectively clap him off).
- Chelsea's manager is an arse.

But at least some respect was earned, even if points weren't. Appreciated the match report on the *Guardian's* website by Paul Doyle, (who's changed his tune about us):

'Norwich, meanwhile, look well equipped to prove wrong those who had them pegged as relegation certainties. After drawing their first two games of the season they were strong and creative at Stamford Bridge. Holt was superb up front and, after a Chelsea defensive blunder, struck a deserved equaliser after Jose Bosingwa has shot the home side ahead. Paul Lambert's team seemed on course for a point, at least, until the late red card and Lampard's successful late penalty and a stoppage time goal from Mata. Holt, the 30-year-old who came late to professionalism but looks at home in the top flight, is in no mood to fall back again.'

I am also starting to worry a little about Jonny. At what point is it wrong for a 31-year-old man to hold a 24-year-old-man in such high regard, to the point that in the middle of House of Frasier you'll shake him by the hand? (Jonny sent me a text saying he'd met John Ruddy in the department store and pressed the flesh, I am sadly only jealous.)

29 August 2011

Thinking that the old colitis might be having a bit of a rock 'n' roll time in my large intestine. Doctors tomorrow for me and perhaps time to go back to squirting liquid up my backside for a couple of weeks. Hey if it works I don't care.

Preferable to the chap in the paper who had a high pressure air hose 'jokingly' pushed up his rectum by work colleagues at a mobile home factory. His backside turned into a balloon. Ouch.

30 August 2011

Colitis is back and I will now begin putting liquid up my back passage, life is a joy.

But while contemplating the deep recesses of my colon sports radio butted in to bring me back to reality.

Loyalty was the topic, someone somewhere is leaving a club after four years having not played for the past two years because of injury. He's leaving and crossing the road to the local rivals. According to the presenter that is the most despicable sign of depravity ever witnessed.

How dare the club spend all that money on getting the player fit again, only for the same club to then decide it no longer wanted him, so he took the best offer available to him during the transfer window. The presenter thought he should have done the decent thing and taken a move to a lesser club as a sign of loyalty and acknowledging how he had been helped.

Thankfully all of the listeners who called-in shot the presenter down in flames, none could give a rats arse where he goes.

It was Owen Hargreaves' possible move from Manchester United to Manchester City incidentally.

31 August 2011

The final day of the transfer window. Fans are going mad to find out who they're team have managed to draft in to fill the gaping holes. News channels are spewing out hot air on every single movement – even managers getting out of their cars is being reported – in the vain hope that something exciting might just happen. It's needless hysteria. And at this point in time I can't be arsed with hysteria, I'm tired, the boy was ill today and I had to look after him. Motherhood is tough, thats why misogynistic men go out to work and leave child rearing to the women. Only spending the odd half day to take complete responsibility and then remark on how easy it was, and it went like clockwork – in reality most men know they couldn't cope with full-time child care.

But through my bloodshot eyes, one thing does sadden me about this last fling into the transfer market: Stephen Hughes has left Norwich.

The midfielder who came on to the pitch during the home League One game against Leeds to run down the right wing and launch the perfect ball into the Leeds penalty area. The ball that Chris Martin stooped down for, to guide beyond their goalkeeper, to send the home crowd into raptures. I'm sorry to see him go, even through the waves of narcolepsy.

1 September 2011

Colitis is definitely playing silly buggers. I was sat on the train into work this morning when the uncontrollable urge to empty my bowels hit. Luckily, although the onboard toilet was supposedly out of order, the door opened. Luckily because if it hadn't my body had decided it was going to relieve itself whether there was a toilet available or not.

Unluckily the toilet door really shouldn't have opened because that toilet was full to the brim with someone else's bodily waste, (why can't public conveniences ever be clean?), but it did save embarrassment.

I don't think you can ever explain to anyone what colitis is like, how it affects your life, the embarrassment and frustration it causes and underlying knowledge that it's chronic and will therefore never disappear. I don't think my family fully appreciate it, no matter how much they try. Hey ho...

2 September 2011

Club or country? The question that most even remotely interested in football ask themselves at least once. For my part I'm as disillusioned with the national team as I am with politics, society and the continuing shrinkage of my childhood sweets – Wagon Wheels use to be so much bigger – but England actually won tonight in Sofia, 0–3.

So now my enthusiasm for Tuesday is growing, although I'm slightly split as Wales will have two Norwich players in their squad.

A trip to Wembley is always a wonder, the home of English football, filled with 'grockles' as my dear old Norfolk mum would say, but you can't have a game of football without an away team.

My mum uses the term in a slightly different manner, more a long the lines of 'We had a day and went to Wells for a picnic. It was great but too many grockles around!'

Well there'll be 8,000 grockles* in town on Tuesday.

*Grockles is a slang term used in the south-west of England meaning tourists according to the internet.

3 September 2011

Social media are a pain for some and a whimsy for others, but you can't beat a bit of light hearted humour to help you through the day, especially when there's an international break so no football to go to. Dan30stm and NittyNattyNora please step forward, their Twitter conversation was as follows:

@Dan30stm if u do a whitbread it means you've 'pulled' (a muscle)
@NittyNattyNora "I'm going for a holty against Ipswich" could mean I'm looking for a threesome
@Dan30stm a girl with saggy boobs a 'wigan' (little support)
@NittyNattyNora amazing. If you pull 2 nights on the trot it's called a lambert (back 2 back promotions)
@Dan30stm If u do a delia u just get drunk and make a fool of yourself...
@NittyNattyNora good call. If you pull on your home you could call it a 10/11 season special or a 90 minute winner
@Dan30stm if you're onto a banker and fcuk it up it's known as a fulham '05!

@NittyNattyNora and If you look like you've lost it with a girl and then pull it back with something you say it's a Hoolahan
@Dan30stm and If it's a ruck with your own mates it's a hughes!
@NittyNattyNora you refer to your pants as you r.martins
@Dan30stm if u end up rucking you've done a Martin!!

You can forgive the use of poor English when you only have 140 characters to type your thoughts. Thoughts can be far greater, wider and all encompassing than 140 characters.

5 September 2011

The most random of nights and the most random of conversations. I'm not going to shy away from the fact that if you work as an automotive journalist you tend to be treated quite well on business trips. Business trips being new car launches, generally in foreign climes and generally conducted at luxurious hotels. The flights that get you to the events aren't too shabby either, if it isn't business class then its a charter flight from the likes of Farnborough airport. A dozen journalists or so all travelling well beyond their means thanks to the lavishness of a car manufacturer launching its latest product.

It was Peugeot's turn this time, a diesel hybrid, which will mean nothing to most people, but is quite unique as I write this.

Peugeot brought us all to Brittany, paired us up with another journalist co-driver, handed us some keys and sent us on our merry way to drive a predetermined route so we could see the benefits of its new four-wheeled stallion.

The thing with launches is that being paired up with another journalist means that you have to find some common ground, otherwise the two hours in the car would be painfully quiet. I tend to fall back on either monotonous car-related chatter, fatherhood and marriage or if at all possible football.

Luckily my fellow hack on the Peugeot diesel hybrid launch had a passing interest in the beautiful game – though his real passion was rugby – which made things easier. He also lived in Lincolnshire and once tried to visit Norwich for the day. Though failed miserably as the day in question the good lord decided to dump mountains of snow on the fenlands. Inane conversation filled the car's cabin.

But that isn't random, what was random was the evening's entertainment. After being ferried across the harbour to what can only be described as a surfer's beach house, music was provided. Traditional Brittany music I think not. A drum, a snake charmers trumpet, an accordion and a set of bagpipes, and the Frenchman on the bagpipes wore a kilt and a sporran.

He also forced everyone to stand up and dance – automotive journalists tend to be of the male variety – by holding hands and moving in a circle. He failed. Miserably.

It was more-or-less a dozen Englishmen stood in a circle, looking awkward holding hands uncomfortably.

But what did come of it was a conversation with a Coventry fan. A Peugeot press relations officer who'd only been in the job for 10 weeks, and was one of the uncomfortable dozen.

He knew Darren Huckerby, Dion Dublin and Cody MacDonald – who we sold to them for £400,000 after buying him for only £25,000.

He took his seven-year-old son to games, as his dad had done with him. Now three generations of his family went to watch the Skyblues together. How wonderful would that be?

My aim now is to convince little George that Norwich is the way forward, and that when he has a son, he too should support the green and yellows. How great would that be? I'll have to convince Jonny and Ben to do the same with their kids.

6 September 2011, England 1–0 Wales

Walk out of Wembley Park station and there it is, the arch. I know it cost £900 million, I know it was three years late and I know it almost bankrupted the construction company, but Wembley stadium is an impressive sight. It's just a shame the national football team is a little less impressive.

Hart, Smalling, Terry, Cahill, Cole, Milner, Lampard, Barry, Downing, Young, Rooney, there might have well have been eleven of me on the pitch for all the joy the game brought. Wales, ranked 117th in the world and England, ranked fourth could only muster a turgid 1–0.

Bloody shame. Steve was back from Saudi, I'd rushed back from my business trip, donned my England shirt and green and yellow trainers in patriotic fashion, and headed back into town.

Flatter to deceive – England verses Wales was a damp squib.

It was how things should be, talking rubbish about Steve's time in the middle east, parenthood and the fairer sex. A sneaky pint in the St Stephens Tavern in Westminster – Fursty Ferret 4.4ABV – and some much needed sustenance.

A speedy trip up the Jubilee Line and then that view from Wembley Park station.

The walk around the ground, taking a snap or two, nattering about past games, up the endless escalators into the rafters of the stadium, catching a glimpse of the bowl, and then finally climbing the steps out into the vastness. Everyone of the 90,000 seats adding to the gobsmacking view. But not the football on the pitch.

I ended up more interested in how Morison and Crofts were doing than any one of the English players.

I needed a joke to bring back some sort of enjoyment, luckily Steve had one which was at least a little amusing:

Q: 'What does a man with a 10in cock have for breakfast?'
A: 'Well this morning I had bacon, eggs...'

Slightly better than my blond joke attempt:

Q: 'What does a blond do after sucking cock?'
A: 'Spit out the feathers.'

Here's to a return to Carrow Road on Sunday, a passionate crowd, players that care, West Bromwich Albion and apparently beef and Woodfords ale pie.

7 September 2011

Jonny's a little toe rag isn't he. There was no signal in Wembley so my mobile phone was useless. But just before we got into the ground I sent the little bugger a picture of what he was missing.

When my phone catches up with itself I received a reply:

'Your (sic) correct about one thing. Your (sic) getting a divorce. You 'on your own, on your own, on your own.'

Of course I replied, 'With a mate, with a mate, with a mate,' I have friends outside of the Norfolk group. To which the sarcastic little giblet said:

'Is that the one who comes on the train to every home game. I also had an invisible friend once...'

I'm going to clip him round the ear when I see him at the weekend, then probably have a drink and give him a hug too. Time for a posterior squirt of prednisolone.

8 September 2011

Charity football, England verses Wales, ex-pros and TV personalities raising money for cancer research, that's what football is about, not sets of fans beating one another senseless. A Wales fan died at the football on Tuesday night. It's only a game people.

9 September 2011

M*@!$& f&@!kers, received a text from Jonny at lunchtime, failed in our bid for Man United tickets.

But on the plus side, M11, A11 65mph, 137 miles, two hours 45 minutes and it's back in Norfolk for the weekend. George and Kana slept in the back which left me to my own thoughts. A meal with the good lady on Saturday lunchtime, dinner with the parents in the evening and then a quick dash up to Cromer for some joviality with the boys during the night. It's true that 48 hours isn't long to spend back in the motherland, especially when there is so much to fit in but it's worth it, every second. I'm also collecting a box full of match day programmes and some City books that my granddad doesn't want anymore.

10 September 2011

I feel sick, sick to the pit of my stomach. I don't think I've ever retched so quickly after watching only 57 seconds of a video. It's a good job I was sitting next to an open window where the fresh Cromer breeze from the North Sea quickly cleared my head. And it'd all started so well too.

It's tough being a family in the big smog where the closest relatives are over one hundred miles away, all the responsibility rests squarely on Kana and my shoulders, meaning there's no break, no chance to pack George off to his grandparents and just relax, go out and have some food and remember what it's like to be a married couple.

But after the long drive up yesterday, Kana and I had left the boy with his grandparents and had a delightful meal in the Rushcutters, a pub on the banks of the Norfolk broads which serves the most delightful traditional food. Not to be too depressingly dull, but Kana had fish and chips and I had a wild boar burger. We even had chance to have a conversation – what job I should do that would a) pay enough money to support the family b) be something I'd enjoy doing and c) fit in with my dodgy guts and a constant need to empty the bowels, (teaching it seems is the answer).

It was then a quick hop back to the folks home for some dinner, though Kana drove so it was more of a death defying terror trip where I sweated like a man on death row waiting for his lethal injection, clutching onto the hand rail for dear life.

Kana, meanwhile seemingly confident, or blissfully unaware, doesn't do roundabouts (there aren't any in her native Japan), and doesn't really do wing mirrors (though these are freely available in Japan), so was neither nervous nor terrified.

Dinner was simple, dry chops, a seemingly speciality of the folks and one that the whole family looks forward to, but it did give further time to the debate on life, the universe and everything. Specifically on how tough things are for young families.

I can't help but feel slightly guilty about the lack of time I spend in each place when we head back to Norfolk as a family, but if you go back you want to do everything. See the family, have some couple time and see friends, and seeing friends is a definite stress release.

If you've known someone for well over 15 years there are no false pleasantries, no pussy footing around certain topics, no awkward silences and no need to try and think up safe topics of conversation. You just get on with the job of being friends.

Firestarter – We become no more mature and still enjoy mixing fire and deodorant.

There is a downside – but only to those looking in – that all pretence of manners and decorum are forgotten and anything goes.

Conversations with Jonny, Twon, Button and Cruso, whether drunk or sober, tend to focus on two key areas: poo and sex.

I'm not sure if it's a male personality quirk or just the group's dynamic, but it takes only minutes for one of the two topics to be broached and from then on it really never abates. Unfortunately both topics mixed to cause outrage this evening.

It started well enough, though I was fashionably late. The beach beckoned, the sea's breeze and bit of star gazing.

Jonny and Button argued about what caused the northern lights, Twon put his two cents worth in and Cruso and I stood there and nodded every now and again. No one ended up in the sea willingly or otherwise, which was good because the North Sea isn't very warm in the height of summer let alone September.

But the lack of practical jokes or stupid incidents didn't last, Button has a set of kendo practice swords, and after a few beers, like every time we all get together, stupidity prevailed and we started getting hurt (apart from Cruso who somehow manages to keep away from being battered and bruised every time).

I blame Twon. Actually no, I blame Jonny. Jonny's the one who always starts the pain infliction, eggs people on and more importantly brings psycho Twon into the fray, somehow winding him up.

Who's stupid idea was it to smack one another on the shins with the kendo swords because 'it won't hurt that much and will be fun'. I'll tell you whose, Jonny's! But for some reason Twon then said he liked it.

Twon got smacked, Button got smacked, I got smacked, Jonny got smacked. Twon got smacked again, Button had a rush of testosterone and asked to be smacked. Jonny the little wind up merchant sneakily cracked Twon without permission, Twon tried to retaliate, Jonny ran way.

It doesn't seem to matter where we are at some point during the evening, whether it's a slap in the face or a punch in the leg, someone ends up getting hurt. But when the dust settles we start hugging and singing.

Tonight included many Queen songs, kicked off with *Bohemian Rhapsody*, *Fat Bottomed Girls* and *Flash*. Followed by a little play-time with matches, deodorant and glue to make pretty shapes on the tiled floor. Being 30 years old doesn't make men anymore mature than a spotty teenager.

And as the evening was spent at Button's flat with access to satellite television we also included watching live telephone sex programming, with the volume turned down making up what the girls were saying. This unfortunately lead to the evening's big finale, all 57 seconds of it. The infamous *Two girls one cup* porn film, which involves sexual use of faeces and vomit. Jonny, Cruso and I hadn't seen it, Twon and Button had. Jonny wanted to know what all the fuss was about. Curiosity thy name is Satan, we unfortunately now know what all the fuss is about.

11 September 2011, Norwich 0–1 West Bromwich Albion

Swine-cock-arse-bilge-pumps, why are referee's such short sighted git merchants? And my shin and fingers are bruised to buggery thanks to the ancient art of Kendo.

12 September 2011

The fallout from two girls one cup continues. Text from Jonny: 'You loved it. I don't think I will eat a Mr Whip ever again. I can stomach most things but that was wrong.'

Cruso wasn't far behind: 'It was sick, just started to forget until you just brought it up, LOL, I think you enjoyed it.'

Admittedly I did send a text out first: 'Nearly 48 hours later and I can't even look at a Mr Whippy ice-cream.'

I am still having flashbacks.

13 September 2011

Hello Frankfurt motor show. Hello sausages. Hello cars. Hello pretty ladies. Hello…

14 September 2011

Tired. Shower, brush teeth, bed. The Frankfurt motor show has absolutely broken me. I have blisters on parts of my foot I didn't know contacted the floor. It was good, and for all the miles that you walk and the number of interviews you have to conduct with big cheeses it isn't a bad way to earn a dime.

After the grief I got from Jonny, Twon, Button and Cruso I did have a brief moment when I almost had the courage to walk up to one of the models lying over a flash car and ask to have a photograph taken with me, just so I could text it to the boys as a big two fingers up. Didn't quite make it, so made do with a long distance shot. One day though, those six foot models will be stood either side of me.

15 September 2011

Random letter from the club and ray of hope on the old Man United. I may have missed out on the first ballet but should there be any returns I could be in luck. I do have to contact the club as they have the wrong email address: james_scottock@yahoo.co.uk – close but no cigar.

I've had far worse, most just go for a rearrangement of the L and T, Scotlock, the worst by far was Smallcock – not good for a gentleman's ego.

16 September 2011

There are some real plonkers in football, more dodgy quotes than you can shake a stick at in Private Eye's *Colemanballs* book published in 1982. A gift from grandad. Are people involved in football really this dim:

'After a goalless first half, the score at half-time is 0–0.' – Brian Moore

'It's been an amazing year for Crystal Palace over the last 12 months.' – Brian Moore

'With the very last kick of the game, Bobby McDonald scored with a header.' – Alan Parry

'If we can stop hooliganism, we can go a long way towards stemming this great tide of people not going to football matches.' – Brian Clough

'He's got three goals in four games – you can't get better than that.' – Stuart Hall

And my favourite:

'Norwich's goal was scored by Kevin Bond, who is the son of his father.' – Frank Bough

17 September 2011, Bolton Wanders 1–2 Norwich

A win by gods, a win. Apparently the first away win in the top flight since Crystal Palace in 1994. That's a long wait, but thank you Anthony Pilkington and Bradley Johnson. Hope *Match of the Day* gives us some praise.

And I want to find out if Hugh Jackman, Hollywood actor, is really a Norwich fan. The internet seems to think he is but I'm not so sure.

He was on a television chat show this evening with Stephen Fry – a director at the club no less – yet nothing was mentioned of the club, not even surreptitiously, leaving me cynical. I've sent a message to @RealHughJackman on Twitter:

'@RealHughJackman the word is that you have a link to @NorwichCityFC is it true, I'm cynical?'

I'm awaiting an answer.

18 September 2011

No word from Hugh Jackman, can only assume he's ducking the question to negate a media storm. But I will give him some more time to respond and perhaps search for his agent contact details, just in case his schedule is so busy that he was unable to access Twitter.

19 September 2011

Hugh doesn't seem very talkative. No matter while I was searching for a better form of correspondence I ended up daydreaming about refereeing.

It's not something that many people would do I would imagine, but it kept my mind occupied for a good 10 minutes or so.

Refereeing is a damned if you do, damned if you don't profession. One of the teams will have a gripe with a decision you make in the heat of the game. The referee against West Brom the other week most certainly did, and I was one of the masses screaming my vitriol, (how did he miss the elbow on Vaughn???). But I do wonder how I'd approach refereeing.

I'd definitely have to have a quiet word with both managers and team captains before the game, set them straight and point out my guidelines for the afternoon.

There'd be none of this first name nonsense, everything would be done with surnames. I'd only respond to Mr Scoltock, I'd call managers by their surnames too – Mr Lambert, though I guess Sir might crop up every now and again for some – I'd only refer to players by their family names, and should anyone want to question my decisions on the pitch they'd have to do it through the captain.

And should someone need a quiet word, I wouldn't allow everyone on the team to surround me, it'd be the player and the team captain if they needed someone by their side. And the final rule would be no swearing. Swear at me and you go in the book. Swear at me again and you go to the dressing room for an early shower. What could possibly go wrong, it'd be perfect, order restored to the game.

20 September 2011

Some bloke called Paul Moon is causing ire among Norwich fans. He's had the audacity to criticise Grant Holt. I'm not sure how he can make an informed opinion considering he lives in Australia and his main loves are racing, cricket and rugby, but an opinion he does have and it's been published on the Betfair website:

'Misguided loyalty to Grant Holt could cost Norwich City

He's strong, determined and committed but Paul Moon doesn't think Norwich skipper Grant Holt can cut the mustard at this level. Heres' why....

It is more than likely that Norwich will struggle to stay in the Premier League this season and one of the reasons could be a misplaced loyalty towards striker Grant Holt.

Holt is an old fashioned centre-forward and one of a dying breed. Previously his style would have been more appreciated in the top league but the game has changed considerably over the past few years. Fluidity, movement and intelligence have noticeably replaced the blunt instrument, physicality and honest endeavour.

In 2011 even better centre forwards in that mould like Joe Royle, John Toshack and Duncan Ferguson would struggle to adjust to the modern game. A more recent example is Emile Heskey (nine goals in 68 games for Aston Villa and seven goals in 62 games for England) who's direct and unsubtle approach has pleased his managers and frustrated fans in equal measure. Andy Carroll and Kevin Davies cannot be described in the same category as both display a range of mobility, movement and skill over and above the aforementioned duo of Holt and Heskey.

To Holt's credit he has been the talisman, team captain and focal point of the Canaries' attack for the past two seasons and in reward, received the Norwich's player of the season for both of them. In the short time he has been with them he has served the club well scoring an impressive 53 goals in 92 appearances in the Championship and Division One. It would be churlish to undermine those goals solely because they weren't scored at the highest level and his strike rate represents a legitimate return, where he has played a major part in getting Norwich to the Premier League. In doing so he has made a real connection with the fans and currently receives their appreciation and adoration.

But now Holt is out of his depth in the Premier League. He is heavy set, lacks pace and the chances of him scoring regularly from open play are remote. He will work hard and put in a shift, he will be awkward and unpleasant to play against but more importantly, he will not frighten or hurt defences. Some players find their level and his is the Championship. It's not an insult to him but he is a typical lower league player who has made the most out of what his maker has given him.

So, to jettison the target man from the starting eleven would cause some disquiet but that is the task facing manager Paul Lambert if he wants to improve the side. There can be no cutting edge for his team with a player of his type as the focal point of their attack.

Lambert is intelligent and fiercely ambitious (he played successfully at Borussia Dortmund while taking UEFA coaching courses in Germany) yet displays inclusiveness and a sometimes excessive sense of loyalty to his players. He surely realises the shortcomings of Holt and the plan could be to phase him out, thus quelling any backlash from supporters should future results disappoint. The decision has a political look about it and it will be interesting to see if he has the courage to make the call early enough.

It was interesting to see Lambert dropping Holt last weekend after playing every game so far and by doing so, they gained their first win in the Premier League. He took that opportunity to praise his replacement Steve Morison and it was worthy of note that Norwich made four bids before securing his services from Millwall for £2.8m. The manager clearly sees something in the player and first indications show he could be the man to take over the primary goalscoring duties.'

Maybe I'll start commenting on water polo, equestrianism and beach volleyball.

21 September 2011

Marvellous manager quote by Mick McCarthy of Wolves: 'Opinions are like backsides. We've all got them but it is not always wise to air them in public.'

Which will make Darren Huckerby's biography pretty interesting, what little gems will be in there about past managers, players and board members – can't wait.

One thing I didn't get in the preamble on the pre-order website was this, it says: 'He is almost certainly unique in having scored goals in every fully professional competition in which an English football club can participate.'

Almost certainly? Does that mean they're not sure, there might be someone else to have done it? Can't they say with clarity that he is unique in scoring in every professional competition?

And the pre-order also throws up a conundrum, you can select your own personal message that Hucks will write on the inside covers. Have to decide what that message will be by 5 October when pre-orders open.

As Hucks replied to my Twitter message £18.99, his life for under £20.

22 September 2011

It's the friendly Cup on Monday, Norwich versus Sunderland, which I won't be attending (damn you all to hell satellite television), but is a wonderful advert for the true spirit of the game.

I doubt many people will ever have heard of the friendly cup, but for the uninitiated there was a wonderful piece on the Rocker Report website. Michael Graham I doff my cap to you sir:

'The Magic Of The Cup - The Friendly Cup

On Monday night at Carrow Road the battle for The Friendly Cup resumes. It is never going to make headlines or spark an open top bus parade through the deliriously happy streets of Wearside or East Anglia, but it is nevertheless worthy of acknowledgement and just a smidgen of pride.

For those who are unaware, Norwich City and Sunderland have competed for the Friendship Trophy since the Milk Cup (League Cup) Final of 1985. The game was dubbed 'the friendly final' due to the warmth and sporting spirit displayed by both sets of fans towards each other. Following the final, won by Norwich thanks to a Gordon Chisholm own goal, supporters in East Anglia launched the Friendship Cup to commemorate the occasion. The trophy has since been contested every season during which the clubs have met, with the spoils going to whichever side gains more points from the two league meetings or whoever wins a cup encounter played when the clubs do not share a division. Therefore, Sunderland will go into this season's encounters in possession of the Friendship Trophy having retained it in an Andy Reid inspired 4–1 League Cup win at Carrow Road in 2009.

Many younger fans at this point may well be wondering what the big fuss was all about. Well-humoured joviality between supporters has become common-place in the modern game, and the advent of the technological age has seen friendly banter between fans a daily occurrence through message boards and social media.

But the football climate in 1985 was very different indeed. At this time, football was probably at its all-time low. It was a game blighted with hooliganism as hot-headed unsavoury characters used the inherent tribalism of our national game to satisfy their own sinister agendas. Amidst a torrent of lurid press reports of crowd violence, match attendance had fallen to the point where perhaps fewer spectators braved the games than ever before. A mere 11 days before Norwich and Sunderland took to the field at Wembley in front of a reported 100,000 crowd, large scale rioting had taken place in a cup tie at Kenilworth Road between Millwall and Luton prompting Margaret Thatcher to set up a "war cabinet" to combat football hooliganism. A mere two months following the final, 39 Italian supporters would lose their lives in the Hysen Stadium disaster when a wall collapsed as a group of Liverpool fans charged their Juventus counterparts. It was an incident which saw all English clubs banned from European competition and the most shameful thing about it was that it surprised no one.

But whilst football was fighting what looked like being a losing battle against the hooligans, Sunderland and Norwich fans steadfastly refused to be dragged down into that world and were there to not only enjoy the occasion, but to create one. Merriment reigned as fans of opposing teams mixed seamlessly before the game, all interested in nothing but the game itself, supporting their team, and representing their club with dignity and class. When southern based 'casuals', the unofficial term for the various hooligan hoards attaching themselves to different clubs, tried to infiltrate the atmosphere looking for a fight, they found no one willing to reciprocate. One Norwich fan recalls, "the jovial atmosphere was severely punctured by an unwelcome invasion of so-called Chelsea fans wielding knives and threatening City and Sunderland fans alike".

The atmosphere would not be punctured for long, however, as behind the Wembley fences – the anti-hooligan weapon of choice for Thatcher's government – pockets of fans were happily accommodated in areas allocated to the opposing club. Fans sang loudly and proudly from the minute the pre-game formalities started on the pitch and carried on until stadium-wide applause broke out when Dave Watson lifted the trophy. Norwich manager Ken Brown would later say:

'Following the game and after approaching each other to offer both condolences and congratulations, fans exchanged club scarves and merchandise as a souvenir of the day. On the London Underground system as supporters began their journeys home, a Norwich chant of "we won the cup" was met with a Sunderland one of "we scored the goal".

In the cut-throat and greedy world of modern football, that there is still room for traditions such as the Friendship Cup is heartwarming. The winner shall receive no prestige, no prize money, no tacky streamer-laden ceremony covered in the logos of corporate sponsors. But the contest shall serve as a reminder of a day when, in times that attending football was potentially literally cut-throat, two sets of fans chose to respect each other and embrace everything good about the game whilst rejecting the bad. In that sense alone, it is a tradition and a competition that celebrates the essence of football in a far greater and more tangible way than the more prestigious competitions could ever hope to, and one that both sets of fans can feel genuinely proud to see their clubs contest.'

I must admit if it hadn't been for a random internet search in the hope of reading a preview of the game I wouldn't have even know about it.

23 September 2011

Using social media to find out what your friends think of you isn't a good idea. I naively and innocently put a question on my Facebook status: Leave me a one word comment that best describes me, using the third letter of your first name. It can only be ONE word.

I'm an idiot. Twon went with Twat, Button went with c***, Jonny went with nob and Cruso thought cock was appropriate. Won't be doing that again.

24 September 2011

Text from Jonny: 'We have been successful for Liverpool'.

I'd completely forgotten we were putting our names into the hat for the game so that was a nice surprise. Anfield here we come, another ground to cross off the list.

Given up with the duplicity with Kana about going to games, so when I found out I just told her straight. I've got balls, I wear the trousers in this house, who's the daddy.

Just have to decide on how to get up there, car, coach or train. Everyone else will be leaving on club canary coach from Carrow Road at 9.30am on match day, living in London I won't be doing that.

25 September 2011

Footballers really are dim, and not always in a way that means they say completely the wrong thing during commentaries. Another ex-City player, though he only had the briefest of stints, John Hartson, has put his foot in his mouth.

When will people realise that Twitter is viewed by the public, anything you say on there is accessible to the world, meaning if you have a lot of followers and are relatively well known you have to be careful about what you say.

Hartson, however innocently, saying 'Nearly home after long drive! Pick up a chinky I think, up early tomorrow taking my son to football!! Swansea under 9s', is going to cause a stir.

It's that word to describe a Chinese restaurant. You can't use it. It's like continuing to say Wog, Nip, Paki, Gypo or Honky, and the hundreds of other derogatory terms in the English language.

People have to realize that saying anything on twitter is like standing on a soap box in the middle of a town square, and I doubt, had Hartson been standing in public view, he would have said the same thing.

26 September 2011, Norwich 2–1 Sunderland

The 'not winning when on television' monkey is well and truly off our back, as is the 'conceded a penalty in every game so far this season' and finally so is the 'when I watch Norwich play on television we lose.'

We've even been compared to Barcelona in the *Telegraph* by Henry Winter:

'On the half-hour, Norwich broke through and what a goal it was, a goal more suited to Nou Camp than Norfolk. Bennett began the move, racing down the right, allowed far too much room by Seb Larsson, who failed to track back. Bennett exchanged passes with David Fox before crossing low for Barnett to tap in. Barnett had been given the freedom of the six-yard box by Titus Bramble.'

Marvellous, truly marvellous. If only I could have been there, but there'll be plenty more chances and it did give the chance for one of Jonny's acquaintances – who is apparently a huge Norwich fan – the chance to go, and it was their birthday so I can feel selfless.

27 September 2011

It's official Hugh Jackman, Hollywood actor is a Norwich fan. He will no longer just be Wolverine from the big-budget X-Men movies, but Wolverine, Norwich supporter.

How do we know? Through the power of Twitter and I'd like to think I had a small part to play in his tweet:

'@RealHughJackman congratulations norwich city…first home win of this EPL season…many more to come!'

It has got the yellow army debating, conversing and nattering. His mother apparently lives in Norfolk and his favourite pub is Kings, in Norwich city centre – though I find that hard to believe.

28 September 2011

I've no idea if this is true, but if it is, it shows that English/British football isn't completely bereft of talent. A chap who goes by the Twitter name of Festivalbuddy said that when Norwich beat Bolton we had 11 British players on the pitch and its the first time that's happened in five years in the Premier League. I guess it could be true:

John Ruddy – English
Russell Martin – English (but he plays for Scotland)
Leon Barnett – English
Marc Tierney – English
Kyle Naughton – English
Bradley Johnson – English
Anthony Pilkington – English
(James Vaughan – English)
Wes Hoolahan – Irish
(Andrew Crofts – Welsh)
David Fox - English
Elliott Bennett – English
Steve Morison – Welsh
(Grant Holt – English)

After Crofts came on for Hoolahan the team was completely British. I guess in this highly globalised world that shouldn't really matter, but in a strange kind of way that makes it easier for fans to relate to the players. And I guess for the players it makes it easier for them to communicate, bond and succeed on the pitch.

Manchester City are splashing the cash trying to win every title and Cup – £200 million on transfers and £100 million on wages thus far – bringing in footballers from all over the world. And maybe they'll succeed but the dynamic of so many nationalities, including the manager, must make it tough for the team to gel, and the egos at the training ground must clash at every turn.

Yesterday Man City played Bayern Munich in the Champions League, (they lost two-nil, maintaining Norwich's record as the only English team to beat Munich in Germany), and the post match talk was all about player antics rather than the game.

Want-away striker Carlos Tevez refused to come on as a substitute, Edin Dzeko, another striker, sarcastically clapped the manager as he was brought off the pitch after 55 minutes.

Maybe it isn't anything to do with multi-national teams and communication and just the money and the egotists it attracts – Tevez is on a reported £250,000-a-week – but I could never see that happening at Norwich.

Modern football is all about big name players which is why Norwich are belittled and disparaged at every turn by commentators, the squad was put together for £?? million, and has been created from players with little or no Premier League experience. The same squad that played Bolton, while mostly British, is also mostly lower League, prior to Norwich the men in yellowed played for a mishmash of teams:

John Ruddy – Everton
Russell Martin – Peterborough
Leon Barnett – West Bromwich Albion
Marc Tierney – Colchester
Kyle Naughton – Tottenham Hotspur
Bradley Johnson – Leeds
Anthony Pilkington – Huddersfield
(James Vaughan – Everton)
Wes Hoolahan – Blackpool
(Andrew Crofts – Brighton)
David Fox - Colchester
Elliott Bennett – Brighton
Steve Morison – Millwall
(Grant Holt – Shrewsbury)

Perhaps not superstars but I know who I'd rather spend my hard earned cash on to watch. And while perhaps not quite in the same vein as Man City, come Saturday these lower League players will be pitting their wits against the superstars of Manchester United.

29 September 2011

Mark Lawrenson, BBC pundit and Liverpool football player many moons ago doesn't seem to be a member of the Norwich City fan club: 'Not that I expect them

(Manchester United) to have a problem on Saturday against the Canaries, where I anticipate a comfortable home win.'

So comfortable he predicts 3–0, still, better than fellow pundit Robbie Savage who thinks it'll be 4–0. We'll see…

30 September 2011

Twitter is remaining a wonder, and the song sung at the final game of last season rings true:

'We're here, we're there, we're every fuckin' where. We're Norwich fans, we're Norwich fans.'

While Hugh Jackman maybe one of the more high profile Norwich fans, there are plenty more out there.

The president of the Automobile Association is a Canary, and he tweeted me – being on twitter is all part of what a good journalist does nowadays it seems. Edmund King, the man who gives an inside view on motoring, politics and the media from the helm of the 'forth emergency service' has got to miss tomorrow's game against United, even though he had two tickets, something to do with his son playing football. Edmund, you may be the president of a well respected company, but you're an idiot. How many people, including myself, would give limbs to be at that game?

But he did raise a good point. Man United fans have taken to wearing green and yellow scarves, though they'll all swear they're green and gold, to make a stand against the current American owners running of the club.

But with Norwich rolling into town there will be choruses of 'We've come to get our scarves, we've come to get our scarves…'

It might also be followed by 'Dave De Gea is a thief, is a thief, is a thief. Dave De Gea is a thief, he nicks doughnuts!'

United's new Spanish goalkeeper was caught stealing a doughnut from a Tesco's the other day. But apparently it's OK, it was just a cultural misunderstanding according to their manager Sir Alex Ferguson: 'He's young and doesn't know the culture of our country.'

Of course, Britain is different from all those other countries in the world where stealing things is perfectly legal.

1 October 2011, Manchester United 2–0 Norwich

Why would I want to visit Sainsbury's at three o'clock on a Saturday afternoon? I'd resigned myself to not having a ticket to today's game long ago, but missing it completely because of a weekly grocery shopping trip.

This is why football loving people need to have a heart of gold and the patience of a saint if they marry non-football loving people.

Kana definitely fits into the non-football loving category. She doesn't see what all the fuss is about and wouldn't care if the sport fell apart at the seams and disappeared from the face of the Earth.

I managed to grab five minutes of viewing pleasure before being herded out of the house – enough to see a Norwich side devoid of nerves and playing some really positive football – a deft one-two between Hoolahan and Bennett sent the winger free into the United box, and only bad decision-making denied Morison the simplest of tap-ins. Another five minutes of radio listening on the way to the supermarket and Hoolahan had a chance to lob the 'keeper – but that was to be my lot – and I'd also like to note that I received two clips round the ear for my troubles.

Kana knew that I would have rather stayed at home, but she politely asked about the game and I told her that I would have been there if it hadn't been for the blasted ticket ballot. Clip one.

I then told her that it wasn't a huge disappointment because I'd been successful in the Liverpool ballot, so would be heading to Anfield on the 22 October. Clip two.

Broccoli, carrots, fish and pork mince aren't my main concerns, on Saturday I only care about one thing and it isn't what we're going to eat for dinner next Thursday.

Still with a smartphone, twitter and a sports news website you're never far away from the latest score. And we'd given as good as we got for over 60 minutes, Pilkington had even had a golden opportunity to put us ahead going one-on-one with the goalkeeper.

But while constantly checking the scores as you pass the vegetable, dairy, biscuit and bread aisles keeps you up to date, it isn't the same. So it was down to *Match of the Day* on the BBC to fill in the holes.

And by god did we look good – I know we lost 2–0 but that wasn't half the story. We defended resolutely. We bossed the midfield and looked full of vim and vigour. And up front we could have nicked two or three goals of our own – and probably would have if Holt had been playing and had lady luck been with us.

Even the pundits praised us. In the post-match analysis there was no mention of United's goals, only how well we played. Not too bad for 'little old Norwich'.

2 October 2011

Fulham 6–0 QPR. I would laugh but I know how that scoreline feels, we needed a win to stay in the Premier League on 16 May 2005, and instead of playing for our lives we capitulated. Brian McBride (twice), Pape Bouba Diop, Zat Knight, Steed Malbranque and Andy Cole all made for a miserable last game of the season at Craven Cottage. (I didn't laugh out loud, but QPR do deserve a little snigger).

3 October 2011

Just realised it's only two days until Huckerby's book is available to pre-order and I haven't thought about the personalised message. This is as difficult as deciding what to have on the back of my shirt (but without the cost per letter).

4 October 2011

Is there something in the water, Chris Sutton, fabled former Norwich striker and legend, has released his biography. Not as in-demand as Huckerby's I would imagine, though it will probably still find its way onto my Christmas wish list, the £17.99 cover price has already been reduced to £11.79.

5 October 2011

A personal message from Darren Huckerby comprising 140 characters, I have an idea. It has to be interesting, memorable and more importantly not too limp wristed and sycophantic. Plus it's only going to be a case of Huckerby copying it, he doesn't actually know who I am, hasn't spoken to me, and probably wouldn't really care if he did.

7 October 2011

Who'd have thought getting Liverpool tickets would turn into such a trauma. Putting your name down on the list with a group of other fans should make life easier. Me, Jonny and Ben all with tickets – simple. Except I seem to have been given a coach ticket, and although I had called the club before and told them there had been a mistake, and I didn't need or want one I've still been handed one.

I had asked the very polite young girl in the ticket office a week ago that I didn't require a coach ticket and she duly told me she would put a note next to my name saying so. But today I receive a text via Jonny from his mate Cleggers who applied for us all: 'Got Liverpool tickets today. They have debited me for four coach tickets so either Junk needs to call club to sort out or he'll need to pay me for the coach ticket.'

Flipping arse bandits. That polite young girl from the ticket office is now off my Christmas card list. Another phone call and more hassle than I could possible want or need (that's probably over dramatic, but a little drama is a good thing I think). Jonny definitely thought I was being over the top, he called me a ballbag and a moaning Minnie. I didn't think my reply was that bad: 'Think next time I'll enter for away tickets on my tod, less hassle. If he's paid by card they aren't going to refund the money to me. Hey ho I'll call them and see what they say.'

What sort of insult is ballbag anyway?

8 October 2011

Text from Jonny: 'Read the Evening News website re Hugh Jackman.'

Turns out that the Hollywood movie star was approached to invest in Norwich – he didn't – how desperate must the club have been to send a letter to him?

All this talk of him being a fan is a bit far from the truth, depending on your definition of a fan anyway. An online dictionary defines a fan as: 'An enthusiastic devotee, follower, or admirer of a sport, pastime, celebrity'.

I don't think this fits Hugh Jackman, which is disappointing. He was interviewed on BBC radio and said: 'I got a letter about a year ago saying, "Being such a huge Norwich City fan would I like to be a celebrity investor?" I said, I think that's a little stretched, I've been to Carrow Road once, my mum took me, so I decided not to invest.'

Not exactly a devotee, but he did miss out. He was asked to invest when we were languishing in the lower divisions and now look at us, which he apparently admitted: 'And since then they're on a run, so what do I know?'

10 October 2011

I may be in a smidgen of trouble. The game at the weekend is not only the first home three o'clock kick-off this season but also my fifth wedding anniversary, which I forgot. My attempts to regain some credibility and earn some brownie points has been hampered by the two Michelin starred restaurants close to Norwich being fully booked. The owners of The Neptune gave me very short shrift in their email reply – 'I'm very sorry but I'm afraid we are fully booked on Saturday'. Whereas Morston Hall, although no more helpful were at least more gracious – 'Thank you for your email. I am very sorry we are already fully booked on the 15th with a private function. If I can offer you any alternative dates, please do not hesitate to contact me.'

I need a plan C.

11 October 2011

Haring down the autobahn isn't the expected place to talk about Paul Lambert, nor is it the ideal situation to mock the afflicted – Colchester – but you have to make do with the lot you are given.

As is so often the case in the automotive industry, most of my time is spent outside the UK, flitting between countries which still have a car industry. And more often than not that means flights to and from Germany.

The transfer between wherever I was and Frankfurt airport (I can seldom tell people where I've been as I have little idea myself. Flights to well known towns and cities mean little when you then have to spend the next hour on a minibus driving to somewhere in the middle of nowhere), for the return leg threw up a curve ball of some sorts.

The chap behind the wheel, Michael, while a car lover was also a football fan. After talking about his love affair with the VW R32 and Golf R – the Golf GTi was OK but it needed to be chipped to eke out whatever power was left in the engine – how the Pheaton was a wonderful vehicle but not worth the cost once you take into account German company car taxes and the ambivalence he felt towards French cars, conversation edged towards soccer in a roundabout kind of way.

Given the need to find an alternative to burning explosive fuel in a combustion engine, range-extender engines seem to be a solid idea over and above pure electric cars and their limited range. A car with both an electric propulsion system for short distances and a petrol engine for when you need to travel cross country. Of course as a London-based journalist with offices in the centre of town, driving electrically would be fine from Monday to Friday, but come the weekend and match days I need to drive a little bit further. Entering that into conversation always leads to the 'who's your team?' question, and today Michael took the bait.

Though he'd never heard of Norwich City, even after regaling him with the story of how we beat Bayern Munich in their own backyard, and City are still the only English team to have managed it, he had heard of Paul Lambert.

The man who played for Dortmund for a season had made such an impact even Hamburg-supporting Michael knew the name.

He had even heard of Colchester United, the speck of a club that we'd poached Lambert from, to the extent that he had a Colchester supporting friend in England that he exchanged football banter with via email. Apparently this friend had once sent him an email detailing every player who'd ever played for Colchester in retaliation for Michael suggesting that Colchester were an unknown, unloved, footballing anomaly. At the top of the list was John Robertson.

That would mean nothing to most, but as an 11-year-old boy Michael had watched Hamburg lose a European Cup Final to Nottingham Forest, and who should have scored the winning goal but a certain Mr Robertson.

I like to think that I've helped Michael out a little. The next time he emails his friend in Colchester, he'll be able to mention how it could have been the Essex club who climbed out of the third tier of English football and reached the Premier League with back-to-back promotions, if only they'd kept hold of Lambert.

12 October 2011

Michael had his facts wrong. John Robertson never played for Colchester. Nottingham Forest yes, Derby County yes, but not Colchester, I can't decide if he's the plonker or his Colchester-supporting friend.

Wedding anniversary plan C has saved me. The Olive Branch in Tunstead. Hopefully the French twist to its menu, courtesy of its Francophile owners, can make up for the lack of a Michelin star.

13 October 2011

Ordered Huckerby's book. Went with 'Upper Barclay, Area EU, Row I, Seat 120. That's where the loudest cheers can be heard...' for the personalised message. Not too weird, not too stalkerish, not too boorish I thought, Jonny on the other hand had different ideas.

Not only did he call me a Norwich geek – which I can handle – and lame – water off a duck's back, but he also said that it's one thing to meet players in Norwich city centre and shake them by the hand to wind up mates but quite another to buy their autobiographies and then ask for, in his words: 'Please address it to Mr Junk, seat number one, row B, and will you lick my willy. How old are you five? You massive gaylord.'

I thought it a little harsh, especially considering this is the same person who has asked someone to get his City shirt signed by the players two seasons in a row, and

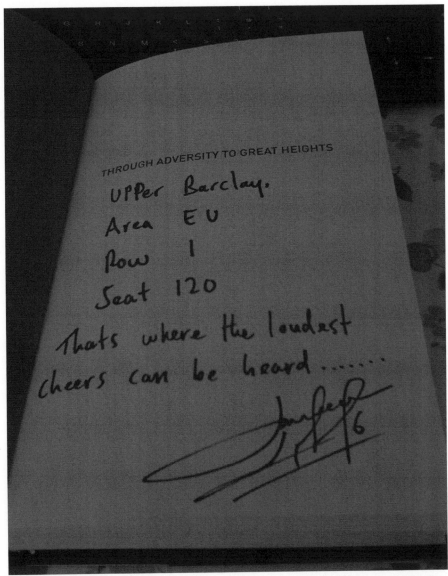

THROUGH ADVERSITY TO GREAT HEIGHTS

Upper Barclay.
Area E U
Row   1
Seat 120

Thats where the loudest
cheers can be heard.......

Personalised - Chosing a message for Huckerby's autobiography was as difficult as chosing what to have on the back of my shirt.

worse than that, when he went to the Goodwood Festival of Speed practically ran after Formula One driver Vitaly Petrov to get his entry ticket signed. Double standards? Me thinks so.

14 October 2011

Has it really been 196 days since Norwich's last competitive 3 o'clock kick-off at home?

15 October 2011, Norwich 3–1 Swansea City

Nine minutes of absolute marvellousness and Norwich were 2–0 up against a team I thought we were going to struggle against. A goal for the Swans against the run of play brought a bout of nerves, but a third strike in the 67th minute and three points were in the bag. Solidifying ninth place.

First Pilkington drilled home from close range after 47 seconds, then before the 10 minute mark Russell Martin ghosted into the box from a Fox free-kick to head home. Game won. Jonny, Ben and I all looked at one another and said it could be a good day. How many would we get, six, seven, eight?

Then we conceded and the swift delirium was replaced by an even swifter dread. Carrow Road, which had previously been bouncing like a rock concert was reduced to a library. The Swansea fans even started singing words to that effect.

Half-time was a welcome reprieve and the second half brought the smiles back.

Pilkington scored his second and that was us home and dry. I didn't understand the songs from the Welsh fans: 'Boring, boring, Norwich.' Why, Because we were winning?

Still you have to feel for them, it's a long old slog from South Wales to Norfolk. Bearable when you're on your way to the game full of hope and expectation, a little less easy to stomach when you've had your happiness-bubble burst by the home team.

The win made dinner in the evening all the more pleasant, a godsend when it's your wedding anniversary. There's nothing worse than being deflated by a defeat – I imagine it to feel the same as a depressive does all the time – it can put a real downer on the rest of the day. And given the occasion could also be a recipe for disaster: the end of wedding related anniversaries.

I'm glad that the Michelin restaurants were fully booked, The Olive Branch was wonderful – my pigeon breast starter was divine, the wild mushroom risotto a wonder for the palette and the Muscat wine particularly delightful.

Kana had a carnivorous streak and had steak, which looked beautiful, though there was a shred of disappointment, as a restaurant with a French twist she wondered why there was no sauce. Apparently she often – inwardly – laments the fact the British don't always have sauce with their steaks. I hadn't considered it before.

We did feel a little out of place, it's a nice restaurant, nicer than expected and we, by which I mean me, wearing jeans and yellow trainers, didn't dress appropriately for the occasion.

16 October 2011

I chatted with my sister – who'd been summoned to Norfolk by my mother – and she made a snide comment about my yellow trainers. I would defend my shoes were it not for the fact that, if I'm perfectly honest, I feel a bit of a prat wearing them if I'm not at a game.

17 October 2011

I'm a little bit buggered, I forgot it's my wife's birthday on the 19 November, the same day we play Arsenal at home and the same day that Christian wants to come with me to watch the game.

No fear we have a cunning plan that involves a subtle build-up in our friendship: introducing our wives to each other so that come the day, we can ALL go to Norwich and ALL celebrate Kana's birthday. It's water tight.

18 October 2011

Huckerby's book has arrived and I'm pleased with the choice of wording in the inside front cover. Not only that but when I tweeted my delight, the big man replied. 358 people looked at the picture I uploaded of his signature on the inside front cover, my previous best was 47 views of a picture of my Liverpool ticket for Saturday – the power of celebrity.

Grant Holt played in the reserve game against Aston Villa tonight. Feel sorry for the number nine. He's scored a huge number of goals for us over the past two seasons in essence getting us promoted twice. Now he's reduced to playing in front of 900 supporters on a cold Tuesday evening, with a teenager telling him what to do; George Francomb, born in 1991, was captain in the 1–0 win.

I didn't realise people were born in 1991. It must be an age thing, people can't be born after the 1980s, it just doesn't seem possible.

19 October 2011

I might have made a slight mistake booking my train ticket back from the Liverpool game on Saturday. I thought that the 19:48 – the last train back to London – would be a safe bet.

Kick-off is 17:30 which means that all things being equal I should have 30 minutes to travel the 2.4 miles (according to the route calculator) back to Liverpool Lime Street station.

The problem being that no one thinks it's possible. I've asked fans on twitter and on the discussion boards and everyone to a man said I was setting myself up for a fall. I really panicked when someone said away fans are kept in after the final whistle.

It wouldn't be so bad but if I do miss it then what do I do. I'll be 220 miles from home, with a very angry wife at home.

20 October 2011

Liverpool Travelodge is fully booked, Premier Inn is fully booked, Holiday Inn is fully booked, Radisson Blu is fully booked, even the Marriott is fully booked on Saturday. I really will be up that creek without a paddle should I miss the train from Liverpool Lime Street the day after tomorrow.

21 October 2011

Made myself cry tears of joy watching Youtube clips of Norwich's promotion season to the Premier League. I feel like an idiot, but less so as I put the links on Twitter and people responded asking if it was wrong to be tearful.

22 October 2011, Liverpool 1–1 Norwich

A two hour train ride from Euston station and I'm at Liverpool Lime Street by 3 o'clock, Jonny and Ben left Norwich at 9:30am and arrived at the same time. Who wants to be on a coach for five hours, at last living in London has an advantage.

For Jonny being on a coach probably wasn't the best idea, at 06:22 the little man texted me to say he was hungover, and at 11:14 he sent me another message saying he was two hours into the journey and had the runs, (he finally knows what it's like to have colitis!). Luckily his coach had an onboard toilet, but imagine trying to take a runny dump when the drivers flinging the thing around roundabouts.

Liverpool, albeit a match day, is just a constant stream of people, old and young, wearing Liverpool branded clothes. Not just scarves and replica shirts, but training tops, hats, tracksuits, coats and every other conceivable item – pants and bras I'm not so sure about. I've never seen anything like it before.

Though the 2.5 mile walk to Anfield from the station saw the branded scousers thin, I don't blame any of the fans, from the first step the route to the ground is up hill.

And the tiredness levels only increased as I took wrong turn after wrong turn, doubling back on myself countless times as I realised my mistakes.

I guess I could have asked someone but I had to find my own way because I was planning on walking back after the game and wanted to time the trip so I could calculate how long it would take me to walk back and also how early I'd have to leave the ground.

After seeing central Liverpool two things stood out about the rest of the city on my wanders: Stanley park seems like a nice open green area. Liverpool isn't a rich place, there don't seem to be that many local shops and half the houses look like they're boarded up and about ready for demolition.

Once I did find my bearings the road that lead down to the ground – Venmore Street – was a microcosm of what the whole city was like.

On the one side was a building site with very little seemingly going on and on the other were terraced houses with metal shutters (though the road did seem to serve one useful purpose – matchday parking for locals).

But at least walking up that road does lead you to the Kop, perhaps one of the most famous football stands in the world.

And the number of people and the type of people milling around the place at 16:15 proved how well known it is. Many a scouser but also more accents and languages than you can hear at the United Nations, and all of them in a shade of red. I don't know if that's a good thing or not, but I guess it's a reflection of how globalised the game is now.

When? - Liverpool was welcoming but they need to check their history.

I had time to take it all in and contemplate globalisation because Jonny's phone is bloody useless, 14 times I tried to call him to let him know I was at the ground, not once did the bloody thing ever ring. I even sent him an abusive text to no avail, 'Oi! Numb nuts'. In the end I had to phone his mate's phone – whose number I luckily had – to get hold of him.

Ben apparently doesn't like crowds (how he manages to watch football with 25,000 other people I don't know), so a visit to the away pub was out of the question.

You'll never walk alone – 3,000 Norwich fans packed into Anfield.

Into the ground it was then for larger and banter. Jonny's idea of banter only consists of calling everyone a homo and jibes about sleeping with our mothers. He talks the talk, but he trips over his shoelaces before he has chance to walk the walk. Jovial beers aside, game time loomed its pretty little head.

Jonny was nervous, Ben didn't say much and I was ambivalent. The famous Anfield atmosphere wasn't really up to much. I think I need to eat more fish because only certain things really stick in the memory, even such a short time after being at the game.

Liverpool have players that pass the ball phenomenally well, their striker, Suarez is an absolute world beater and my ambivalence turned quickly to match Jonny's nerves after they'd hit the woodwork the first time.

But Anfield is quiet, once the fans have sung *You'll Never Walk Alone* (which drones on for far too long), they're practically silent.

So it didn't take long for the the Norwich faithful to start pulling their chain: 'Where's your famous atmosphere?' we teasingly sang.

The Liverpool fans shouted with joy when Bellamy scored in the dying minutes of the first half, but they soon settled down afterwards. Bellamy, who started his career with us, was rightfully booed during the game. Not harshly, but in the manner that befits a player that left, is on the opposing team and is actually quite dangerous – as proven by his goal.

But neither Liverpool's players, nor their fans were expecting Grant Holt. The man that spent most of his career in the lower leagues, is now on the biggest stage in the domestic game. And while he may not be starting from the first whistle, he's causing all sorts of mischief when he comes on for his obligatory cameo.

Two defenders and a goalkeeper couldn't stop him powering in a header. He leapt above Jamie Carragher, Glen Johnson and Pepe Reina, before leaving them on the floor and turning to celebrate with the net rippling behind him. The man most of the Kop hadn't heard of had silenced them (if it's possible to silence a library).

Jonny went nuts, Ben went red in the face screaming with joy and I jumped up and down like a loon on day release. Out of 44,931 fans in attendance only 3,000 were euphoric, the remaining 41,931 were gobsmacked.

That 60th minute strike left me with 10 more minutes of nail-biting tension until I had to hot foot it back to the station for my train. And the more I thought about it the more I groaned with disappointment that I was going to miss a single moment of the action.

Holt could have had a second. Morison drew the defenders to him, Pilkington crossed, Holt sent his header back across the goal but somehow Reina flapped at it and pushed it away. And that was where my match finished.

And what do you think Jonny had to say about me leaving on the stroke of the 70th minute?

'Ben and myself have had a conversation and decided that the homo of the day award goes to…You for leaving 20 minutes early. You are a complete tosspot.'

I love having friends.

But I wasn't the only one who had to drag myself away. Sat on the train back to London was a Liverpool fan bellowing down his mobile phone, telling whoever was on the other end that he had to leave at half-time to make the long hard walk back to the station in time for the last train back to the big smog. Another Liverpool fan who sat next to me – randomly from Malaysia but studying for his A-Levels in Somerset – had left early too. Though the sneaky bugger had jumped in a cab in the 89th minute so got to see most of the game.

My one reflection on that train ride home is that Liverpool fans come from a diverse cross section of society. And not that it's a prerequisite to supporting a club, but there weren't many scouse accents among the fans travelling in my particular section of the train.

Jonny's long coach trip back to Norwich did contain at least one interesting fact. He spoke to someone who was at the Chelsea match. A five minute conversation and a short slide show of this chaps football photographs and whose face should turn up. Mine. Some strange man, who I've never met before, and am never likely to, has a picture of me at Stamford Bridge.

23 October 2011

The evening after the night before and the newspapers love us:

'What is remarkable about Norwich is the tenacity with which they stuck to their own style. Even when Liverpool were piling into them at the death, they kept trying to pass their way out of difficulty. Considering that every member of the team was playing outside the Premier League last season it showed admirable self-belief.' – *The Telegraph*

'One year ago Blackpool were the newly promoted entertainers accepting the congratulations of Anfield. Norwich may not have emulated their success but nor do they look on course to repeat their ultimate failure.' – *The Guardian*

'Norwich City deserve great credit. They defended heroically and never abandoned the slick passing game which secured their return to the top flight on the back of successive promotions.' – *The Liverpool Echo*

'And once again so called 'inferior' opposition had discovered there was nothing invincible about Liverpool in their own backyard with a draw Norwich boss Paul Lambert fully deserved to celebrate.' – *The Daily Star*

And what has rounded off the praise is an email from Alastair Florance from Lotus, who, after a few months, obviously still feels guilty about the advertising opportunity I gave the company on international television. How many people watch ESPN?

He's invited me to attend the Norwich verses Blackburn game as a guest of Lotus and after some deep thought I've decided to say yes.

I wasn't sure at first – sitting at a game not being able to sing with the other fans or shout at the referee isn't my perfect idea of football viewing but the opportunity to rub Jonny's nose in it can't be passed up. Who know's maybe a free matchday programme, cup of tea and cucumber sandwich can be followed up with a sneaky meet and greet of some of the players. And with the wonder that is the smartphone with inbuilt camera I could take some snaps of me and the squad, and send them to Jonny in a blink of the eye.

24 October 2011

Instead of it being a chance to wind Jonny up, the lucky git has worked his way into my cunning plan. Alastair offered me a guest for the game on Saturday, and against my better judgement I offered it to the dwarf-man. I need to learn to say no.

25 October 2011

Starting to wish I hadn't invited Jonny. How am I meant to rub his nose in it if he's sat right next to me. Also if I get one more text from him asking if all the details are finalised I'm going to scream blue bloody murder.

I sent Kana the match schedule for all the home games today after being told that she is never able to do anything because I'm always at the football. Now she knows when the games are she can sort out meeting her friends, going to the salon or whatever else women do when they want a bit of alone time while I stay home and look after George. That is what you call a balanced relationship.

That balance could be destroyed as Kana is arranging the trip to Japan which could see us return to the UK on the 27 December, the day of the home game with Spurs. Do I say something?

26 October 2011

Alastair from Lotus won't be able to make the game on Saturday, but has delegated mine and Jonny's wellbeing to his colleague, Tracey Parnell.

27 October 2011

It dawned on me today that this Saturday I will be one of the prawn sandwich brigade that Roy Keane so openly despised as both a player and manager.

It hadn't occurred to me before, but Tracey sent through the joining instructions for the Blackburn game.

- All guests should arrive at the Gunn Club entrance before 1pm (ground floor, between the Barclay stand and the City stand – see attached map).
- Guests need to state to the steward at reception that they are with Lotus for the Directors Box – you will then be handed a match ticket and directed to the Gunn Club Restaurant.
- Food will be served from 1pm, table service applies. It's recommended to order food as soon as possible.
- After the meal, one of the NCFC Hosts will escort guests to the Directors Box seats for the match
- At half time, tea and coffee will be served in the Director's Lounge, this is located back in the stadium through to the right hand side
- After the match, you will be escorted back to the Gunn Club where there will be a Man of the Match interview and a chance for Lotus to have a group photo with him

There are two things that balance the fact that Jonny and I will be dining with the hoi polloi of Norwich. Firstly from the director box I should be able to see Delia and perhaps get a sneaky picture, and who knows maybe Stephen Fry will be there. Secondly, I'm guaranteed to meet a city player and get a snap.

My main concerns at this point revolve around not owning anything other than jeans and trainers and wondering if I'll be allowed to take my green and yellow scarf in with me. I jokingly told Tracey that she needn't worry about me turning up in flip-flops and a Hawaiian shirt but at this rate I may have to.

28 October 2011

After what can only be described as a fashion show I have decided to wear a suit to the football. It feels wrong, but if the great and the good of the footballing world are going to be in attendance then I should really make the effort to look presentable.

I originally thought that a trouser, shirt and v-neck jumper combination would suffice but my wife assures me that it's far too casual for such an occasion. These prawn sandwiches had better be good.

29 October 2011, Norwich 3–3 Blackburn Rovers

Chuffing nora. How pants were we today. A 94th minute penalty isn't the way I want to gain a point, no matter how exquisite the delirium after the ball hits the back of the net. Grant Holt buried it, but for the majority of the match I was sitting on my hands and biting my tongue, the director's box is no place for the usual reactions Jonny and I give from our Barclay stand seats. And I doubt people would expect verbal naughtiness to come from someone in a lounge suit.

All the online media have identified this game as being dramatic, I would suggest that it was coronary inducing.

A sublime shot 20 yards out from Blackburn's starlet Junior Hoilett broke the deadlock in the third minute of stoppage time at the end of the first half. Disappointing but it was such a sweet hit you couldn't begrudge the lad his time in the spotlight. Then came the second half, Morison brings it back to 1–1 with a marvellous finish from the edge of their box. Robinson stood no chance in goal.

Ruddy did stand a chance with Blackburn's second – and he looked as frustrated and narked off as the fans – as Yakubu drilled a shot in and beat him at his near post. Ruddy should have had a stronger hand.

And woeful defending let man-mountain Samba in at the back to nod in unmarked. Norwich 1–3 Blackburn.

At that point everything was looking a little less than rosie. It didn't matter that Tracey had arranged for a first-class train ticket up to Norwich. It didn't matter that we'd had a lovely three course meal before the game. And it didn't even matter that during the half-time teas, coffees and biscuits that Jonny and I had seen Delia Smith not more than three metres from us. During the 64th minute of that game not even the padded seat and carpeting on the director's box floor was enough to make me feel anything less than empty inside – though I still appreciated the armrests.

I would, however, like to think I held it together better than Jonny, who, knowing he was in with the well mannered Norwich fans, kept his swearing to a few sharp gasps underneath his breath and shortened the f-word to 'kin: 'What the 'kin hell does he think he's doing' or words to that effect. But with a mountain to climb, he began adding the F-U-C to 'kin. By which point I didn't really care.

But there's a reason I'm in the stands and not pitch side, my decision-making is useless. Paul Lambert on the other hand is a tactical genius.

Three substitutions: Holt on for Bennett, Crofts on for Fox and Jackson on for Pilkington and by the 82nd minute it was 2–3. All three subs were causing mayhem in the Blackburn half, enough to give other players space. Johnson picked up the ball and ran with it. I was screaming at him to pass to Tierney who was making a run down the left wing ready to cross the ball into the box, instead Johnson kept running until finally shooting. A fortuitous deflection and the ball ballooned up, looping high above Paul Robinson in the Blackburn goal, and slowly, slowly coming back down before nestling in the back of the net. Director's box or not everyone to a man went berserk. Eight minutes to save the game.

And saved it was, a serendipitous penalty award by the referee. The ball went high in the air after Holt, Nzonzi – another Blackburn man-mountain – and Crofts all went for it. Nzonzi thought he was being fouled, and raised his arms to appeal, but as the ball came down it struck him. Handball.

Short arse – A happy family of Lotus guests for the Blackburn game. Jonny is shorter than Hoolahan.

I really couldn't give a monkey's uncle if it was harsh, if the referee doesn't blow for a foul, it isn't a foul, and as a footballer you should play to the whistle.

Only Holt was taking that kick, I held my breath, Jonny rubbed his incredibly furrowed brow, others next to us couldn't bear to look.

But when the Barclay erupts you know you don't have to worry. I yanked my scarf off and started waving it over my head, jumping up and down, screaming and shouting. Saved from humiliation, the ground was a cacophony of chants, laughter, singing and screaming. Utter jubilation. A draw that felt like a win.

And from the diabolical to the sublime, the relief of the Holt scoring the equaliser was rounded off by meeting Wes Hoolahan after the game, shaking him by the hand and having a picture taken with our diminutive midfield star.

Although everyone invited by Lotus agreed that he must feel like a piece of meat being dragged in front of everyone for photographs and he'd probably much rather be back with his teammates in the dressing room, the minute they had the chance to get an autograph and press the flesh they went for it, me included. You have to take these opportunities. He did look thoroughly perplexed by the whole thing and bored out of his mind. But what do I care, I have a signed programme and a grainy picture of me and Wes.

30 October 2011

Praise from Mark Lawrenson? Former Liverpool player, long standing BBC *Match of the Day* pundit and purveyor of all opinions reserved for the 'big' clubs, said something positive about Norwich City. I don't think I can believe it, but it's true, I saw it with my own eyes and heard it with my own ears:

'Because it's Norwich, and it's sleepy Norfolk and everyone's nice when you got there, some teams go there and think they can't be very good. We're sometimes guilty of being a little ignorant of some of our teams. Norwich are a difficult team to play against. They've gone to Stamford Bridge, Old Trafford, got a point at Anfield. They've created loads of chances against all those teams.'

Makes a change from his usual drivel. Only at the beginning of August he was telling all who viewed the MSN Sport website how none of the promoted teams would do well this season. We just don't have the budgets to attract the caliber of player able to make an impact in the big league. Sometimes you just feel like screaming 'NO! THERE ARE PLAYERS OF IMMENSE QUALITY OUTSIDE THE PREMIER LEAGUE JUST WAITING TO SHINE ON THE BIGGEST STAGE IN THE COUNTRY!!!' Maybe he'll listen one day. Credit where credit's due, he did get one other thing right: 'There's no 'I' in team, and if you spell it out: Together Everyone Achieves More' – Mark Lawrenson.

31 October 2011

Disaster. I spoke to my mother and she may either be going to visit my sister in Lincolnshire on the 19 November or going to a pub quiz the day we play Arsenal at home.

A selfish mind isn't likely to change, like a leopard isn't likely to change his spots, my first thought was that if she isn't in Norfolk it's buggered my chances of being able to see the game.

I'd concocted a cunning plan so I could see the match. I had booked a table at Dunston Hall – the à la carte restaurant has been awarded an AA rosette – for the evening, and was going to send Kana into the city with cash in hand to buy herself something nice for her birthday while I snuck off to Carrow Road. Meanwhile George was going spend some quality time with his grandfolks. Double arse and buggery. The plan to bring Christian to the game was always doomed to failure.

Plan B may have to involve a Travelodge and a fast food restaurant.

1 November 2011

It's official Norwich have the best football kit in the Premier League. Football-shirts.com (never heard of it) polled football fans as to which kit they thought was the best. Of the 1,321 people who voted, 6.1 per cent liked Manchester United's, 7.1 per cent Newcastle's, 11.3 per cent went for Manchester City's, but a resounding 75.5 per cent went for our brilliant Errea number. I'm happy but sensing a conspiracy.

2 November 2011

Sent Tracey and Alastair a thank you email for the invitation. Tracey has pre-ordered the matchday programme for the next home game which will feature the group photograph taken with Lotus's guests and Wes Hoolahan and will pop it in the post.

3 November 2011

We're back on for Arsenal, kinda. My sister is coming down to Norfolk, so she'll babysit George while my mum pits her wits against others at the pub quiz and Kana and I head out in the evening. I just have to convince Kana of the positive aspects of me attending the football while she picks out a lovely birthday gift.

4 November 2011

Being removed from Nelson's county not only effects how involved you can get in match days, namely drinking, it also means extra parts of being a fan pass you by. If I'd been in Norwich tonight I could have taken part in the fan's forum and bombarded the panel with questions about the club, where it's going, where it's been and where we are. Instead I had to rely on twitter for updates. Not quite the same but needs must when the devil drives.

Lee Coolahan, I'm not sure if that's his real name or just a strange amalgamation of his own surname and Wes Hoolahan's — fan's are a strange breed — was my window on the world. Lucky git had Paul Lambert, David McNally and Alan Bowkett sat in front of him.

All in all it sounded quite an eye opener. Three seasons in the Premier League and we'll have a 35,000 seat stadium, the men in the boardroom have even been in London talking finance for any possible expansion plans.

My eyes were glued to Lee's twitter feed:

AB: in next two years we will pay off all our debt. 35k capacity is still the self-funding aim. 3 consecutive years still the aim.

AB: however careful consideration around ticket sales and economic / demographic factor

AB: we would look to develop City stand. Likely to have that stand unavailable for 1yr if we did go ahead. PL has to do his job first!

AB: must resist urge to jump too soon on stadium development, despite capacity pressures. Will not risk financial future.

AB: You don't know how close we came [to meltdown] 2 1/2 years ago

No I didn't and I don't like the look or sound of words like 'meltdown' especially when they're linked to Norwich!

DM: Statistical evidence that we could fill 35k needs to be there. AB and I believe we can though.

DM: a couple of years ago, 50 per cent of tickets were subsidized

PL: hates 'sacked in the morning's chants. "It's the reality of the game today, but its severe."

PL: Norwich fans demand you win more than not. I'm not frightened by that though

AB: WBA chairman gave us advice at the start of the season - "get used to losing!" Feared the expectation before the Blackburn game

PL: footballers are really thick! Attention spans nonexistent, so too much analysis of games is not needed.

PL: chief scout is Colin Jackson. Been in place for a while now. Promoted to Head Scout since August

DM: Jan is difficult time to add to squad, but money is available

PL: already been thinking about Jan targets. Don't want to dip like Blackpool did, must keep momentum.

AB: hospitality best in League 1. Great clubs.

PL: loved managing at Anfield. History and tradition. Doesn't fancy Yeovil and Walsall again...

DM: would like to put seats in corner in front of hotel if we could. Not very easy at all though. Unlikely to happen before Spring.

AB: Premier League looking at ways go monetize gambling on football to the benefit of PL clubs.

DM: government will at some point come down hard on 3pm pub footy viewings. Not just a rights issue,but more protecting football in UK

DM: we will continue to lobby hard for earlier declarations of newly chosen Sky games.

DM: BBC Look East spat is down to CMS transfer reporting. Close to resolving the issue, but not there yet.

PL: you would not believe the effect the crowd has on the players.

PL: hate the feeling in crowd that we think we can just turn up and win.

One day I'll get to one of these forums myself and ask a very pertinent question that will get the board and manager thinking, until that time I'll have to make do with Lee and Twitter.

5 November 2011, Aston Villa 3–2 Norwich

Arse burgers of the highest order, we lost!

I was never likely to go to Birmingham to watch the game but I never thought of the consequences of being invited to lunch by Christian and Emma. Away from the television and radio and unable to check the scores on my phone put me in limbo. Unable to stay up-to-date and unable to concentrate on polite dinner table conversation I was left to nervously twitch in the corner.

6 November 2011

People are stupid, a loss and some fans are determined to find someone to blame. In this instance it is either Barnett for his dodgy backpass, Ruddy for not committing to clearing Barnett's dodgy backpass, Hoolahan for giving the ball away too often, or Lambert for picking the wrong team: how dare Holt start the game.

Some wonderful discussion board article titles included such gems as: Lambert called it wrong today, to panic or not to panic, Lambert stop making the same mistakes, defensively…sieve like and Hoolahan needs dropping have adorned the internet.

Nestled within these threads were a plethora of insights. Someone called Kick-it-off said, and I quote, 'He [Hoolahan] just didn't care and couldn't be bothered yesterday, his attitude was terrible and his performance even worse.'

I've often said from the stands on a Saturday that the reason I'm watching from afar and not involved is because I don't know toffee about the ins and outs of the game, a sentiment Jonny often attests to as I call something wildly wrong and shout blue bloody murder, only to look a fool.

Screaming from the stand that Johnson should pass to Tierney, only for Johnson to score during the Blackburn game being just one example.

As for Hoolahan, he has just been nominated for Irish overseas player of the year, so he can't be that bad. Not to mention that, after relegation to League One, he was given torrents of abuse only to – with the aid of 30-plus goals from Holt – drag us back to the Championship, and then on to where we are now.

7 November 2011

No sooner had I thought I'd side stepped the trip to Japan in December then Kana brings the topic back again, this time I think I am destined to miss the festive fixtures. There'd better be some way of seeing them on Japanese TV. And it will give me the opportunity to convince some of the in-laws to start following Norwich, broadening their horizons and stemming the sales of Manchester United, Liverpool and Arsenal shirts in Asia, if only a little.

Thankfully I should be back in the UK in time to see QPR, and as it's at Loftus Road, Kana can have little reason to stop me going. But it's a heavy price: Newcastle, Everton, Wolves, Spurs and Fulham could all be scrubbed from the 'to watch' list.

8 November 2011

So that's Japan booked then. From the 10–28 December we'll be in the land of the rising sun. I might be missing the Newcastle and Spurs games at home but I'll be taking a break from the rat race, stress and the hum-drum for two and a half weeks.

It struck me that although I'll miss the chance to go to see Norwich in the flesh to make up for that I might be able to go to a game or two in the J-League, or even the Club World Championship thingamajig – Barcelona are in town – so not all is lost.

9 November 2011

The J-League season finishes in three weeks, so I won't be going to any games there. I had a squiz at the FIFA website to see what the go was for the Club World Championships and I can't make head nor tail of it.

I can get as far the price per ticket depending on which section of the ground you sit, it's anything from ¥7,000 – ¥30,000, but once you click on the 'pay now' section it goes all Japanese.

It's a killer because before it all goes Japanese the line-up is tempting: the competition features CF Monterrey from Mexico, the CONCACAF Champions League winners, Santos FC from Brazil, the CONMEBOL Copa Libertadores winners, Auckland City FC from New Zealand, the OFC Champions League winners and possible whipping boys, FC Barcelona from Spain UEFA Champions League winners as well as the winners of this year's AFC Champions League, the CAF Champions League winners and a club from Japan's J-League, representing the host nation.

At the moment the Japanese qualifiers could be Kashiwa Reysol, my home team from when I lived in the country as a wide eyed and bushy tailed graduate. Not only are they my home team but they also play in yellow. As people in Japan would say; *dosuru*? (What should I do?)

10 November 2011

Tickets for the Club World Championships are sold out unless I want to spend five hours on a coach travelling halfway across Japan to another stadium.

Luckily the Emporer's Cup – the Japanese equivalent to the FA Cup – is in town and there are two rounds of the competition while I am in the country, so with a bit of luck there'll be a game close enough to the in-laws home for me to toddle off to and watch.

I've only ever been to one Japanese football game, and while the quality wasn't great, the ability to drink beer in your seat and eat rather bad hotdogs makes the experience interesting. And the flag waving supporters with drums and chants that last the entire 90 minutes make the atmosphere enjoyable.

Which is a good thing because not everyone seems to be enjoying the season. Some could say there's an air of pessimism floating around the Norwich discussion boards. Luckily there is some sense being spoken. Rudolph Hucker, seems to be a purveyor of logic when he types on the Pink'un website, though the title of his article sent a quiver of fear through the body:

It's about to get a whole lot tougher

We have had an excellent start to the season but things are about to get a whole lot tougher and this is why.

Promoted sides have an initial euphoria and a newness established sides sometimes fail to cope with; that doesn't last forever and this was the feeling underlying the last two games.

The season has been stop-start, matches have been few, but from Saturday week until January the games will come thick and fast. This benefits the bigger squads and if a side gets on a bad run the games can run away from them.

We have had five ideal sides come to Carrow Road so far and we have, in an historically un-Norwich like way, dealt with them well: West Brom aside. The harder home games are about to come and home form is going to be much harder to maintain; this can be difficult for supporters to cope with and crowd tension can be corrosive.

Conversely, most of our away games have been at grounds where nothing was expected. We emerged with credit and got points from our 'peer' sides but we will need to continue to take points from sides around us as we go to their grounds.

There are very few points separating 8th and 20th and any side can rise or fall alarmingly.

The next game up is, of course, Arsenal. Points will be difficult to come by (shame we didn't play them a month ago) and if they lose our players will go into the QPR game feeling the pressure and needing to deal with collating one point over a month. It has been pointed out before that resilience is key in this league and players have to deal with adversity which can come in waves. They are about to be tested.

We need to get to 20 points at least by the New Year because our season builds in difficulty towards the end and the second half of the season will be far more challenging than the first. This means we need 7+ points and looking at the fixtures these will be hard to come by – after QPR it's Man City away.

Our squad is thin. There really isn't much quality outside the first team and three of the subs. Further injuries and suspensions will be particularly detrimental and this goes back to the intensity of games in December.

So, it looks like I'm all doom and gloom and just see Norwich City falling off in the way described by the arrogantly annoying David Gold on Five Live tonight. But, there is another way to look at it.

We are about to start the season proper. Gone is the unseasonal warm weather and the long days. It's going to be cold, gloomy, floodlit and atmospheric. It's about to feel like proper football again and this Norwich team don't mind adverse conditions. I expect the crowd to respond too and for atmospheres to get bigger as the games feel bigger, more important and with more of an edge. QPR home for example is going to be a cauldron.

We create chances and have goals in us so we always have a chance. We haven't been thrashed but haven't kept a clean sheet and the latter is vital to where we play next season. We have to believe PL will improve our system defensively.

We must not write the Arsenal game off and we must not believe a negative result defines our season. Despite our comfortable looking position and good start the upcoming games are individually vital because there isn't much leeway.

It's no good getting plaudits for attitude after losing or leaking goals while having a go – that's Blackpool. There is a thin line between keeping forward momentum and slipping into the bottom three and unless we get some results the next 8 games could put us on a slippery slope familiar to many including ourselves.

So, Norwich supporters, you have no real choice but to back what you have got and help them to continue to overachieve. There is no time to coast, no throwaway games and little margin.

It is about to get a whole lot tougher; are you up for it?

12 November 2011

England beat Spain 1–0 at Wembley, with Spain playing a full strength squad. After the turgid game against Wales I wasn't expecting that. Hopefully they continue that sort of form against Sweden and then on into next year and the Euro 2012 Championships.

Shame I missed most of it, spent the evening in a quiet pub, which unusually for a pub nowadays had no televisions in it.

13 November 2011

So according to Cesc Fabregas, Spanish midfielder maestro, formally of Arsenal and now Barcelona, England were too negative and begrudged us our win:

'At the end of the day, you want teams to have a go at you and test you and see what happens. We knew, especially after we saw the first XI that they put in, that they were going to defend basically the whole game. Even when they were winning, they had Welbeck up front alone and everyone just defending.'

So a team knowing that the opposition is technically superior should set themselves up to play an identical game, and more likely than not allowing the other team to tear them apart. That sounds sensible doesn't it.

How about playing the tactic that will help you get a result, how about Spain should have played the game that would have got them a result rather than bemoan the fact that England defended resolutely and then snatched a goal.

Would the Spanish players have preferred England to have played like Holland did in the World Cup Final, when the Dutch more or less only tried to kick seven shades of wotsit out of Spain.

At the end of the day according to Fabregas, you want teams to test you and see what happens. Well Spain were tested. They were tested by seeing how they coped with a team that was well organised and determined not to concede and Spain failed. For all the prettiness and possession they didn't do the one thing you have to do to win a game of football. Put the ball in the back of the opposition's net.

Not that the Spanish press were all that fussed about England's style, by all accounts they were just as disgusted as their star midfielder:

'England turned Italian to beat Spain,' said one Spanish commentator.

'It didn't matter to Capello that he was playing at Wembley in front of his own fans. He got his team to lock themselves in their own half and wait for a miracle. The selección was a victim of the ultra defensive, mean tactics that Barcelona have suffered so often. Wembley is only for Barça,' the *Catalan Daily Sport*.

'Capello parked the bus: ACCIDENTAL DEFEAT. For the same reason that there are albinos in Africa, snakes with two heads and Japanese over two metres tall, England beat Spain at Wembley,' the AS.

And those involved in Spanish football lined up to belittle England's effort:

'The result was unjust,' – former Atlético Madrid defender Miguel-Angel Ruiz.

'Spain deserved a different result. England won with very little. I'd be more worried if I was English' – Angel Portugal, ex-sporting director at Real Madrid and coach of Racing Santander.

'Rarely has a team won so much with so little.' – Marca's Amalio Moratella

And Santiago Segurola, one of Spain's most respected commentators, said that England could end up falling victim to the 'mirage of victory'.

But they're missing the point, as Fabregas eloquently said, 'But this is the way they want to play and it worked for them.'

It did work for us, and if it continues to work for us, I'm all for England parking the bus again and again and again and again and again and again and again and again.

14 November 2011

Twitter is alive with rumours that Chris Martin is leaving us on loan to Crystal Palace. The Beccles boy who scored more than 20 goals in League One is off for some match time in south-east London. I wonder if I'll see him walking around Bromley.

15 November 2011

Chris Martin has gone until January. According to the official club website:

CITY striker Chris Martin has joined Championship side Crystal Palace on loan until January 2, 2012.

Martin joins the London-based club with the Eagles sitting in sixth position in the Championship table and chasing promotion to the top-flight for the first time since the 2004–05 season.

The 23-year-old has made four appearances for the Canaries in the Barclays Premier League so far this season, with the last coming in the 2–0 defeat to Manchester United at Old Trafford.

The Beccles-born hitman, along with Wes Hoolahan and Grant Holt, formed a devastating trio in City's League One title-winning campaign of 2009–10, hitting 67 goals between them – Martin grabbing 22 in all competitions that season.

Martin then made 30 more appearances for City in the Championship last season, scoring four goals as the Canaries gained promotion.

Paul Lambert commented: 'Chris needs to get some games, and that's why I decided it was the right thing to send him out on loan. Palace have made a good start under Dougie Freedman this season, and if he does play it will be at a good competitive level, which is important.'

He's going to miss Swaffham.

16 November 2011

The toys have been put back in the pram. The BBC and Norwich have buried the hatchet and will now talk to one another.

18 November 2011

I won't be at Carrow Road tomorrow. It's Kana's birthday and a poorly little man means any chance I had of getting to the game has been taken away.

My only hope now is that the Partridge in Bromley is showing the game, old man's pub with real ales and Sky Sports on multiple big screens…

19 November 2011, Norwich 1–2 Arsenal

Robin Van Persie, Theo Walcott and Yao Gervinho showed us how to attack. I've never seen our right and left-back's look so scared. I guess pace really is key to winning games.

I didn't get to the Partridge, had to make do with the internet. Both Kana and George had a nap, so I was on call just in case anyone needed medicine, wet towels and hot water.

Jonny, who had control of my season ticket, was surprisingly understanding about my non-attendance, his first text after I told him about why I wasn't going was a simple 'That's fair enough'. It soon changed.

An hour before kick-off he sent a slightly more Jonny-esque text: 'Coach and horses. Sunshine. CHB, chip butty on order. Lovely. By the way the boy being ill is acceptable. The missus birthday? Priorities!'

I doubt he's that brave with his own wife, I bet he kowtows down to her all the time. Billy big bollocks when he's on his own and a shy little lamb when he's at home.

He was a bit positive after the game, whereas I thought we were shown a footballing lesson – in attack anyway – Jonny thought we had competed with Arsenal throughout the game and was disappointed not to get something. He reckoned 50/50 possession, the BBC disagrees and puts it at 38/62.

Ah well, roll on the 26 November and QPR.

20 November 2011

Jonny is a hypocrite. He may not be attending the QPR game as it is his nephew's birthday on the same day. After the grief, all be it in a joking manner, that he gives anyone that misses, or contemplates missing, a game and I get a text from him saying 'The decision lies with the missus'. I ask you, what sort of man is he?

21 November 2011

It seems that Grant Holt is not only loved by Norwich fans. He might be the messiah at Carrow Road but according to Girlonaterrace.com and the everyday musings of a female football fan, he's also loved by the supporters at Rochdale.

Why I love…Grant Holt

I'm going to go down the route of sensationalism here, merely to get you interested. Grant Holt touched my boob, fact. Did that get your attention?! Ok, so I haven't explained how or why, but he actually did and that's my claim to fame when it comes to Grant Holt and I'm sticking with it!

As the title suggest; I love Grant Holt and I make no secret about that. My schoolgirl-like crush to the side, Holt is just simply awesome. I always think of him as a proper lower league striker; he's strong, determined and intimidating, and that's what I love in a player, so to see him playing in the Premier League is just fantastic. I'd certainly love to see the faces of some of the defenders he comes against that's for sure.

He's definitely a love or hate player…you'd love him playing for you, but you'd hate him playing against you. And I'm quite sure that anyone who's been lucky enough to have him play for them will agree.

Surely, Holt's story is what every boy dreams of. He worked his way up through the Leagues from non-League to the Premier League, making a name for himself as a hardworking goalscorer along the way. I'm also pretty sure I've read somewhere that he's one of very few players to have made a step-up through the Leagues and scored at every level that way or something like that!

It's hard to believe that just a decade ago Grant Holt was a 20-year-old playing non-League football, he'd started his career at Workington netting 11 goals in 11 appearances, before spells at Halifax and Barrow, struggling to achieve his dream, then the sudden death of his father halted his career. It was at that point that he headed to Singapore for four months; I sometimes try to imagine Grant Holt in Singapore but to be honest I struggle and I get an image of several Karl Pilkington-esque moments in my head.

On his return to the UK he signed for Barrow after he'd played a few games on loan previously. It was his time in Singapore and his career at Barrow that would be the start of his career. From there he went on to score a goal every two games before being snapped up by Sheffield Wednesday in 2003. But he didn't live up to expectations and I'm pretty sure Wednesday fans are the only ones who don't have particularly fond memories of him as being a fans' favourite.

And this was where my love affair with Grant Holt began, as in 2004 he signed for Rochdale where he went on to make 75 appearances and score 34 goals, continuing his impressive goal scoring record that he proved in non-League football. We were also lucky enough to see Holty play alongside Rickie Lambert at Spotland too and I'm quite sure that playing alongside a player of such quality improved his game even more. After becoming a fans' favourite at Rochdale, which is quite an understatement, he obviously caught the eye of bigger boys and in January 2006 he left us for Nottingham Forest for £300,000.

Although he made a slow start and his uneasy relationship with then manager Colin Calderwood, he finished the season as the club's top scorer with 18 goals in all competitions and the Player of the Season award. In the summer of 2007 his transfer request was refused and the rest of the season didn't work out as planned as he was regularly played out of position on the wing. In March 2008 he spent a short loan spell at Blackpool in the Championship making four appearances before returning to Forest where he wanted to fight for his place.

In June 2008 he dropped back down the Leagues and signed for Shrewsbury Town where he was yet again to make a name for himself, scoring on his debut with a penalty as well as scoring five of the seven goals in their 7–0 against Wycombe. He ended his time at Shrewsbury with 20 goals in 43 appearances and caught the eye of Norwich City making his move to Carrow Road for £400,000 in the summer of 2009. And as they say, the rest is history.

To this day he has scored 56 goals for Norwich City in 95 appearances in all competitions and has helped lead them to the Premier League. Back in 1999 he was playing for Workington and working in a warehouse I am led to believe, fast forward to 2011 and he's a scoring against the likes of Chelsea and Liverpool in the Premier League.

He's the perfect example of a successful footballer who has gone round it the right way, putting 110 per cent into every game and refusing to let setbacks hinder him. To those that doubted him when Norwich were promoted, I'm loving seeing him playing against the big boys and proving them all wrong.

And Grant Holt even became such a cult figure that he trended on Twitter with #grantholtfacts...ok so they weren't real facts, but it shows just how much he's loved (and also hated!) by football fans. If you want some real facts...he has scored on his debuts for Sheffield Wednesday, Barrow, Nottingham Forest and Shrewsbury Town. FourFourTwo also stated that in he was the player to cover the greatest distance per game in League One and Two with an average of 4.8km per match.

And on a sideline from football, a lot of football fans will know about his Movember efforts last year that were so impressive that a range of Grant Holt Movember merchandise was created! He still looks cool with a porno style mustache, what a man!

I know this blog post is entitled 'Why I love...Grant Holt', but whenever I've tweeted about him I've always got so many responses from others with equally as much love for the guy too. So, while writing this I asked my followers to summarise why they love Grant Holt in one sentence and here are a few of them:

@upthedale27 'Grant Holt – one man army, dragged Dale through games at times, turned 50-50s into goals goals goals!'

@minreds77 'I love Grant Holt cos he is hard working he's been to the bottom and worked his way up 2 the premier league'

@ChaffRAFC 'Best striker I've ever seen at Dale. Could boss a good back four on his own. Great goalscorer, big target man. Awesome.'

@Grandy84 'I love Grant Holt as he has captained Norwich City through two epic promotions.'

@BornOffsideBlog 'Grant Holt: scores old school headers and floors three Liverpool players in the process. Woof.'

@epouvatail '11 goals in 14 victories at 16 years of age. Workington – champions. Cheers Grant.'

@RichWhite2008 'The fact he has worked up the leagues and commitment to club been great, averaging goal every two games where he been.'

@dezzy1907 'I loved Grant at Dale cos he was like a striker from the 70s but had a touch of class too.'

@A_R_Orr 'I'd say hes so great because of his never say die attitude and his pure love for playing the beautiful game.'

@douthcd 'Cos he looks like he's gonna be shit but he isn't'

@Richard242 'Because he always plays with the spirit and commitment that every fan would show given the chance'

@Jamie_McNamee 'A Player who lacks top end skill but has an eye for goal. A work horse in which a team can place itself up on his shoulders.'

@BurrowsAbout 'Always gave 100 per cent, the kind of striker defenders hate playing against and great at winning free kicks and pens.'

@jackweddercop 'Think its great how he has worked up the divisions to reach the Premiership, shows desire and work-rate.'

@Serbzkii 'Because me and my friends simply refer to him as "Daddy Holt" ...what's more to say? Haha.'

@StAkBAFC 'Every boy's dream, to go from scoring at Holker Street to scoring at Anfield'

@JimCorinthian 'Delivered at every level, played with the same conviction.'

@elhayo 'He doesn't moan when he's dropped and he plays like a fucking animal when he gets the chance.'

So all together now....WE LOVE YOU GRANT HOLT...or something like that!

If you've read to the end of these ramblings about my love for Grant Holt then well done, and if you're still wondering how he came to touch my boob then I'm sorry but it's not as seedy as it sounds…although I do have a photo of said incident somewhere. It was all very innocent (unfortunately for me!) and happened while having a photo taken and I'm quite sure it's only me who remembered the touching but yes, Grant Holt touch my boob – fact!

22 November 2011

You can't ever please anyone all of the time as the Pink'un message board so wonderfully shows. One poster just isn't a fan of Delia Smith and would rather we had much richer owners:

'Yes, we know you love City and you're intentions are good BUT…you can't cut it financially.

It's not investment we need, its a ruddy serious rich owner. Did we want Tony Fenandous to invest or did he really want total control? If it was the latter I wonder if it was blocked by HER or the board?

The Premiership is a rich man's playground now and survival can't be done on the cheap anymore imo. This is why QPR will survive ie money.

Could that have been us? Only Delia knows the answer to that question.

So, time to put your feet up woman, you've done ok…sometimes! now for the sake of our future Premier status, sell up!

I thought and hoped we could survive with you, but sadly, I now realise the stark truth of it all.'

Will people ever be pleased with where we are and how quickly we've arrived. We're playing Premier League football for goodness sake.

23 November 2011

Rich backers don't make for a happy ship. Our friends down the A140 have Marcus Evans who's bankrolled the team in blue and white to at least the tune of £8 million plus all of the players that he's brought in. Not that I can explain it very well, but City Penguin on Pink'un (the message board that fill every cynics fantasies but also mixes a little bit of sense).

'It's not quite as bad as it looks to be fair to them, Marcus Evans bought 32million of the debt for 8 million and can only sell this for what he bought it for, but that doesn't help with the extra 34 million they now owe him in non-interest bearing loans in that period. So really their debt to him is 40 million, not a small sum of money!

The rent rebate is a funny one, they were only paying 15k a year rent on their ground, the council have done a review and now charging 111k and want back dated rent to the sum of 650k, which apparently the club cannot afford. So much for money bags.

Yes Evans can only sell the debt he bought for the same amount but that doesn't stop him charging interest on the full amount, in effect he is gaining interest on 24 million pounds of credit to Ipswich that he never had to pay. So in real terms the interest payments are 4 or 5x higher on than they should be, and compounding.

Ipswich model was to spend big (mainly on wages)on the back of interest free credit after the 32million they owe M.E from his purchase of the club. In doing so they have amassed another 34 odd million in debts in roughly 3 seasons, while making quite substantial profit in the transfer market. The playing squad is now ageing and this market values of the team greatly depreciating and wont be able to raise anywhere near the likes of revenue like they have in previous seasons.

If we assume continuation of debt rises of roughly 13million pounds per year as a conservative estimate, would be higher if player sales had not been a large source of revenue. Then in a further 3 years time debt levels would be around 100million. At this point even promotion to the premiership wouldn't really be able to save them as increase in the playing budget would be very large. At which point asset liquidation would have to take place, oh but they already don't own their ground the fsmain way of raising cash for struggling football clubs so are really on the brink.

Ipswich NEED promotion within 3 years or it will all end in tears unless they find another person wanting to throw money into a bottomless cesspit.'

George hasn't done a poo for the best part of three days. His mother is worried. I am worried but not showing it in the same way as Kana, which isn't going down well. The boy needs laxatives.

24 November 2011

My back is giving me all manner of hell every time I move. I blame children and the inventors of the child's car seat and cots. Neither of which allow you to lift and lower your child without performing some sort of contortionists pose. Unfortunately I am not that supple and after lifting George once too often my back has failed me. There is a plus side to all of this, it now means Kana isn't allowing me to lift a finger around the house until I am better. She is apparently worried that I may cause irreparable damage and she will be left, quite literally, holding the baby.

I tried to explain to her that the doctor said it would heal within a week and that I should just take paracetamol to numb the pain (I would have been prescribed codeine but that can inflame the bowels, so stronger painkillers are off the menu), but she doesn't believe me.

The doctor completed a very rudimentary examination of my back and legs. He got me to lie on my back and he lifted my leg, keeping it straight, which hurt. He then bent it at the knee while lifting it which didn't hurt.

This is, in his wisdom, a sure sign that my sciatic nerve is being irritated by a disc in my spine that has moved out of place while lifting the boy.

I should believe him, even for a doctor who works at the South Lewisham Group Practice he seems to know his stuff. He saw my yellow socks and immediately asked if I was a Norwich fan. Of course I proudly said yes.

He asked as he saw an advertisement in some medical journal for a GP position in Norfolk. Apparently rather than focus on the beautiful countryside, the laid back way of life or the general pleasant working environment that the fine county offers, the ad suggested the best reason to apply for the role was because Norwich were in the Premier League. Are all doctor's football fans, is it a requirement of being a general practitioner?

25 November 2011

Panic and mayhem today, Kana and my mum had to take George to the hospital because he hadn't done a poo for a week. Kana took him to see the GP who said he really needed to go to see a specialist. Laxatives weren't working and he had a hard lump halfway round his large intestine.

Kana told me she was going to the A&E, and also said I needn't leave work to go to the hospital with her as my mum was down in London helping babysit the lad. But after five hours of not hearing anything my concern got the better of me and I dashed back to the London borough of Lewisham, with my back in tatters, to find out what was going on (I perhaps could have saved myself the pain had either Kana or my mum bothered to answer and/or switch their mobile phones on – I tried calling dozens of times to no avail).

Thankfully George cleared his system out while they were waiting to see the doctor. Thank sweet jesus for lactulose oral solution: 10ml and you'll no longer suffer from chronic constipation.

A much more relaxed cup of tea at home, with an empty son sleeping peacefully in the bedroom, Kana told me her Fulham-supporting friend's husband had bought their son a Fulham replica kit. Brilliant idea, George will love his green and yellow Christmas present (shan't tell Kana it's £35).

George's bowel movement also means that tomorrow's game is still on, as is meeting the boys afterwards.

I learned something new about football rivalry today. Christian, a Parisian, supports Paris Saints-German, PSG have a hatred of anything to do with Olympique Marseille. PSG fans apparently shout something along the lines of Marseille, Marseille on t'encule. I'm going to translate it online tomorrow when I'm more awake to find out what it means, I'm guessing it's something similar to 'always shit on the old blue and white'.

26 November 2011, Norwich 2–1 QPR

Holt and Hoolahan saved the day. Hoolahan crossed, Holt scuffed the ball into the back of the net, Norwich stay safely mid-table.

I hate these games, they've got to be the worst in terms of nerves, expectations and heart palpitations. And it's because winning is such a strong possibility.

It doesn't matter if you play Arsenal, Manchester United, Liverpool or any of the other big clubs because you never expect to score any goals or gain any points, but against the teams of a similar size and those that you were promoted with the pressure of expectation grows. In my case, and Jonny's, it manifests itself as palpable nervousness.

It didn't help that pre-match I had to drive my mother from London back home to Aylsham, then meet my father for lunch before getting to the game.

Lunch was more complex than it should've been. Not the act itself, that was enjoyable, but trying to pick a place to meet and eat with someone who doesn't head into the city very often on matchdays or otherwise, so is unaware of the deluge of people that hit the streets.

A quiet lunch cannot be had at:

The riverside development and any of its bars or pubs.

The Complete Angler, it's the official away fans pub.

The Coach and Horses, it's a nice pub but full to bursting with football fans.

The Red Lion, further away from the ground but equally full of football people.

Prince of Wales Road, you wouldn't take anyone there any of the time day or night, football or not.

The Nelson Hotel is a football hotbed too, but as I park there before games it proved the easiest option. Father and his better half, Bridgette, were sat waiting surrounded by people in yellow. It was a strange juxtaposition.

My father the Ipswich-lad, schooled at Tower Ramparts and who lived in the Swan Inn with my grandmother, a frequent watering hole for the Ipswich team of 1961–62.

It's perhaps not strange that I'm a Norwich fan having lived in Norfolk all my life, but the opportunity was there to follow a very different team.

Yes my grandfather is a Norwich fan and could often be found in the River End, and when he was making deliveries for Palmers (that well-known department store in Great Yarmouth), be it in Nelson's county or in other parts of the country he'd often whip round the addresses quick sharpish before heading off to a game should the gods be smiling on him and Norwich were playing away to a team he was in the general vicinity of.

But to have had a grandmother who was so close to the team down the A140 could have meant a very different life for me. Serving beers to a team that won the League and was managed by the one and only Alf Ramsey and had players of the calibre of Leadbetter and Crawford. Stranger things have happened in this world.

How many Norwich fans can imagine catching the train down to Portman Road decked out not in the yellow and green of Norwich but the blue and white of Ipswich? The only advantage it would have at present is the shortening by 40 minutes of my journey from south-east London.

Thankfully having a father who can't necessarily be described as a football enthusiast meant that the chances of following Ipswich were slim, and now rather than forever harping on about the trophies Ipswich won during the club's glory years (and neglecting the years of mediocrity and self loathing), I'm happily and firmly sat in the Norwich supporters club. Parental obligations fulfilled at the Nelson, off to fortress Carrow Road.

There were a lot of police around, must be a London club thing, horse poo all over the place, but no helicopter hovering over head or dogs on leashes – a sure sign that something particularly wayward could happen at any moment.

I thought we were in for a nerve free afternoon when Russell Martin made the net ripple in the 15th minute, but for some reason this season Norwich just can't keep a clean sheet. And in the 59th minute QPR equalised.

It was a stupid, stupid goal. Someone, for the life of me I can't remember who headed the ball back to Ruddy, but before it reached him Barnett decided to attempt a clearance. It was too weak and the ball ended up going straight to Jamie Mackie who drilled the ball at goal. It rebounded off the post, but only as far as Young who couldn't miss. I long for a 1–0 win against someone, anyone. Are we going to go the entire season without a clean sheet?

So thank god for our saviours Grant Holt and Wes Hoolahan.

Morison battled his way into the QPR box before floating a cross to the far post, where Holt's header was blocked on the line by Derry. The ball pinged out to Crofts who found Hoolahan on the right side of the area, and his cross into the six-yard box was bundled in by Holt for his fourth goal of the season. Cue pandemonium on the terraces.

Three points is three points, but to gain them against relegation rivals is often as sweet, if not sweeter than banking them against the bigger teams, because it helps you keep your nose in front, important come the final days of the season.

Pandamonium wasn't quite had on the streets of Norwich after the game, driving and sensible celebration aren't easy bedfellows.

I'd stretched out my drinking allowance over the afternoon in the form of two pints of beer.

Fruit-based drinks don't have the same effect and the equation is worsened when those around you are mockingly (in my tiny mind), downing copious amounts and becoming steadily more jovial.

Jonny was so far away with the fairies that he started getting bullish and decided that he should assert his masculinity by playing his 'I'm a better driver than you and I could beat your skinny arse on a race circuit' – the choice of vehicle is yours.

Perhaps he could, but considering he screamed like a girl on the drive down to the Goodwood Festival of Speed, when apparently my braking distances were too short coming up to, among other things, roundabouts, I can't help but think the little man is all mouth (my testosterone levels got the better of me and I said as much to him, in fact I even think I added some rubbish about having some time on a number of race circuits through work).

By 9pm I'd had enough of the fruit juice and drove home leaving Jonny, Twon and Cruso to carry the torch and burn the midnight oil. Next time I'm in Norwich I'm not drinking anything other than alcohol.

Marseille, Marseille on t'encule does not mean always shit on the old blue and white, it means something else entirely. I don't even think I can bring myself to write it down and I'm not sure you'd get away with chanting something similar at an English ground.

27 November 2011

I was going to write something convoluted and tedious, but then I read the news:
Gary Andrew Speed, MBE, 8 September 1969 – 27 November 2011. Was found dead at his home aged just 42. He was a former Welsh football player and

manager. He was captain of the Welsh national football team until he retired from international football in 2004. He remains the most capped outfield player for Wales and the second overall, having appeared 85 times at senior level between 1990 and 2004.

Apparently it was suicide. Depression is a difficult thing. He leaves behind a wife and two children.

28 November 2011

I think that both my back and my guts are going to be the death of me. I'm up every 10 minutes to go to the loo but every time I bend to wipe my arse I have a spasm of pain through my spine. I'm glad there are no security cameras in my home otherwise I may well find myself an internet sensation or on *You've Been Framed.* Sciatica and colitis why are you doing this to me?

But while my digestive system battles it out to see if I sit on the comfy sofa with a cushion to ease my poorly back or the porcelain throne I'd would just like to say that today marks the one year anniversary of the our demolition of Ipswich Town, 4–1. And with that in mind I'd like to recount the words of the fans at Carrow Road:

He scored three goals against the scum, Grant Holt, Grant Holt,
He scored three goals against the scum, Grant Holt, Grant Holt,
He scored three goals against the scum, and Wesley scored another one,
Super Grant Holt Norwich's number nine!
Nanananananananana
Nanananananananana
Nanananananananana
Super Grant Holt Norwich's number nine!

In celebration I have purchased a DVD review of last season so I can watch the goals over and over again, and a Norwich City mug so I can have a relaxing cup of tea while the waves of happiness wash over me.

29 November 2011

Ehime FC verses Urawa Red Diamonds at the Saitama stadium is where I'll be on 17 December. I may not be able to make the Newcastle or Tottenham games but I will be getting my fill of football while I'm away in the land of the rising sun.

Now I'll be honest I know absolutely nothing about Ehime FC, haven't even heard of them before. But after some internet checking I can say with some certainty that they are a J-League Two side based in Ehime prefecture which is in north western Shikoku. They have no star names and a single Brazilian and South Korean playing for them, but their manager is Croatian. The rest, according to Wikipedia is as follows:

'The club was founded in 1970 as Matsuyama Soccer Club and renamed itself as Ehime Football Club in 1995. For many years it competed in the regional and prefectural league, as Matsuyama was represented in the Japan Soccer League by the local club belonging to the Teijin company.

Ehime F.C. was promoted to the Japan Football League in 2003. After winning the JFL championship in 2005, Ehime now plies its trade in J. League Division 2.

On November 28, 2007, Ehime pulled off a major shock by consigning the Urawa Red Diamonds, the AFC Champions League 2007 winners, to a fourth-round exit from the Emperor's Cup courtesy of a 2–0 win on Urawa's home soil, Urawa Komaba Stadium.

In 2008 Ehime absorbed local club Ehime Shimanami F.C. as their reserve team, and now the latter are billed as Ehime F.C. Shimanami.'

The fact that they have beaten Urawa before in the Emperor's Cup could make for an interesting atmosphere at the Saitama stadium – although strangely in Japan teams often have more than one home, so the game could be held at the much smaller Urawa Komaba stadium. But no matter where it is it should be a good.

Urawa are the best supported team in Japan, and the fans have a reputation for being boisterous, drunken and mad, a Japanese equivalent to the Millwall mob minus the violence.

I exchanged a few messages with someone on Twitter who'd been to a game who said I should keep an eye out for the 'were gonna fuck you up' banners. Who'd have thought the typically reserved Japanese have their own brand of football thuggery.

Kana doesn't understand my excitement, but I'm going to go, have a few beers, chat to some locals and see what's what. And for balance, Wikipedia provided some learned tit-bits on the Reds:

'Mitsubishi Motors established a football club in 1950 and in 1965 it formed the Japan Soccer League along with today's Sanfrecce Hiroshima, JEF United Ichihara Chiba, Kashiwa Reysol, Cerezo Osaka and three other clubs who have since been relegated to regional leagues.

Mitsubishi first won the JSL championship in 1969, as a break in Mazda/Sanfrecce's dominance (and also with the fact that Toyo were in Bangkok, Thailand, competing in the Asian Club Cup); their runs up the first division were sporadic but steady until the 1980s when they fell into the Second Division. In 1990 they were promoted as JSL 2 champions, and thus were ready when the J-League implementation began in earnest.

Mitsubishi were the first Japanese club to complete a domestic treble, when in 1978 they won the title, the Emperor's Cup and the Japan Soccer League Cup.

The club has enjoyed mixed fortunes since the J-League advent. The club finished bottom of the league for the first two seasons of the J-League with an average crowd of under 15,000. In 1999 they suffered relegation to the second tier of Japanese football yet again. The team has since improved in form in recent years, starting with a 2003 victory in the Nabisco Cup.

In 2006 Urawa clinched their first professional league title by defeating runners-up Gamba Osaka 3ñ2 on December 2 before 63,000 supporters. This came after two close calls in the previous two years. In 2005, they finished 2nd, one point behind champions Gamba Osaka. In 2004, they finished 3rd in the First Stage and won the Second Stage. Having qualified for the two-match J. League Championship decider, they lost on penalty kicks to Yokohama F. Marinos.

Urawa were back to back Emperor's Cup winners in 2005 and 2006. Winning the title for the first time since establishment as a professional team, they defeated Shimizu S-Pulse 2–1 on January 1, 2006, and retained the title in 2007 with a 1–0 win over Gamba Osaka. This win also completed a league-cup double. In the 2007 tournament they were defeated at the first hurdle by J2 outfit Ehime F.C.

In 2007, despite a seemingly unassailable lead of seven points with four games remaining, Urawa picked up only two points from their final four games. This run included losing at home to Kashima Antlers; the team who would leapfrog Urawa on the final day of the season to claim their fifth J. League title. Following their capitulation in the fourth round of the Emperor's Cup to J2 outfit Ehime F.C., Urawa had to be content with their 2007 Asian Champions League title. Urawa recorded their first international title after overcoming Iranian team Sepahan F.C. 3–1 on aggregate. The victory made them the first Japanese side to win the title since the competition was reorganised from the Asian Champions Cup in 2003. In the Club World Cup of the same year, Urawa became the first AFC team to finish in third place, beating Tunisian …toile Sportive du Sahelside on penalty kicks in the third / fourth place play off.

In 2008, Urawa attempted to win their second consecutive Asian Champions League Title and progressed to the semi finals where they were defeated by fellow Japanese and J-League rivals Gamba Osaka 3ñ1 on aggregate.'

I'm keeping my fingers crossed that Urawa win, go through to the next round where they'll meet Kashiwa Reysol – my local team from my time in Japan – that could be a spicy affair.

30 November 2011

QPR tickets for the 2 January applied for, Loftus Road here I come.

1 December 2011

It's done, a Norwich City mug has been ordered and to accompany it the review of the 2010–11 season DVD. Next on the to-buy list, George's first replica kit, but at £35 he may have to wait as at the rate he's growing he needs new clothes daily and I doubt Kana will agree to him wearing a Norwich shirt every day to nursery – no matter how awesome he looked.

3 December 2011, Manchester City 5–1 Norwich

Shrugs shoulders What can you do. Manchester City were the one team I feared could give us an absolute hiding and it became a reality.

4 December 2011

It seems not everyone is at ease with our loss to Man City. It doesn't matter that the team in blue are top of the table, have already blown Manchester United away at Old Trafford 1–6, and are more than likely to win the League at a canter given current form. Not for 'Rock the Boat', it was a disaster, an embarrassment, the worst thing to have happened this season:

'I don't know why the team bothered to travel up to Manchester because today most of them didn't bother to get off the bus once they arrived. There's one thing about showing respect to the opposition but it's a totally different matter going out there thinking you're going to get beat. I thought we were the team that always gave it a go? Well today we didn't. Apart from a five-minute flurry around the hour-mark substitution we had all the enthusiasm of a dentist's waiting room.

Yes we know it was Man City but if you're going into the game with a never-say-win attitude you're going to get rolled over. And we did. Our worst performance in the Premier League to date. We sat too deep. With dithered on the ball. We showed too much respect. Some of the team looked as though they would rather have been somewhere else at 3pm. And it was not a question of if but when will Man C. score. We just gave them three points on a plate this afternoon. Our attitude was all wrong.

And what was wrong with Ruddy? Had a representative of a Far-Eastern betting ring approached him before kick-off? He was reponsible for four out of the five goals conceded, and his glaring fumbling of the ball for the second proves he has all the credentials for an England goalkeeper.

Shockingly inept performance today. Hope it was a one-off.'

I can't help but feel he's overreacting. A win against Newcastle on the 10 December and everyone will be happy again.

We have Burnley at home in the third round of the FA Cup. How glamourous. My money was on a trip to Crystal Palace – though my heart wanted a home tie against Ipswich so we could have the derby game back on this year's planner – but I guess as we've already played them once this year we we're let off.

Given our Cup credentials I guess Burnley can be described as the first team to qualify for the fourth round of the competition. Oh how nice it would be to go through to the latter stages, but it just isn't going to happen, if memory serves, Leyton Orient knocked us out last year.

In fact, I think the only time we have made any progress in the FA Cup in recent times is when we were in League One. Starting from the bottom of the pile and beating Paulton Rovers 0–7. Heady days.

I did enjoy the chants from a Cup game against Chelsea in 2005, 'You've got a Russian crook, we've got a drunken cook'. That was the last time we reached the fifth round.

5 December 2011

Oh for the love of everything holy. The fall out from the weekend's game continues, this time people want Ruddy's head. A mistake it seems isn't allowed, because fans never make mistakes in their day-to-day lives.

It's god awful when things go wrong for players and you sit there flabbergasted and unable to believe what is going on. My stepfather often makes the point that given the riches that professional footballers are awarded they should be able to score goals at will and as a goalkeeper save every shot going (how that balances out in a game I don't know). But in my defence of players making mistakes, that's the beauty of the game, human error. A person's fallibility is just as much a part of the rollercoaster ride that is a football game as a players moment of magic.

Lionel Messi does some stupidly audacious tricks when he's playing for Barcelona, it's almost as if the ball is stuck to his foot at times, but Ruddy's howler against Man City, or today, Pepe Reina's cock-up against Fulham, (he didn't manage the simple task of catching the ball and Clint Dempsey pounced in the 85th minute to score Fulham's winner), mean you never know which way a football game is going to go. And Reina is supposedly one of the best goalkeepers in the Premier League.

It can be galling as a partisan fan, but it can also make things feverishly exciting for a neutral.

6 December 2011

How bloody selfish of them. Christian and Emma are leaving their jobs, packing their things up and leaving this blessed country. They're going to explore the globe before settling back in Christian's native France. Twats. That makes my chances of getting a ticket to the Arsenal away game slightly less sure. Christian on t'encule, Christian on t'encule!

7 December 2011

I may despise Christian at the moment but he'd like to go and watch the Chelsea game at Carrow Road with me before heading off. His birthday's in January as is mine so it could be a double celebration for him.

8 December 2011

There seems little hope that my Norwich DVD and mug will arrive before I jump on the plane to Japan. Is this going to be a re-enactment of the replica shirt saga. I thought Diane at the club and I had come to some sort of agreement, I was obviously wrong.

9 December 2011

Bags packed, passport, wallet, mobile phone and car keys in a safe but obvious place. Tomorrow Heathrow, terminal three.

10 December 2011, Norwich 4–2 Newcastle United

Hello Tokyo!!!

I'm eternally grateful to Christian for texting me the result so I had it when we touched down at Narita airport. I'd spent most of the 12 hours at 36,000ft wondering whether or not we'd been hammered by the Geordies.

11 December 2011

I'd forgotten how wonderful Japanese electric toilets are. Not only do you get a warm seat to rest your weary rear on, but once you've done your business then at the press of a button a stream of warmed water will delicately clean your posterior. I would say it's a colitis suffers dream, but surely anyone who goes to the loo has to appreciate the technical marvel. I must look into getting one when I'm back in the UK. There must be a company somewhere that imports them.

I failed miserably in my attempt to find highlights of the Norwich verses Newcastle game online – worse it seems all live streams for 3pm kick-offs have disappeared from the respectable websites I used after an injunction was served on the Greek satellite company that used to show them – so have had to make do with the match reports from a variety of newspapers. I am growing a little tired of the same old adjectives being associated with Norwich: workman-like, industrious, tenacious, pugnacious, it's as if we have no quality in the team whatsoever.

Mind you if even our own manager calls Grant Holt unorthodox then I guess there's little hope that the wider world are going to perceive us any differently to a team of hardworking but technically lacking players.

According to the *Daily Telegraph*: 'Grant Holt's brace plus Steve Morison's fifth goal in six games eased the way for Paul Lambert's hard-working side. Norwich were a touch workman-like, while there was precision and guile at times from the visitors –

In control – Japanese toilets bring pleasant relief for everyone.

despite their lack of a recognised centre-back following injuries to Steven Taylor, Fabricio Coloccini and Mike Williamson, as well as Cheick Tiote's absence.'

The *Daily Mirror* went for some colourful use of tired clichés: 'All that was required, on a chilly afternoon at Letsby Avenue, was for the Bernard Matthews tendency to carve open the Toon's depleted back four repeatedly and serve up a treat. It wasn't as easy as falling off one of Saint Delia's yule logs. Even with 10 men after Dan Gosling's red card for a rash lunge at Russell Martin, Newcastle were as game as poultry. But if the wheels haven't come off Alan Pardew's unlikely crusade for a place in Europe, the tyres are flat, the hub caps have gone, the wheel nuts are loose and the axles are groaning. In the absence of Steven Taylor, Fabricio Coloccini and Mike Williamson, Pardew's diddy men couldn't cope with the aerial threat of carpetbagger Grant Holt and his sidekick Steve Morison. Three of Norwich's goals came from set-pieces and the other was a present from the delinquent Gosling. It was a twitchers' paradise: the Canaries ruffled the Magpies' feathers, Newcastle's goose was cooked by Gosling's dismissal and Pardew got the bird.'

Newcastle's striker, who admittedly scored two very good goals was a little hasty in his underhand comments about our style of play, Demba Ba said: 'Against Norwich, I don't think we had a good game. We could've done better but conceded the first goal in a bad moment and it put all our heads down. Defensively was the key as they were playing long balls and it was difficult for Danny Simpson to compete against Holt or Morison. I don't know if other teams who come here are going to struggle, but, if they need advice, they need to put the bigger lads on the pitch and they'll be fine.'

Does no one understand tactics, not even the players? Any team that came up against opponents that had no first choice centre-backs would use powerful strikers and pepper the box with crosses. I know players aren't necessarily the brightest but surely Ba must understand that.

Kashiwa Reysol were on the television. They beat Mexican side Monterrey on penalties to make the semi-final of the Club World Championships. They're up against Al Sadd next. Not the best show of quality on the pitch but it did make me that little bit more excited about the Urawa game on the 17 December. Not sure about the quality of banners at the games, the Kashiwa supporters had a huge sign draped over the edge of the hoardings which read: 'We are Kashiwa Stupid!'

I may have travelled halfway round the world, but at present the furthest I've ventured is the living room.

12 December 2011

Funny thing time zones, Chelsea beat Manchester City 2–1 on the 11 December in the UK, but from where I sat – jetlagged to buggery – it was 6am on the 12 December.

It apparently takes one day to adjust for every two hours difference in time, so I'll be over my very early morning starts in four and a half days. Until then the only thing keeping me going is J-Sports – the Japanese equivalent of Sky Sports – which is showing repeats of the main games from Saturday. So far I have seen Manchester United beat Wolves 4–1 twice and will probably be watching Chelsea beat City again tomorrow.

Thankfully as the stream of repeats continue until the next batch of games, the highlights programme showed Holt's two goals in all their glory, Morison's headed number and the bundle that was Hoolahan's effort against Newcastle.

I really am going to have to make it outside into the wider world, but as this is Kana's holiday and a chance for her to see friends and family I'm going to take my opportunity to do as little as possible for as long as possible.

13 December 2011

I've asked Jonny to buy me the *Canary* magazine that has just gone on sale. It's probably just another way to eke out as much money as possible from the Norwich City football fan, taking advantage of the clubs new found status as a top half Premier League team, but I don't mind admitting I'm a big enough mug to have bought into it. I could order one and have it sent to Tokyo, but I don't trust the Royal Mail to get it here in a timely fashion and I don't think it's worth spending £8 for the postage.

14 December 2011

Darren Fletcher has taken a break from football because of ulcerative colitis. While I'd never be pleased that someone has had to take a back seat from doing something they love because of the disease, it's a good thing for other sufferers in so far as it brings colitis in to the media and everyone's view – for a little while at least. And it also brings out other famous faces who suffer from ulcerative colitis – Sir Steve Redgrave, multi Olympic gold medal winner, or how about England international rugby player Lewis Moody and we can't forget our own famous colitis sufferer Russell Martin.

The only problem is some of the coverage isn't always spot on, not even by the delightful BBC. Its reporter was still mentioning words such as 'recovery'. Unfortunately there's little chance of a recovery at the moment and the best people can hope for is to keep it under control so it doesn't affect their lives too much.

Strangely the best reporting came from the *Daily Mail*, who had an interview with Sir Redgrave. He was diagnosed 10 weeks before the 1992 Olympics.

Apparently 1 in 500 people suffer from some kind of inflammatory bowel disease, with colitis it means inflammation and ulceration in the colon and rectum, which can produce symptoms of urgency, bleeding, diarrhoea, pain, profound fatigue and anaemia, as well as vomiting.

Can you imagine being stuck in a rowing boat with those symptoms, let alone competing for your country at the highest level, and winning?

As he said: 'Perhaps I was one of the luckier ones. I wasn't usually vomiting and I didn't have uncontrollable diarrhoea, which some people suffer from. That would have been a bit inconvenient in a boat. But I was going to the toilet about six or seven times a day and my athletic performance was severely affected.'

But Fletcher hasn't done too badly in his career so far, and I'm sure a well paid footballer isn't going to be short of medical attention.

The man is only 27 and has already made 300 appearances for Manchester United, 58 for Scotland, scoring nearly 30 goals. Not forgetting the four Premier League titles, two League Cups, one Champions League and World Club Cup.

15 December 2011

There are two very good reasons that I like coming to Japan. The first is obvious, half my family (through marriage), live here, the other is the chance to eat yakinikku, a Korean-style barbeque.

Thinly sliced bite-sized pieces of beef sizzling in front of you, you decide when the meat is ready to eat and chose from a variety of sauces to dip the meat in, sweet, salt, lemon, they're all divine. There's no place for rabbit food eaters at a yakinikku restaurant, only go if you like red meat and beer.

Kana's cousin Chie and husband Isao gave some enlightening insight into the world of Japanese football and what is acceptable behaviour for a husband.

I always think of the British and Japanese being very similar; both island nations, both universally disliked by their neighbours in the wider continent and both very proud. While the Brits like to think we invented most of the world's modern technologies, the Japanese are happy to know that they've improved most of those technologies and made them marketable.

I don't think the Japanese have improved football, but their brand of hooliganism is definitely developing beyond what we expect from the likes of Leeds, Millwall and others.

The Urawa Reds game is only a couple of days away, and during some beer-fuelled conversation with Isao (I have to admit that due to my light grasp of the Japanese language, Isao's even lighter knowledge of English and the fact we're both men and rarely utter more than half a dozen words during the day, conversation was initially lacking but a couple of beers soon loosened the tongue), it transpires that wearing my Norwich shirt to advertise the club at the game may not be a good idea.

Urawa Reds while being the best supported team in the country, a country that frowns upon people stepping out of line, is also the team with the biggest number of troublemakers.

I can't believe that they're on a par with the nasty elements in some European clubs, but they're bad enough to make Isao concerned about me standing out in a yellow football shirt in a sea of red.

Urawa, according to Isao, once won a game, but the manner of the victory was so poor in the fans eyes that the Urawa Ultras surrounded the team bus after the game, letting their feelings well and truly known to each and every player.

So perhaps appearing to be a Kashiwa Reysol fan (finishing higher in the League than Urawa, not to mention winning the Championship is a big no-no), at first glance isn't a good idea.

It is slightly reassuring that there is a badboy contingent in the Japanese game, the 2002 World Cup there, which was bloody marvellous, all the talk was about English hooligans, and I was constantly asked if I was one. During that tournament, the Japanese fans were causing havoc in Osaka after breezing through Group H (it consisted of Belgium, Russia and Tunisia), much to the shock of the locals. I had a wry smile on my face. But while the Japanese might well have that exterior air of smartness and uniformity, there are parts of the culture that divert quite drastically from Britain, not necessarily in a bad way, but in a 'we wouldn't do that over here' way.

There are booby bars the world over, go into certain pubs in London and all you have to do is put 50p in a pint glass, when the glass is full a girl comes out and does a strip show. Go to a slightly more up market establishment, pay a little more and you can have your own private dance. But in Japan there are certain places you can go to – all above board – pay your money and actually touch the women's breasts while having a conversation with them as they're sat next to you. It's a mix of a hostess bar and Stringfellows.

Isao loves them, I presume his wife less so, but it is all done out in the open and he talks quite enthusiastically about it, and Chie knows he goes. I don't get it.

I understand the culture of expensive hostess bars in Japan. They're used as a business tool by some. You pay a lot of money to take a client to one of these places, talk business, have a drink all the time in the company of very attractive women.

The women for their part earn a lot of money, but do nothing other than talk. They're well educated, worldly wise and spend their time making sure they know what is happening around them, be it economics, politics or even sport, visit the cheaper, seedier side of Tokyo if you want less knowledgeable women and less talking.

Isao's choice seems to be somewhere inbetween. Talk, look and touch but without the highbrow conversation or the end game. I got the look from Kana when he suggested we should go and have a look together.

16 December 2011

Grant Holt could have ended up at Colchester United! He was given the chance to join them down in Essex when we were in League One, thank Christ he didn't otherwise he could have been one of the players who scored in that 1–7 mauling we received in the first game of the season. Paul Lambert was the draw according to the interview in *The Sun* newspaper: 'It's a good job I didn't go to Colchester because he buggered off after three weeks. I spoke to him but then when Bryan Gunn got sacked, he came in and I thought 'Thank God'. Now, I'm happy and settled down. I've just bought a house in Norwich with my wife and kids and I think when you're settled, you enjoy your football.'

Luckily instead he's played 100 games for us and scored more than 50 goals, the guy's a gem.

17 December 2011, Everton 1–1 Norwich (Urawa Reds 3–1 Ehime)

Well that wasn't quite Premier League quality, I don't think it was even Championship level, but nonetheless: Road Trip!!! It's 50 miles from the in-law's home in Tokyo to the Kumagaya Athletic Stadium in Kumagaya. The sprawl of Tokyo gives way to the never ending flatness of the Kanto plain and Saitama prefecture, with the distant mountains surrounding everything like a wall. And all the time Mount Fuji sits there, looking down on all around it. That 3,776m peak is absolutely enormous, and considering it's 90 miles away, you can see it as clear as day from just about anywhere. I used to work in Chiba prefecture, that was 110 miles away and you could still see the bloody thing.

戦

日本サッカー最大のトーナメント

天皇杯

4回戦・準々決勝・準決勝・決勝
第91回 天皇杯全日本サッカー選手権大会

Little beauty – Japanese matchday programmes are artistic affairs.

So I was a little disappointed when Isao took five minutes to spot the tallest mountain in the country after I shouted out I could see it. I shouldn't complain. Isao sorted out the tickets and went to the game with me while we were chauffeured by Chie, so all in all it was a winning day out.

Sing up – the Urawa fans give it some gusto.

You can't see much from Japanese motorways, once you go through the toll gate it's 3m high concrete walls for as far as the eye can see, but once you get out of Tokyo and onto the local roads things open out.

If you can forget the mountains in the distance it's a little like being in the flatlands back home, albeit a 10,500sq mile area.

And compared to Tokyo it's barren, all three sat there wondering what the hell people did both for work and for pleasure apart from working the land.

It could be part of the reason that Urawa fans are so, comparatively, nuts. With nothing to do why not get a bit lively at the football.

And the closer we got to the stadium the more white and red stickers appeared in the back windows of the cars driving past us, the more flags we saw fluttering off the car's aerials and the more nervous Isao got.

He needn't have been worried, Urawa fans might have a reputation but compared to the sorts of toss pots you get at English grounds, the harsh atmosphere at the Old Firm derby and the ultras in Italy, it's a family atmosphere. I think the worst thing that happened was some old lady, unbeknownst to me, telling me off because I, as a neutral had the audacity to say that Urawa's defence looked a little suspect.

The game was dire. Urawa were shocking for a top division team, and the only thing Ehime had was their number 27, who was a tricky customer, but surrounded by a teammates who couldn't hit a barn door.

But however bad they were, you have to support the underdog so come the second half Isao and I moved away from the hot-under-the-collar old lady who disapproved of my critique and sat with the Ehime supports. All 150 of them.

While the show at the Kumagaya Athletic Stadium may have been disappointing, back home Norwich are still racking up the points. Thank Christ for Grant Holt. Another goal in the 28th minute and he's turning into quite the seasoned Premier League striker:

'Out of the blue, the Canaries took the lead in the 28th minute when Holt scored his seventh goal of the season. From a free-kick on the right given for a foul on Hoolahan, Fox crossed towards the far post where Morison knocked the ball on to Holt, who, with his back to goal, turned Heitinga splendidly and rolled his shot left-footed just inside the post.' – *Pink'un*

Oh, and while the quality of the football on the pitch might have been lacking, Japanese matchday programmes are full-colour A4, quality.

18 December 2011

Paul Merson, that wonder of a pundit on Sky Sports has had to eat his words about not only Norwich but also Grant Holt, not only did he predict us to lose 3–1 to Everton but he also thought that Grant Holt wasn't built to play in the Premier League.

'He's a clever footballer, he's brainy, he sees the full picture. I didn't think he'd have the pace but they don't play in a way where they need the pace. They've got attacking midfield players that will make runs beyond him so he doesn't have to run the channels as much and he holds the ball up; he brings people into play.'

Maybe Merson, who played for Arsenal, Middlesbrough, Aston Villa, Portsmouth and Walsall (he also had a single game with Tamworth), will figure out that the reason he was sacked as Walsall manager was because he wasn't very good at judging players or building a team, and that he needs to be a little more considered with his opinions before writing teams off. Pundits should listen to Mick McCarthy, who once said opinions are like arseholes, we've all got them but we shouldn't air them in public.

The in-laws got excited though. J-Sports had the highlights of the game on and when the yellow shirts of Norwich hit the screen everyone turned round to watch. I'm spreading the word that Norwich are in the big time.

I've not been able to find any match reports for yesterday's game between Urawa and Ehime, the best I could do was in the *Japan Times*, an English language daily which gave a far reaching insight: 'Elsewhere, Yosuke Kashiwagi sealed a 3–1 win for Urawa Reds against Ehime'.

The Urawa Reds official website did a little better, at least the manager was honest, it wasn't a good performance.

'I can't think of a game that was worse than today's. Our players were not able to go into the game, in addition we could not express anything on the pitch.'

19 December 2011

It's done, Norwich have deducted £35 from my bank account, so I'm sitting in the upper tier of Loftus Road on the 2 January.

20 December 2011, Wolverhampton Wanderers 2–2 Norwich

I don't mind being away from the UK, everyone needs a holiday, but that was meant to have been quite a match with both Jackson and Surman scoring and I didn't see any of it.

23 December 2011

Back to Wikipedia again to find out something about the teams I've spent ¥2,000 on to watch in the next round of the Emporer's Cup, and to find out how to get to the stadium.

First Kyoto Sanga. Of course I've heard of the city, it's in every guide book and where every tourist heads to see a real life geisha, but the football team I haven't got the foggiest about.

Wikipeda says:

'Kyoto Sanga FC (京都サンガ FC *Kyōto Sanga Efushī*) is a Japanese professional football (soccer) club based in Kyoto. The word "Sanga" is a Sanskrit term meaning "group" or "club", often used to denote Buddhist congregations. This reflects Kyoto's tradition of Buddhist temples (seesangha). The club was formerly known as Kyoto Purple Sanga with "purple", the colour of the team uniforms, an imperial colour reflecting Kyoto's status as Japan's ancient imperial capital city. It was decided however that, from 2007, the team will simply been known as "Kyoto Sanga". They are the oldest club competing in the J. League.'

As for Shonan, which I swear sounds more Irish than it does Japanese, I know one thing – it's where perhaps Japan's most famous player of recent times started out, Hidetoshi Nakata according to Isao. Apart from that, I'm stumped. But wiki reliably informs me that:

'Shonan Bellmare (湘南ベルマーレ *Shōnan Berumāre*) are a Japanese professional football (soccer) club, currently playing in the J. League Division 2. The team is located in Hiratsuka, in the west of Kanagawa Prefecture; their home stadium is Hiratsuka Athletics Stadium in Hiratsuka. The name *Bellmare* is derived from the Latin "bellum" for "war" and "mare" for "sea". *Shonan* refers to a coastal area that includes Hiratsuka.'

So it should make for a cracking game at a ground that can hold 25,000. Isao doesn't seem to think so and continues to laugh at my choice of teams and game.

24 December 2011, Kyoto Sanga 1–0 Shonan Bellmare

What the hell was that. It was like watching football being played by a load of primary school kids. Eleven players on the pitch, all of them chasing the ball around in one big group. The quality on the pitch was mirrored by the quality watching from the stands.

Showpiece – Kyoto v Shonan wasn't of the highest quality on or off the pitch.

There were less than 5,000 people at the ground, a mixture of people with nothing better to do, loners and *sakka baka*'s (literally translated as football idiots) according to Kana and her family.

After riding the Tokyo trains for 40 minutes I had no idea where I was but knew I had about 10 minutes to travel 1.5km to the Todoroki Atheltics stadium.

My main problem was that there were no buses running outside the train station and no taxi rank. The map I had in my pocket was useless as my father-in-law's printer had run out of ink, so it was more faded than a 1,000-year-old scroll and even if it had been any good road signs and names were at a premium. So I did what any self-respecting man would do and didn't ask for help but used the wind and the tides and a wing and prayer to get me to where I needed to be.

Truth be told I found a taxi after five minutes and after gracing the driver with my Del Boy Japanese set off to watch the glory of the 91st Emperor's Cup, glory in this instance being another way of saying turgid rubbish.

25 December 2011

It's perhaps a little wrong of me, but although we sit happily in ninth place in the Premier League table as everyone tucks into their Christmas dinner, I have a little knot of panic sitting at the back of my mind.

Blackpool, who Norwich forever seem to be compared to, including by myself, were also placed similarly this time last year, but ended up getting relegated.

On the 25 December 2010 Blackpool had played 16 games and amassed 22 points, fast forward to 2011 and Norwich have played 17 games gaining 21 points. But then I could well just be being pessimistic.

But it dawned on me during my Christmas day nacho burger in the middle of Tokyo that the speed with which we've scored goals and points in the first half of the season is going to have to be maintained in the second half too. (That's actually obvious and what every pundit under the sun says every year, but clichés become clichés for good reason.)

There was actually a match report from yesterday's game in the *Japan Times*, though it was taken straight from the Kyodo news agency so is lacking the human touch and intellect of a typical Sunday newspaper read back home:

'Kyoto Sanga filled out the Emperor's Cup semifinal bracket as the J2 side continued their scalping of the J. League with a 1–0 win against Shonan Belllmare on Saturday. In a tactical tussle between two sides coached by former national team assistants, Brazilian striker Dutra netted the only goal midway through the first half for Kyoto, which had sent holders Kashima Antlers packing in the previous round.

'Sanga, who will face J1 heavyweights Yokohama F Marinos in Thursday's semifinal at Tokyo's National Stadium, will be joined in the last four by J2 champions FC Tokyo. No J2 team has yet to win the Emperor's Cup.

'"It was a tough game for us," said Kyoto coach Takeshi Oki, who worked under Takeshi Okada as Japan reached the second round at last year's World Cup. "We wanted to attack more than defend, but they wouldn't let us get forward. We've got Marinos next, and we'll do everything to try to beat them."'

26 December 2011

Today's nacho burger tasted even better than yesterday's, but it wasn't quite the same as eating leftover turkey and ham. Next year it's going to be a traditional English Christmas.

27 December 2011, Norwich verses Tottenham Hotspur

For a game that is meant to be on satellite television back home there is no sign of Norwich's game being aired in Japan, even though J-Sports is nothing more than another part of Rupert Murdoch's little media bastion.

The disappointment is already taking over as it means a sleepless night wondering if we've managed to resolutely rebuff the Spurs attacks, of which I think there will be many, and perhaps nicked a winning goal from our sole attack – a cheeky tap in or scuffed shot will suffice.

Christian's big idea of watching Chelsea has been shattered. Tickets went on sale to super members at 9am this morning, UK time, but sold out within 45 minutes, which means no chance of a season ticket holder getting one.

Norwich really need to speed up the ground expansion plans because we've been full to capacity for many a year now, even when we were plunged into League One. Now I have to think of an alternative male bonding experience we can do before he selfishly leaves the UK at the end of January.

28 December 2011

Piddling bollocks, **Norwich 0–2 Tottenham Hotspur,** and by all accounts we stood little chance of gaining anything from the game, Spurs dominant from start to finish, Gareth Bale running the show and scoring both goals.

And to make matters worse, the flight back from Japan was flying into a 100mph head wind which extended our stay at 36,000ft from 12 to 13 hours.

The good news is that although disappointment is two-fold, there was a postcard on the floor when I did get back home from the mail man saying he'd tried to deliver a parcel while I was abroad, which can mean just one thing: my Norwich City mug and 2010–11 Season Review DVD aren't too far away. And to brighten the soul even more a ticket for the QPR game on the 2 January is also held in my sweaty palms.

29 December 2011

I think Diane at the Norwich City FC warehouse really has taken a disliking to me, I have my new mug, but the DVD was wrong. Instead of sitting back to watch the highlights from a season that ended in promotion, I will have to watch Norwich's first demolition of Ipswich. Now although Demolition Derby is a DVD I wanted to purchase it isn't the one I wanted at this point in time.

But my disappointment pales into insignificance compared to some of the fans spouting doom and gloom about the last Norwich game. Not only is it doom and gloom but also indignation.

A chimp chant at Gareth Bale was apparently sung out by many hundreds if not thousands of Norwich fans. Now, this is a problem on two counts. Firstly those that are livid that after having to hear those chants from the home fans Bale should celebrate the first of his goals in front of the same fans – paybacks a bitch – calling him arrogant and antagonistic.

'I used to like Bale a lot, my second favourite non-Noriwch player after Messi. But his celebration, was pathetic. Did he think he won the World Cup? He's more arrogant than C. Ronaldo. Old 'arry doesn't help, saying how wonderful he is every week. Why can't some of these footballers take a leaf out of Messi and Xavi's book, you don't have to be so arrogant and self obsessed to be a good footballer,' said a certain Ginger Pele.

Don't see it myself, if you dish it out you have to be able to take it as well. Secondly the debate is now raging about what chanting and taunting is justifiable and what oversteps the mark. What would have happened had Bale been black?

I can say that I saw one of the 2011 Emperor's Cup finalists. Kyoto Sanga have made it to the Final of the competition after overcoming Yokohama F. Marino's 4–2 in extra-time. It's what the Cup is all about, giving lower League teams the chance to achieve grandeur.

30 December 2011

There is some sanity in the world, but it has come from the least likely of places. Jonny was quite clear with his thoughts on the game against Spurs, when even the most level headed of fan was saying that Gareth Bale was an arrogant git and being less than positive about the team overall.

Jonny's wise words were refreshing; yes Spurs were good, but they were playing a team that has risen from League One, some of our fellow supporters seem to forget this point – anyhow they were decent – worthy contenders for the Premier League title. I hope he isn't going to make a habit of being so honest.

The midget has also said he's going to wear a flat cap tomorrow because it's a bit chilly up in Norfolk, I knew he wouldn't be able to resist the temptation to follow my lead for long (two years to be precise), football and watching from the terraces is made for flat caps; they keep your head warm, keep the wintery sun out of your eyes and make you look stylish and mature.

31 December 2011, Norwich 1–1 Fulham

That has to have been one of the most frustrating displays from the team this season but we're 10th in the Premier League at the halfway stage. I know Fulham were a very good team – at both defending in numbers and time wasting – but we looked decidedly lacking in ideas and ability. Inside I was fuming but unlike some of my fellow fans I wouldn't boo the team based on just a single, difficult, game.

Not that the quality on display today stopped the crowd roaring with joy, and relief, when Simeon Jackson netted the equaliser in the 94th minute after a nice turn and cross from Elliott Bennett.

It should have been such a marvellous day, as the Japanese would say *ohisashiburi* (long time no see) Carrow Road. I hadn't been to the ground since the QPR game on the 26 November. I'd wangled my way into Kana's good books by waking up earlier, looking after the boy so she could have a lie in, taken her into Bromley to have a wander round the shops and then set off up the motorway. (And as a little bit of a pre-game build up exercise I had a small competition with Jonny to see who had the most Norwich-related memorabilia. It was text-war).

The Essex countryside had whistled by as I trundled up the M11, Essex turned into Cambridgeshire, Suffolk and then Norfolk as I crossed the border.

Things were looking even brighter as, although a fellow contender for relegation and therefore a rival, Blackburn had downed Manchester United at Old Trafford 2–3. A United loss gives everyone a warm fuzzy feeling inside.

There's a large section of the yellow army who don't agree with the building of a hotel in the corner of the ground, but whether they're right or wrong it does make a useful watering hole pre-game, I just wish they'd diversify their range of beers in the bar – wife-beater isn't my first choice of tipple and makes me run to the toilet more than a pint of CHB from the Coach and Horses.

Strangely Jonny didn't bother drinking pre-game before I arrived as he too was looking to earn some brownie points with his missus as he's off to the QPR game on Monday. He's going to be having a cheeky beer or two before boarding club cabbage and heading to London I reckon, the cheeky little drunk.

But the game, oh the game, why do we bother. Ben's crystal ball gazing had told him that this would be our first clean sheet of the campaign. Well after six minutes he was proved wrong as Fulham's Orlando Sa ran through the middle of our defence and rasped a shot past Ruddy.

From our seats in area EU, row I it looked like the parting of the waves by Moses, we just didn't have any energy, any foresight or any determination to close him down.

There was a lot of effing and blinding, not only from me, Jonny and Ben but also from everyone around us. The players, the ref, Fulham's annoying stubbornness and most of it was focused on David Stockdale, Fulham's 'keeper who had been away on loan at Ipswich.

From the moment they took the lead he took what seemed like decades to take a goal-kick, constantly shifting the ball position, changing the side he kicked from and taking achingly long to run up and actually kick the bloody ball. Morison was the centre of our own frustrations.

He didn't run into the box, he didn't chase balls and he just looked knackered the entire time he was on the pitch. Thank god for the half-time changes: Holt, Jackson and Bennett and an injection of urgency. The pressure finally built, Fulham's idiotic time wasting from the minute they scored finally came back to bite them on the arse: five minutes of stoppage time.

The rest is now written in the annuls of time, well the free press anyway:

The *Daily Telegraph*: 'Talk about brinkmanship. Simeon Jackson waited until the death throes of this match, and indeed the dying embers of 2011, to pounce with the header that rescued a most improbable point for Norwich City.'

The BBC: 'Norwich's second-half pressure finally told as Simeon Jackson's injury-time header denied Fulham only their second away win of the season.'

The *Guardian*: 'Paul Lambert had spoken of a successful 12 months for Norwich City but then Fulham rolled up and nearly claimed only a second away win to send the Scot and his men into 2012 on a dissonant note. But instead Simeon Jackson, with virtually the last kick of City's footballing year, headed an equaliser deep in added time to salvage a point that, following his side's second-half renaissance, always appeared likely.'

Sky Sports: 'Simeon Jackson's injury-time equaliser ensured Norwich avoided defeat at the end of a memorable 2011, as Paul Lambert's side grabbed a 1–1 draw with Fulham at Carrow Road.

The *Daily Star*: 'SUPER-SUB Simeon Jackson rescued a point for the Canaries with a sensational leveller in the fourth minute of stoppage time to break Fulham hearts.'

The *Daily Express*: 'SUBSTITUTE Simeon Jackson salvaged a crucial point for Norwich City with a sensational leveller against Fulham in the fourth minute of added time.'

Not that the Fulhan manager, Martin Jol seemed to agree with the sentiment from the press that we deserved a point from the game. He spent more time lamenting that fact that we dared put balls into the box and that his team should have scored more than just the solitary goal. I must give some credit to the Fulham fans who turned up to support their team, and spent £43 to do so, they didn't sing much, but when they scored they did have a sense of humour; 'We're winning away from home, you must be shit.'

Pre-match build-up – Competing with Jonny in the memorabilia stakes.

But what I, and Jonny, have learned from this game, and won't be repeating in the remaining fixtures, is that both my thermal leggings and his Christmas jumper bring bad luck to the team. Ho hum, next stop QPR.

1 January 2012

Happy New Year. It's time for the January transfer window to open and for teams to be linked with a plethora of players they either don't want, can't afford or who just don't want to move. Who'll be spotted in the car park of Morrison's supermarket, at the petrol station at the Thickthorn roundabout or having a meeting with club officials at Dunston Hall.

Lambert's already said he wants Kyle Naughton on a permanent deal, which should make every fan happy. And to add to that heady feeling, after watching *Match of the Day* on the BBC Alan Shearer reckons we'll survive the drop and stay in the League for another season, as does fellow pundit, Mark Lawrenson. So, whoever Lambert does bring in should do the business for us.

On the other side of the world Kyoto Sanga lost in the Final of the Emperor's Cup to FC Tokyo. That means that although Kyoto lost, and FC Tokyo will take the remaining spot in the Asian Champions League, it's still the first time that a second tier club has won the competition and entered the continental competition.

Could you imagine the likes of Barnsley, Coventry, Derby or any of the other teams in the Championship competing against the likes of Barcelona over here in Europe?

2 January 2012, Queen's Park Rangers 1–2 Norwich

Why is it that Joey Barton has to be at the centre of everything that QPR do or don't do, and on this particular day it has distracted attention from a very hard earned three points for Norwich.

If the stupid boy wasn't such an apparently obnoxious thug he could use his sprinkling of talent to play football rather than get himself sent off for violent conduct.

If you let the red mist descend after a challenge then you deserve to be taking an early shower, and I don't care if your manager, Neil Warnock (an anagram of whose name is Colin Wanker), thinks the referee's been conned. Shoulder barging an opposing player and squaring up to him isn't a sign of affection.

And Colin's post-match interview didn't exactly help matters, it's all very well to speak up for your players but to be so disrespectful of the opposing team is just plain wrong. These are Colin's words verbatim:

'It's not easy to speak about it if I'm honest without getting carried away. It seems to happen every single time we play Norwich – getting people sent off wrongly and all the decisions going against us. I thought my lads were fantastic and it takes a lot of stuffing out of you. What's that they say? Cheats never prosper. Bradley Johnson has never been headbutted at all. Not in a million years. Okay the heads are together but the movement of him going backwards has conned the linesman. The referee hasn't seen it. I think he has guessed. Because the lad has gone back you presume he has been headbutted. Then to rub salt in the wounds he starts rubbing his nose as if he is feeling for blood. I think it's a disgrace personally. There was two vicious tackles on Joey which were never booked. I find it amazing.

No, I don't think Paul Lambert is like that. But I've seen Bradley Johnson do that a few times in the past so it doesn't surprise me. He's done great if you think you can wind somebody up. Joey could've avoided the situation but football is football. He is not daft enough to headbutt somebody with all the cameras around. I've not got any confidence in the appeals procedure. I just think all round we have been mugged and conned. The referee has not seen it so you can't blame him. To get a fellow professional sent off; I think he should be done.'

But it's bitterness because QPR have spent an awful lot of money and now hang precariously at the wrong end of the table only three points clear of the bottom three. And based on yesterday's performance it's no more than they deserve.

Norwich set up strangely with Simon Lappin and Adam Drury down one side and Russell Martin and Anthony Pilkington down the other, that left Bradley Johnson and Elliott Bennett in the centre with Grant Holt and Simeon Jackson up top. It didn't seem to work.

We had a lot of possession but did nothing with it. There wasn't that spark of imagination a player like Hoolahan brings to the team when he is pulling the strings from the centre of the pitch.

Bennett for all his ability is much better hugging the touchline, getting chalk on his boots and taking on full-backs while getting balls into the box.

Pitch invasion – QPR 1–2 Norwich, remembered for Joey Barton's antics.

And it showed, the industry was for nothing because after 11 minutes Barton popped up to thrash home QPR's goal, from their first real attack.

Still it didn't stop the away fans singing 'On The Ball City' to rally the team, and I particularly enjoyed the rendition of 'My garden shed.' For those not in the know it goes like so:

> My garden shed (my garden shed),
> Is bigger than this (is bigger than this),
> My garden shed is bigger than this,
> And so is my conservatory,
> My garden shed is bigger than this…

(It pertains to the size of Loftus Road, which holds only 18,360 fans but is rarely full).

And then in the 37th minute the referee brandished his red card and send Barton for an early shower. I thought something might happen. Barton was running alongside Zak Whitbred as QPR moved forward in attack, they seemed to tangle and Whitbred went down, Johnson then ran across him and seemed to have a nibble at Barton for hitting Whitbred. It was then that Barton lost his cool, firstly shoulder barging Johnson before squaring up to him and leading with his head. It was a red, you can't do that in the modern game. It wasn't as if Johnson went down rolling around in the throws of death, he turned and rubbed his nose.

Play carried on for a few seconds before, for some unknown reason, the referee blew his whistle. I don't remember anyone screaming at the referee about the incident, but every fan, as you'd expect, wanted the red card. Maybe his linesman did see it, maybe the fourth official had a word in his ear. You'd need to see his match report to know that.

QPR were down to 10 men for the remainder of the game, and surely it was only a matter of time before our numerical advantage turned into goals. It took five minutes. Pilkington hit a left-foot shot inside Paddy Kenny's left-hand post from just outside the area for his fifth goal of the season. I clapped as I was sat on my own, but the young lads down the front were jumping up and down like loons, I was with them in spirit.

The second goal took an age. Lambert stuck with his original line-up until the 66th minute before bringing on Wes Hoolahan, David Fox and Steve Morison, which made the world of difference.

Then ecstasy; in the 83rd minute Pilkington's cross from the left was knocked back at the far post by Bennett for Morison to drill home from eight yards. Fists pumped, and my throat went horse from screaming.

I saw Jake Humphrey on the way out of the ground, he might be the face of the BBC's Formula One coverage, but I felt no need to have my photo taken with him. In retrospect I probably should have as it would have been one over the little man – Jonny loves motorsport. Still walking behind well known people is better than chasing them like paparazzi, which is probably what Jonny would have done.

3 January 2012

It seem every man and his dog has an opinion about Barton's red card, from former referees, to players and managers, even those in the press and media are debating whether it was a legitimate booking.

Graham Poll, infamous for dishing out three yellow cards to one player in a World Cup said it was unacceptable as the match officials didn't see the offence. Robbie Savage that divisive former Welsh player said it was wrong, while QPR are going to appeal the decision.

It perhaps wouldn't be so bad, but would there be the same outcry had it been one of the other QPR players, or perhaps if roles were reversed and Johnson had attempted to head butt Barton.

According to Barton, perhaps not, who labelled Johnson a 'no mark' in one of his tweets after the game. He also called him 'Boris Johnson from Norwich'.

In fact, he wouldn't stop banging on about the subject, his timeline was full of personal insight into the whole episode, which then turned into a debate on the advantages of introducing video technology:

'Well feel for the officials, they've been conned. Admitted to me at HT they never saw it. I was pulled back 1st, then kicked 2nd!'

'Linesman definitely never saw it, all he seen was Johnsons reaction. My head doesn't move forward at all. Ridiculous decision seen 25 replays.'

'Why dont they copy rugby and cite incidents instead of taking a blind stab at decisions. Theres too much money involved for guesswork.'

'I wonder how long it is before a football club sues a referee for making a bad decision? Theres too much at stake to not have technology.'

'Someone has to set the precedent to stop the game from being ruined, maybe i'll be the 1st one. Can players sue referree's?'

'It's only archaic dinosaurs who don't like change that don't agree with technology. Right that's it, my 2nd Big Issue column is going to be…'

Barton has previous, he fell over very theatrically after being slapped very softly across the cheek by an Arsenal player when he was at Newcastle, getting the guy sent off, making him slightly hypocritical. I did try and raise what I think is the more important point with Master Barton, that it's the players feigning injury that is the real issue, but as he has nearly one million followers on Twitter I don't think he saw my tweets directed at him.

In Barton's mind the introduction of technology would allow match officials to quickly replay an incident and make a decision based on video evidence. The counter argument is it would slow the game down too much. But in my mind the problem that referees have is that they can't ever be sure if a player has really been badly tackled or the victim of violent conduct because players spend so much of their time rolling around on the floor clutching their ankles, shins, faces, shoulders, you name it they hold it, after the mildest of touches from an opposing player. Players need to re-learn integrity. It's embarrassing watching players roll around on the ground like they've been shot, especially when that begins to trickle down into the lower leagues, the Sunday teams and even the school kids.

I remember the 1990 World Cup semi-final between England and West Germany, and what is etched on my mind is the image of some German players doing cartwheels down the pitch after being tackled. That for me is where this disease that afflicts the beautiful game began.

If you only go down after a truly heavy tackle then a referee will instantly know that something isn't right and be able to deal with the crime accordingly. Yes there will be instances when neither the referee or his linesmen will be able to see what has occurred – they don't have eyes in the back of their heads – but they'll be minimal.

Save the technology for the goal line, where deciding if a ball has crossed the line or not, something that can happen in a split second and you may actually need a reply. For the rest of the 90 minutes just get players to show some respect to themselves, their fellow professionals and the fans.

4 January 2012

The mood has turned decidedly sour for some QPR fans as they begin to think of Norwich in the same way some at Leeds do. Their message boards are alive with incandescent hatred for us:

'I ****ing hate them. Hate Paul Lambert and the fact that despite being the most boring man I have ever seen interviewed he is a good manager.
Hate Grant ****ing Holt, the fat cheating, diving bastard, who somehow manages to score against us every time despite possessing no skill whatsoever.
Hate Bradley Johnson, the scumbag.
Hate their tactic of screaming at the referee and conning him.
Hate the way the media goes on about them – 'Yeah, Norwich, such a great family club. Proud history. Love them'. Erm…what exactly have they ever achieved?
Hate the way the media makes them out to be 'the Blackpool of this season'. No they're not – they play boring 'sideways' football and cheat.

Hate their stupid yellow and green kit, which makes me want to puke.

Hate their logo.

Hate their ground, particularly their stewards.

Hate the fact that we always give them both tiers of the School End despite them giving us a tiny allocation every year.

Hate the 'Norwich mafia' a.k.a. Delia Smith, Stephen 'overrated' Fry, Simon Thomas, Hugh Jackman and that god-awful band The Darkness. Wouldn't be surprised if they were involved in these biased refereeing displays, the SCUM!

Hate the way their supporters campaigned for us to be docked points so that they could get their six-fingered hands on our trophy. Scum, scum, scum!

Hate their stupid anthem, whatever it's called.

Hate the way their fans sing 'green army!' – that's Plymouth Argyle, you ****s!

Hate their city.

Hate their farms.

Hate their tractors.

Hate every single member of their Board of Directors.

I HATE THEM!'

No reading between the lines with that particular point of view, quite the vociferous thought chain.

5 January 2012

I'm just a little bit disappointed that there have been no rumours about players coming into the club. The window has been open for five days now and not a dickie bird. Even that annoying club from West London have made a bid for Chris Samba, the goliath Blackburn defender, all £5 million of it.

There have been a few interesting rumours on the least reliable website fans use: football-rumours.co.uk.

Arsenal are set to make a shock move for Norwich 'keeper Ruddy with Almunia and Mannone out of contract in the summer.

Eight Premier League club scouts watching Jordan Rhodes tonight including Norwich. Norwich looks like a likely destination for him after they have a good relationship as there manager Lee Clark used to be at Norwich.

Sunderland forward Frasier Campbell to Norwich £1 million.

Norwich are after highly rated Shrewsbury striker Tom Bradshaw.

Nicky Maynard to go to Norwich for £4.5 million.

Peter Whittingham has been spotted in Norwich!

Norwich Boss Paul Lambert is set to bolster his attack by making a move for Southampton Striker Rickie Lambert. The deal is expected to be finalised within the next few days. Lambert is also looking at a loan move for Leeds winger Robert Snodgrass with a view to a permanent deal in summer should Norwich avoid relegation.

Norwich boss Paul Lambert is looking to bring in Dortmond striker Lucas Barrios.

Norwich City are set to sign promising Colchester United left back Ben Coker for £350k.

I wonder how many of them will be true when the window closes at the end of the month.

6 January 2012

Paul Lambert has finally come out in defence of his players after the huge amount of venom directed at them by Neil Warnock. It's taken longer than I wanted, he should have been jumping down Warnock's throat from the minute he heard the drivel coming out of the man's mouth:

'I think some of the comments labelled towards Bradley Johnson have been ludicrous. He is my player and he is certainly not a cheat. If you are going to label someone then have a bit of substance to it. If you go face-to-face with someone then there is a chance that things can happen. I certainly don't think it is a full-blooded headbutt. That is not the issue I have a gripe with – it's the comments after. I know in the heat of the game things can happen. One; Bradley Johnson never went down so for somebody to say he did is totally wrong. Neil did his talking on the television. I am just responding, but my player is not a cheat. He played with great discipline before and after the incident. But those aftermatch comments were wrong. Maybe when you get beat you start to look for excuses and end up blaming everybody else. My lads were excellent on Monday. They played with an enthusiasm and discipline in their game. If you are going to criticise them make sure there is some substance. I have no issue with Joey Barton whatsover. He scored a really good goal, a really good player. Don't have a problem with him or the incident, but I have a problem with other people speaking about my players.'

But while Lambert may well have eventually stood up for his player, Johnson has got into a little bit of trouble. All the lads are going to watch the darts after the game on Monday, a few images were tweeted, one of which included Johnson holding a board up that he'd scrawled 'Barton, your breath stinks' on. Perhaps not the most intelligent thing to do, even if it was funny. That incident has apparently been dealt with in-house.

I wonder if he'll get dropped to the bench for the game tomorrow when we take on the mighty Burnley in the FA Cup?

One incident that won't be dealt with in-house is the abuse that Tom Adeyemi had thrown at him by certain aspects of the Liverpool crowd when he was playing for Oldham at Anfield tonight. Someone apparently shouted at him, calling him a 'black bastard,' which caused a certain amount of distress, the crowd then started singing a song about Luis Suarez just to add insult to injury.

Adeyemi's only a young lad, just finding his feet, he's out on loan from Norwich learning his trade, and he's subjected to that.

There's been a furore surrounding racism, with Suarez calling Patrick Evera a *negro*, John Terry apparently calling Anton Ferdinand the same and now this.

Twitter has been awash with people either agreeing or disagreeing about the level of abuse footballer should tolerate considering their wages, I think this has crossed the line. In fact, it's so far over the line that you can't even see the line.

Liverpool have issued a statement, which is decent of them I guess:

* **Liverpool FC apologises for upset and distress suffered by Oldham player Tom Adeyemi**

* **Club reaffirms commitment to work with game's ruling bodies to fight discrimination**

* **Reds vow to take strongest possible action against unacceptable behaviour**

Liverpool Football Club has been forthright and resolute for many years in its stance against racism and any form of discrimination.

The Club has worked actively to combat discrimination and has been at the forefront of social inclusion and community activity in football, winning awards and commendations for its work throughout the world. And this Club is determined to continue its part in working with the game's ruling bodies and the other organisations active in this area.

Whatever the outcome of what is now a police investigation, all of us are deeply sorry for what happened on Friday night and our players and our Club pass on our sincere regrets to Tom Adeyemi for the upset and distress he suffered as a result of the matter at hand.

Our supporters are renowned throughout the world for their outstanding commitment, passion and fairness. They are drawn from nationalities across the globe with widely diverse backgrounds and heritages. The actions of any one individual do not represent our fans. Their stance on these issues is just as resolute as the Club's. We have a very clearly stated public stance on discrimination and intolerance with dedicated staff that work hard daily on programs in this important area.

Regarding the incident that occurred on Friday evening, we have given Merseyside police every possible assistance we can and will continue to provide the necessary support to their investigation in order to ensure this particular incident is dealt with properly. We will continue to take the strongest possible action(s) against unacceptable behaviour during our matches.

7 January 2010, Norwich 4–1 Burnley

I don't speak Portuguese, but what NorwichBrasil said on twitter translates quite easily once you know the score:

'E como prev', o primeiro gol do dia na FA Cup é Can·rio, e advinha quem foi? Super Holt. Em cabeÁada venenosa, assistencia d Surman.'

And his entry for the second goal wasn't too difficult to figure out either:

'GOOOOOOOOOOOOOOOOOOOOOOOOOOOOOOOL JACKSON, DE CABE«A, 2 A 0 PRO NORWICH.'

He wasn't too happy about Burnley's goal:

'Gol de Jay Rodriguez. em cabeçada. Norwich 2 - 1 Burnley - 17 min'.

But normal service was resumed when Surman scored our third:

'GOOOOOOOOOOOOOOOOOOOOOOOOOOL DE SURMAN. GOL DO GAROTO'.

And the fourth, after Holt and Jackson were replaced by Morison and Wilbraham:

'STEVE MORRISON ACABOU DE ENTRAR E J¡ VAZOU O BURNLEY. FAZENDO O QUARTO GOL CAN¡RIO EMPURRANDO PRO MEIO DO GOL, EM CRUZAMENTO BAIXO.'

Maybe I should make the effort and go to the next game – depending on who we're drawn against and whether it's a home or away tie. Imagine if it's QPR.

8 January 2012

West Brom in the Cup, well that's slightly underwhelming, but on a positive note Neil Warnock has been sacked as manager of QPR, throwing the club into turmoil and adding another team to the mix of possible contenders for relegation, easing every Norwich fan's nerves.

It seems saving the R's from relegation from the Championship one season and then winning promotion as champions wasn't good enough for the owners. As much as I find Warnock an obnoxious man it's a sad reflection on the game that a successful manager can be given the elbow so swiftly – the team aren't even in the relegation spots.

9 January 2012

QPR are looking at bringing in Mark Hughes to replace Warnock. Not as bad an idea as many might think, even if he did walk out on Fulham because the club didn't meet his ambitions.

And what will it take for Hughes to save QPR from dropping through the trap door and back into the Championship? £30 million.

Yes, Hughes would need to spend an extra £30 million on new players to save them from relegation. How must that make the current squad feel?

And that statement makes what Lambert has done at Norwich even sweeter. On a miniscule budget he's managed to drag Norwich up through the leagues and into the top half of the Premier League. It makes you wonder what he could achieve if he was handed £30 million.

10 January 2012

I've conceded, I'm keeping the DVD of the 4–1 demolition of Ipswich, my reasons are two-fold:

1) I can't be bothered to pay for the return postage, (I really am that tight).

2) I've already watched it and so have broken the seal.

Diane from the club won't feel my wrath, and the club it seems will be making more money from me when I wander over and buy the DVD I actually wanted – the 2010–11 season review.

11 January 2012

Season ticket prices are apparently being increased by 12 per cent for the 2012–13 season. I think that means my seat should cost about £450, which if we're still in the Premier League seems like a bargain. That means £25 a game, which when casual tickets to watch the big games can cost as much as £45 this season (so presumably add 12 per cent for next season), is an absolute steal.

12 January 2012

I am under pressure to meet up with the boys for a drink after the Chelsea game on the 21 January. Now while that may not seem like the biggest social disaster in living memory, it puts me in a conundrum, should I go and have a drink or 10, which will undoubtedly be a bloody good laugh, should I take the good lady out to dinner, at Delia's obviously to celebrate my upcoming birthday, or should I head straight back to my mothers and have a family dinner?

Now as mentioned the positives of going out for a drink with friends are obvious, but there are some drawbacks mostly related to the relationship between copious amounts of alcohol and my delicate digestive system.

Dinner with Kana is always an acceptable evening, but as she has just bought me a rather expensive folding bicycle I don't think it would be too gentlemanly to then ask for her to buy me dinner as well, as much as I would like to eat at Delia's restaurant. I guess we could go to every Norwich City footballer's favourite eatery and try Nando's.

The next choice is a family dinner. Nothing wrong there, a good home cooked dinner and a catch up on local events, but quite selflessly I think, it's nice for the grandparents to spend time with George without his parents about.

With mum and dad in view he tends to levitate to us, if Kana and I bugger off he's slightly more gregarious and gets proper bonding time. Maybe I should draw straws.

13 January 2012

QPR are now apparently in for Steven Pienaar from Spurs, they're also after Samba from Blackburn and Alex from Chelsea. While I think they've got a cat in hells chance of actually signing any of them, it'd be nice if we were actually officially linked with someone, instead of the tittle-tattle floating around the discussion forums.

My only solace is found in Paul Lambert's words: 'We have a structure we think might stabilise it, but you still have to get players in who you think can try and help. You'd love to be linked with people who cost £10 million or £12 million and pay the wages, but we're not – that is the reality of it. Because you are in the Premier League, people assume that we can do what QPR can do, but we can't. The money they are talking about, we can't compete with that.'

14 January 2012, West Bromwich Albion 1–2 Norwich

The internet is a wondrous thing, you can read the match reports from the Sunday papers on Saturday. Unfortunately it seems our hard fought victory today wasn't as illustrious as Norwich fans may think.

'Norwich mugged West Brom yesterday – leaving Baggies boss Roy Hodgson looking for another advertising hoarding to bang his head against,' according to the *Sunday Mirror*.

While the *Express and Star* (never heard of it), said: 'Two sucker-punch goals from Norwich condemned West Brom to a third successive Premier League defeat despite a goalscoring return by Shane Long.'

We did look a little suspect in defence – I couldn't make the game but I found a watchable stream online – with Ayala hacking down a WBA player in the box for their goal, and numerous last ditched tackles, blocks on the line and reliant on some super saves from John Ruddy.

Still a cracking volley from Andrew Surman for the first goal (Jonny seems to think that by somehow hating him he has placed a positive curse on Surman making him good), and a wonderful run down the left wing and cross by Holt for Morison to head home the second. As long as you can score more than the opposition then who cares if you still haven't kept a clean sheet this season.

Last week I quite enjoyed the Portugese tweets from NorwichBrasil, this week NorwichCityFCBR was just as enthusiastic but a little harder to understand, and the translation services online leave a lot to be desired. *Dois gols feitos por Surman e Morison por contra-ataque fazem com que os can·rios liquidem os Baggies por 1x2 em pleno Hawthorns,* became: Two goals made by Surman and Morison by counterattack cause the Canarian settle the Baggies for 2 teeth in full Hawthorns.

I don't know what that means.

15 January 2012

Twitter gave me two interesting insights today. Firstly happiness can be measured against whether you own a jet ski or not and came via Alice Bhandakravi, (whose followers I am steadily starting to equal, she has 1,917, I have 1,539), care of someone called Damian Victory: 'Money doesn't buy happiness? Well it buys a jet ski. Have you ever seen a sad person on a jet ski.'

I can't argue with that.

Secondly the Norwich phenomenon is growing, Dan Walker, BBC sports presenter tweeted this: 'By the way…forget Spurs…Norwich are going to win the league! Maybe not but they've been brilliant this season.'

16 January 2012

Still no transfer news, halfway through the month and there's nothing, nada, absolutely zero.

And a club faces disappearing from the football map. Cheerio Darlington, your 25,000 seat stadium that cost £18 million, was possibly the worst decision you've ever made. Today your manager and playing staff were all made redundant.

17 January 2012

No players in, but players are leaving. Ritchie DeLaet has had his season long loan terminated by the club. So he's off back to Manchester United, while Oli Johnson has had his contract cancelled by mutual consent.

Johnson joined from Stockport in January 2010, scored four times (two of which came against Southend, getting us out of jail and winning the game), in 23 appearances for the Canaries, of which 19 were as a substitute.

18 January 2012

We've got a new player! Jonny Howson, the Leeds United midfielder and captain is coming to Carrow Road to enjoy some Premier League football. Leeds fans aren't happy, they're blaming their manager Simon Grayson and owner Ken Bates. Some are even further in despair:

'I really don't understand. I'm only a youngster, still in my teens. But this isn't the Leeds United I was told about.

'Elland Road was described as a fortress, crowds of 50,000, frightening the opposition, even being described as being as good as a goals start! We had the best away support in the country, packing out anywhere we went and then accordingly smashing it up. I heard tales of great games and legends, scoring 4 past giants such as Liverpool, locking horns with the likes of Barcelona and Real Madrid in the finest competitions. 7,000 fans travelling to the San Siro and witnessing a 1–1 draw. I hear tales of Revie and Billy, Norman Hunter and the wizard that was Eddy Gray.

'So now, at an age where I can attend the matches alone, I travel when possible to watch the Mighty Whites, but the thing is, we are not. We aren't a force. Elland Road isn't a fortress. There are no legends. There are no heroic matches. Just the same broken promises and bull**** churned out week on week. My 'boyhood heroes' have gone. Beckford, Gradel and now Howson. My three favourite players have all walked away. But I don't get it.

'What on earth happened to Leeds United?'

Makes you happy that Norwich are on an upward spiral and now using Leeds as a feeder club.

19 January 2012

Bugger, the Chelsea game is a 12:45 kick-off, sodding Sky. That could have been a major cock-up had Jonny not asked. Not a lot going on if you arrive for a lunch-time kick off at 3 o'clock.

David McNally tweeted that season ticket renewal forms would be arriving tomorrow. I did reply to ask if the interest free monthly payment option was still available, but he hasn't replied yet.

I also tweeted the *Pink'un* the same question, and also if the rumour about ticket prices increasing by 12 per cent was true, they haven't replied either. Losing faith in twitter, Hugh Jackman never replied either.

20 January 2012

The build up to the big game tomorrow continues, but rather than look forward, I thought I might have a little look back. To 2006 to be precise.

Since Norwich lured Howson away from Leeds there has been lots of arguing about why he'd move from a 'big' club like Leeds to a 'small' club like Norwich.

One of the criteria for Leeds being a bigger club was the number of fans it has, according to a survey conducted in 2006, Leeds at that time had 928,000 supporters, making it the ninth most popular club in England. Norwich had 458,000 and was placed 15th.

Our enemies on Saturday, Chelsea were the fourth most popular team six years ago with 1.4 million fans, but more interestingly Chelsea supporters, when compared to the average UK football supporter, were:

More than twice as likely (164 per cent more likely) to have been to a beauty salon or spa in the last three months.
More than twice as likely (139 per cent more likely) to be underweight.
84 per cent more likely to agree 'I wear clothes that will get me noticed'.
64 per cent more likely to agree 'It only feels like a holiday if I leave the UK'.
63 per cent more likely to be aged between 25 and 34.
56 per cent more likely to be renting their current residence.
54 per cent more likely to agree 'I was born to shop'.
50 per cent more likely to agree 'I choose a car mainly on its looks'.
44 per cent more likely to see their main goal in life is to have 'A prosperous life'.
28 per cent more likely to agree 'It's important to have a full social life'.
20 per cent more likely to be single.

21 January 2012, Norwich 0–0 Chelsea

What's the best way to wind up Chelsea fans? Tell them they're all a bunch of wankers. Or at least that's the view of the Barclay anyway.

'Team full of wankers, you're just a team full of wankers…'

Not exactly the most eloquent use of the English language but it got the message across, as did the follow-up chant of: 'We've got a famous cook, you've got a Russian crook.'

Most of this game is going to be remembered for Torres missing a golden opportunity to score for Chelsea, scuffing his shot from only eight yards out. But that's the rest of the nation who only saw the game on *Match of the Day*, for every Norwich fan, this game was the first clean sheet of the season, against a team that had been assembled for many, many millions of pounds and who are managed by a 34-year-old who thinks he's the next Jose Mourino, but is just a shadow of the 'Special One'.

But we could, and perhaps should have won the match. Raul Meireles should have been punished for a handball on the edge of his own box, but what seemed even worse was the officiating by Mark Clattenburg – my least favourite referee – who was overly-officious and didn't let Holt take a quick free-kick which put Pilkington clean through.

How can someone place the ball on the ground and then kick it be accused of benefiting from a travelling ball?

So close but a well deserved point, and now we're ninth and on 29 points, 11 more to go until we are theoretically safe from relegation.

Went for the family dinner option.

22 January 2012

I missed it yesterday, but the front cover of the digital version of the *Pink'un* posed an interesting question; One Fernando Torres (£50 million, 30 League games and three goals), or 125 Grant Holts, (£400,000, 104 League games and 52 goals)?

It was a theme that didn't just have the local press talking, the *Independent* thought it a good topic to cover too.

Richard Rae might find comparisons odious but it didn't stop him from comparing the Norwich and Chelsea strikers:

'At Carrow Road today is surely one of those times. On one side will be Fernando Torres, the former Atletico Madrid and Liverpool striker for whom Chelsea paid £50m, who has scored two Premier League goals in 16 appearances this season. On the other will be Grant Holt, the former Barrow and Shrewsbury forward for whom Norwich paid £400,000, who has scored seven in 20.

'Unfair? To Holt and to his teammates, definitely. The Cumbrian's return for the Canaries is impressive, but if there is one thing the Premier League considers it has learned about Norwich this season it is that the whole is greater than the sum of their parts. Less readily acknowledged seems to be the fact that those individual parts are of a considerably higher quality than many people were prepared to admit.

'Holt is a pretty good example. Given the quality of the goals he has scored and the assists he has provided this season, one of these days people might stop referring to him as "old-fashioned". Not many who were at The Hawthorns last Saturday to see him sprint down the left wing before curling in a perfect cross for Steve Morison to head home City's second-half winner against West Bromwich Albion would continue to place him in that category.'

I've returned to London with the DVD I had ordered online but which never materialised as the club thought better and gave me the 4–1 victory over Ipswich DVD. I now own the 2010–11 season review. One in the eye for Diane.

I also bought a plaque for the boy's room, it includes a nice big image of the Norwich crest and 'George's Room' printed in big bold letters. Kana isn't impressed, she was hoping to decorate his room with Winnie the Pooh, but thankfully George likes the big yellow bird.

23 January 2012

It's my birthday, and I've celebrated by renewing my season ticket. They have indeed increased by 12 per cent. In total I'll be paying £471 or just over £39 a month to watch games, it's a little of a pinch but as it's really the only thing I spend my money on other than bills, I guess it's worth it (and as I've renewed early it's cheaper than the £547 I would be paying should I have held off renewing until the 7 April). Knowing I'll be back watching from the stands next season fills me with joy. I also have a pair of green away socks, which I shall be testing for luck value during the next city game. Life's good.

It's also good if you're a Norwich goalkeeper or defender as both John Ruddy and Zak Whitbred made it into ESPN's team of the week

24 January 2012

Jonny has renewed his season ticket. That just leaves Ben. Will he give in to family pressures or will he join us in the 2012–13 season? Only time and his wife will tell.

25 January 2012

So when it comes to the promoted teams, only Swansea and Norwich are worth watching, and more than that, we both bring a little bit of Spanish and German respectively, to the Premier League.

That's the view of Michael Cox in an article on the ESPN website anyway, and he's a journalist that I might start playing closer attention to, especially when he says things like:

'The performances of these two [Norwich and Swansea] this season has been remarkable, and fascinating on a tactical level too. That, rather than the title race, the battle for Champions League places or the relegation dogfight, has been the best thing about the 2011/12 Premier League season so far.'

And that was only the end of the article, the beginning and middle were equally as complimentary. How can you argue with someone who seems to understand how we go about the game so well.

The reason that Norwich play with the mind of a German is purely down to how Lambert went about gaining his coaching badges – in Germany under the tutelage of Erich Rutermuller, the man in charge of the German FA's coaching course. As for

Swansea's Spanish link, that is down to their manager, Brendan Rogers, being obsessed by the Spanish (and Dutch), way of playing the game.

Which influence on each team's style of play will be more successful only time will tell, but for me, just as Cox has suggested, it's Lambert's pragmatism rather than Rogers' willingness to stick to the rigid, but aesthetically pleasing, passing style, that will is better suited to staying in the Premier League.

'Although the diamond seems Norwich's natural shape, he has also played a 5–3–2, a 4–4–2 and a 4–4–1–1. The Scot is a more pragmatic manager, looking at the opposition's shape and adjusting his side accordingly. After the draw against Chelsea at the weekend, Lambert indicated he had been entirely happy to allow Andre Villas-Boas' side the majority of the ball. "They had the majority of possession, which they're entirely entitled to," he said.'

26 January 2012

It seems that the habits of some fans who attend games at Carrow Road is proving a little irksome for some. Arriving early, leaving late, getting up to use the little boy's room, bringing bags, it's all become too much for Ilovedelia on the not606 discussion board:

'I just want to put this on record for all to read. It's for the so called supporters who arrive late, leave early, go to the bar or pie shop 10 minutes before the end of the first half, come back their seats 10 minutes after the second half has started, bring the biggest rucksack they can find which only has a can of coke in it apparently, breathe alcohol fumes in my face as they push past, bring 3 month old babies and really small kids who get bored after the first 15 minutes, and start to leave 10 minutes before the game ends......

WHY DO YOU BOTHER?
If you're more interested in drinking, eating pies, having a picnic or showing off your new baby, then go and do it somewhere else! I'm there to watch the football, and I'm fed up with having to constantly get up to let you wander about. Here's a few pointers: Eat before you get to the ground, likewise with the drinking, have a pee before the game starts, leave the enormous rucksack at home, take your kids to Bedlam for the afternoon, and get some breath freshener!

Thank you for your attention.'

Now part of me agrees with the sentiment, it has to be one of the most annoying things when someone gets up and pushes down the aisle, it puts you in the predicament of not wanting to move in case you miss something but not wanting to be a belligerent arsehole and not move. And who am I to speak with my digestive problems? If I need to dash to the loo, I need to dash to the loo. But given the team's track record of scoring late goals, those who leave early – for whatever reason – get no sympathy (I didn't get any when I left Anfield early).

27 January 2012

I missed this, but Grant Holt is an absolute gent, and is the epitome of why the majority of Norwich fans currently feel so close to the team. On his way to London for a bit of stress busting fun with Adam Drury he tweeted from the train:

'What's that funny smell. Strange place.' He was travelling through Ipswich at the time.

Can you imagine some of the prima donnas who earn millions every month plying their trade with the big teams doing something like that? Probably not. And to make himself even more 'one of the boys', in a recent interview with *The Guardian* newspaper, he told everyone what car he was driving when he first joined Norwich. Not an Audi, Range Rover, Bentley or any of the other vehicles that have been tainted by the title 'Footballer's car'. No he spent his time driving the 300 miles between Norwich and his family in Carlisle in a Peugeot 307 and put 45,000 miles on the clock in his first year at the club. Can you see Wayne Rooney doing that in his wanky pimp-mobile?

And this from the man that has scored 62 goals for Norwich and helped drag us from the despair of League One to the wonder of the top flight in two years (he's still got a long way to go until he beats Johnny Gavin as our all-time leading scorer – 132 goals in 312 appearances between 1948 and 1958).

28 January 2012, West Bromwich Albion 1-2 Norwich

We're going to win the Cup, we're going to win the Cup! I repeat we're going to win the Cup!

It wasn't on TV, it wasn't on any internet streams, but it wasn't a classic so I didn't miss anything. We scored two – one for Holt and one for Jackson – which was more than the opposition. West Brom might feel hard done by, but I'm happy we're one step closer to playing at Wembley in the oldest Cup competition in the world.

29 January 2012

Leicester at home in the fifth round of the FA Cup. The Cup games might be maligned by some but when you haven't progressed this far for the last seven years then it's nice to get a step further to Wembley. And if there is one thing I would love to experience as a Norwich City fan it is a trip to Wembley. A sea of yellow and green, on the ball city belted out in the capital city at the home of English football.

Survival this season might be the aim for the club, and while I want the team to stay in the top division, there's not much better than the romance of making it to a Cup Final. And Leicester at home is probably about as winnable a game as you're going to get at this stage of the competition. Arguments and brownie points permitting I might get to watch this one in the flesh – unless they show it on the television in which case I might have to reassess.

I wonder how much FA Cup Final tickets will cost, the League Cup – a much less prestigious event – is priced at £90 for the best seats in category one, £72 for category two seats, £56 for category three and £40 in category four.

Last year the most expensive ticket was £115 and the cheapest £45, how much do you think the FA will add on this year, 10 per cent, 15 per cent, 20 per cent? Depends how desperate they are I guess.

30 January 2012

More than 200 people queued up to buy one of the few remaining tickets for the Manchester United game in three weeks. Some of the nut cases had been in line from 4.30am. I'm not sure if that is dedication or stupidity, and I'm not sure that the people in the line were Norwich or United fans.

Mr Swatman, who was number six in the queue told the local paper that: 'It is Manchester United, so it will be really good to see them. We wanted to be guaranteed a ticket so we got down there early.'

I don't know how to take that, surely if you're a Norwich fan you'd go to any game not just one against Manchester United? Isn't only wanting to see the current League champions a little one-dimensional?

I wonder if Mr Swatman went to watch the likes of Yeovil, Leyton Orient and Bristol Rovers when we were in League One, or dragged himself to Carrow Road to see Crystal Palace or Barnsley last year in the Championship. But I guess if nothing else he's putting more money into the club's coffers.

31 January 2012

That's it, I give up we aren't going to sign anybody else before the transfer window closes. There have been rumours, spurious and otherwise, floating around all day. Grant Holt was meant to be on his way to Rangers, and if you believe Fox Sport Chris Sutton was making his way to Blackburn for £5 million (I think the American's are 15 years behind the footballing times).

As for those coming in, well how about Jordan Rhodes from Huddersfield or finalising a permanent move for Kyle Naughton? Neither of which seem to be happening.

The only rumour that seems to have any grounds whatsoever is that we might be stealing Ryan Bennett from Peterborough United. I say stealing, he could well sign but then loan him straight back as he's only a young lad.

I'm going to bed. Even David McNally isn't sure that we'll be getting anyone else in. He twittered not five minutes ago: 'We are attempting to do some business before the deadline but it cannot be guaranteed with so little time left.'

Maybe when I wake up tomorrow morning something interesting will have happened and I can get back to looking forward to the game against Sunderland in the evening.

We may not be spending the millions that QPR seem to be (£4 million for Lazio's French striker Djibril Cisse or £3 million for Nedum Onuoha from Manchester City), but at least we seem to be acting sensibly rather than panic buying I guess. Time will tell if it's the right way: either we'll stay up or end up back in the Championship come May.

1 February 2012, Sunderland 3–0 Norwich

Let's move on swiftly shall we. That was, even through the blur of an atrocious internet stream, the worst performance of the season. Yes, Sunderland's first goal was an absolute peach – and scored by Fraizer Campbell, returning after a long-term injury – but the Norwich boys were rubbish. Even Lambert was rubbish. Not much marshalling from the technical area and changes to the formation made too late to be effective. All in all a horrendous evening to be a canary, especially the 800 or so who made the 500 mile round trip on a cold winter's night.

Some fans went straight to the discussion boards to lament our rubbishness.

'Totally bottled it today under his "master" and he was certainly shown as the school kid. Wrong line-up, why no wingers? Crofts is so poor need at least fox in his place so we can actually make a pass in the middle. As we all saw it was clearly going wrong first half why no subs at half time it needed something to change? Then I was going to complain about Wilbraham being put on instead of Jackson however Wilbraham was far better than our other strikers today. Ahh this was such a poor performance it was almost embarrassing that others could watch this on sky. We are a long ball team with no idea's!'

Others were more able to take it in their stride, but can't we just move on...

2 February 2012

I'm back in the Director's Box to see the Bolton game, Tracey at Lotus has invited me (and Jonny) back. This time no pratting about I'm going to get a photo of Delia Smith, Michael Wynn-Jones and anybody else who I can get near. I hope the Man of the Match isn't Wes Hoolahan again, no offence, but it'd be nice to get a bit of variety.

Alastair Florance is going to be attending along with six other people who I've never heard of. At least the joining instructions are clear:

– All guests should arrive at the Gunn Club entrance before 1pm (ground floor, between the Barclay stand and the City stand – see attached map).
– Guests need to state to the steward at reception that they are with Lotus for the Director's Box – you will then be handed a match ticket and directed to the Gunn Club Restaurant.
– Food will be served from 1pm, table service applies. It's recommended to order food as soon as possible.
NB – *Our hospitality package covers all food and beverages consumed before the match*
– After the meal, one of the NCFC Hosts will escort guests to the Director's Box seats for the match.
– At half time, tea and coffee will be served in the Director's Lounge, this is located back in the stadium through to the right hand side.
– After the match, you will be escorted back to the Gunn Club where there will be a Man of the Match interview and a chance for Lotus to have a group photo with him.
NB – *If you would prefer to leave straight after the game please let one of the NCFC hosts know.*

And I'm more prepared for the dress code – no jeans or trainers are permitted – which means brown shoes and trousers for me. And a green and yellow scarf.

3 February 2012

It looks like fashion murder but I'm going to don yellow socks tomorrow. I've tried them on, and while yellow doesn't go with a black suit and brown shoes – not by any stretch of the imagination – I feel it my duty to wear the colours even while in the Director's Box. Nobody will see them anyway as my feet will be under the table during lunch and everyone will be looking at the game when we're outside.

4 February 2012, Norwich 2–0 Bolton Wanderers

It's difficult to describe football players without it sounding homoerotic but if I was a striker I think I'd rather be like Simeon Jackson than Grant Holt. Jackson had a blinder of a game today and rightfully scooped the Man of the Match award.

He's short, stocky and powerful, which is what I like to think I would be like should I be reborn and come back as a professional footballer.

After today's game I realised just how naughty Holt is when he's tangling with opposing players. Nothing vicious, just naughty; leaving a leg in, backing into defenders, anything to get an edge, but it's why opposing fans dislike him so much.

Smart finisher – Sitting in the director's box with the Lotus family and Simeon Jackson.

Jackson is slightly more cultured and also relatively eloquent considering he's spent the vast majority of his life focused on kicking a sphere of leather around a football pitch, which while requiring talent doesn't require a high amount of intelligence. During the post-match interview he made a joke about how tall Zat Knight is – he's 6ft 7in but looks about 8ft – which everyone chuckled at.

And now we've bagged another three points we're closer to a Champions League spot than the relegation places – though Jackson reckons we should still focus on staying in the League (another chuckle).

There is also another reason to appreciate the diminutive striker, I shook him by the hand and Jonny didn't. So now I have one up on the nuisance that is Jonny bragging about who he's seen and spoken with.

In fact, more than that I can now openly mock Jonny because he left the game early – after all the grief he gives people for that sort of thing (me and Liverpool), the little swine does the same thing.

His loss, he missed a photo with Jackson after the game and probably more important than that, he missed our second goal. A poaches effort from Pilkington after an audacious turn and shot by Russell Martin.

We scored two but we should have had a hat full. Bolton weren't up to much, and even though everyone was nervous after both Ayala and Whitbred went off injured all Norwich did was attack.

Something did make me chuckle, two things in fact. Firstly, Paul Lambert squeaks a lot when he's shouting out orders to his team. I hadn't noticed during the Blackburn game, but it's as if he's a 16-year-old whose testicles can't decide if they prefer being high up or low down. And if his voice is hitting the sort of notes that shatter glass, how on earth can the team hear what he is saying above the noise created by 26,000 fans? Perhaps he's the human equivalent of a dog whistle.

Secondly, for all the praise Lambert receives he's as blind, biased and down right idiotic when he shouts at the referee as any fan sat in the stands. Midway through the second half and he's shouting blue bloody murder for an offside decision that even me, in my completely inept rants from my chair, could see was nowhere near offside. Jonny had a jolly good chuckle at Lambert's expense too.

The day also showed the two extremes of reactions to the bitter cold. In the Bolton dugout Owen Coyle was wearing shorts and a jumper seemingly oblivious to the meteorological conditions, next to me Tracey was wrapped up from head to toe in winter clothing, shivering.

If it hadn't been for the pre-game schedule; three course lunch, polite conversation, and social drinking, I think she may have turned into a block of ice.

After speaking to Alastair about the ESPN shoot, I feel a little guilty about labelling the Lotus employee as a grease monkey – though in my defence it was in a pique of rage as I'd missed out – as who wouldn't jump at the chance of being on the television. And the person who took my place was by all accounts very grateful for the chance to appear on international television, even if they were a little nervous. Perhaps I can count it as a selfless act of generosity and let it lie now.

I didn't have the balls to ask Delia Smith for a photograph. Arse.

5 February 2012

Decision made. I am going to selflessly give up my chance to see Norwich play Leicester in the FA Cup allowing someone else to take my seat.

I say selflessly, it's more to do with the costs involved; £25 for the ticket plus petrol money, plus parking, plus refreshments could make for a costly afternoon's entertainment. Much better to give someone else the opportunity to watch the game, someone who isn't a season ticket holder and who can't get hold of tickets for the regular season games for love nor money.

I would like to add that should Norwich progress further in the competition I won't be looking at cost implications merely handing over my credit card details. I want to visit Wembley, and that experience, as the television commercial is constantly reminding us, is priceless.

6 February 2012

It's official, there shall be no gloves in the Norwich squad, even if the temperature drops below zero. Snoods and hats are also included in the equation.

Thankfully Lambert doesn't want the players to resemble fashion models, which Pilkington was more than willing to tell the nation in an interview in *The Sun*:

'We're not allowed to wear gloves – even in training – and the same applies to woolly hats and scarves. And as for snoods, don't even think about it. But what you wear isn't important – it's performances which win you points and that performance against Bolton spoke for itself. Three points is the best insulation against the cold and you can tell by the way we fought for each other that the team spirit here is massive.'

And it's proven on the pitch. When Martin came in to plug the gap at centre back on Saturday he took off his undershirt and ran onto the pitch with only his jersey on. How often do today's Premier League players do that when the ambient temperature is -2°C?

7 February 2012

Disaster. Homeland Security Investigations has seized the website that so many fans use to watch Premier League games online. That could make life a little more stressful, not being able to see the matches will mean more biting of nails and checking of the internet when I'm dragged out of the house around the supermarket/shops/out into the big wide world by Kana.

8 February 2012

Fabio Capello has quit as England manager. The Italian who came into the job in 2008 to rescue our national team from the utter shambles it had become has left the building after the FA board decided – without his input – that John Terry should no longer be captain of England while he is waiting to stand trial for his alleged racist abuse of Anton Ferdinand.

Capello who has won 66.7 per cent of his matches as the England manager, and with a track record of success: four Italian League titles with Milan, one with Roma and two with Juventus (though these were revoked during the match fixing scandel that tore the Italian League apart), two La Liga titles with Real Madrid plus a Champions League winners' medal, he didn't like being undermined by his boss's when it came to decisions about players.

I have to admit that it's a little strange, Capello sacked Terry once for having an affair with an ex-girlfriend of an ex-teammate because he thought, as a strict disciplinarian, that it was bad for the sport and bad for the team. Yet, alleged racial abuse seems to be OK.

Never mind, now Capello has gone all eyes are turning to Harry Redknapp, the man who has just got off a fraud charge for not paying his taxes, who is the bookies favourite to take over and lead England to glory in the European Championships this summer.

9 February 2012

Fulham tickets are on sale. Not directly to Norwich fans, but if you sign up to the Fulham FC website you can buy tickets for the match on the 31 March in the neutral stand next to the away fans.

I didn't even know neutral areas existed, but I guess this is a club based in Fulham and owned by Mohammed Al-Fayed, hardly likely to be filled with knuckle-dragging hooligans.

I suggested to Jonny that it might be a good way to avoid the disappointment of missing out in the ballot for tickets whenever Norwich decide to put them on sale. I'm still waiting for him to get back to me as he was taking a crap when I called him (he sent me a text to let me know he was squeezing one out. Always the charmer).

In other news our left-back has been banned from driving for 15 months. Kyle Naughton it seems thinks driving at 53mph in a 30mph zone is OK, as is driving at 96mph on the A11 near Wymondham. Mind you I guess at least he was driving an Audi, fine cars.

10 February 2012

Leicester fans are up in arms about the number of tickets that have been allocated to them for the FA Cup game on the 18 February. Usual practice would see 15 per cent of Carrow Road's capacity given over to away fans for a Cup game – 4,000 tickets – but after a meeting of the Safety Advisory Board only 2,400 seats were handed over.

It does seem a bit harsh. Leicester took 8,000 fans to Nottingham Forest, their local rivals, and didn't have any trouble, yet 4,000 Foxes in Norwich is seen as a risk.

11 February 2012, Swansea City 2–3 Norwich

I really am starting to despise going to Sainsbury's on a Saturday and my own stupidity for ever losing faith in Norwich.

It took 23 minutes for Swansea to score their goal, at which point there was little chance of us getting anything from the game.

Even on my newly found website – which lacks some of the quality of the one which was shut down by the US authorities – it looked as if Swansea were going to pass us off the pitch, much as they had last season at the Liberty stadium.

As was said before, Swansea do pass the ball well and like to get into a rhythm not too dissimilar to Barcelona. Little did I know that Norwich's German machine was going to turn the game on its head within 16 minutes of the second half whistle being blown.

'Russell Martin sliced an attempted volley high into the air, but Ward somehow managed to hook the ball back from the byline across the face of goal, where Holt headed home', according to the *Pink'un*.

And then not five minutes later: 'Bennett teed Pilkington up for the shot and his goal bound effort was diverted past Vorm by defender Taylor.'

A smidgen of luck with the goal to give us the lead, but apparently the third goal was the result of far better build up play.

'The Canaries scored for the third time in the 63rd minute and it was Holt again with a clinical finish. Surman picked out Bennett and his pass was perfectly judged for Holt to drill a low right-foot shot past Vorm,' said the *Pink'un*.

Damn and blast, I shall never be seen again walking up and down the frozen yoghurt aisle when Norwich are playing either home or away. And I shall never again lose faith in the boys.

12 February 2012

While Swansea's manager, Brendon Rogers, was able to praise Norwich for yesterday's result, his players were less willing to commend us.

Rogers said: 'Congratulations to Norwich, they have come here and ended up getting the three points and this is a tough place to come. That is also a big credit to my players that this far into the season, well into February, we have only lost two games at home for a promoted team. We'll move on and take our medicine.

I was disappointed because when we score two goals at home we don't expect to lose the game. It was a close first half. We scored an outstanding goal and nearly went 2–0 up but for an excellent challenge from Elliott Ward on Danny Graham but then we go to sleep in the first period of the second half.

Norwich is a team who score goals so when you go to sleep and you don't do your job they will punish you.

But from that moment when it went to 3–1 I felt we came back into the game and were probably unfortunate at the end not to get something from it.

We had chances to score goals. We had a penalty and we looked to have another clear penalty when the lad handled the ball from the cross in the box.

I know Norwich from the past few seasons and they are very much like ourselves. They play without any fear. They have good players who score goals and we didn't deal with that.'

It's just a shame that Rogers' little (and I mean little he's only 5ft 5in) midfielder maestro Nathan Dyer, doesn't listen to his manager, his post-match comments were a little less gracious:

'I don't want to comment on the refs, but I felt on Saturday we maybe didn't get as much protection as we would have liked. There were a few too many kicks. We're not the type of team to be crowding the referee so maybe we're a bit naïve in not protesting to the referee as much as we should. That's our nature, we just want to get on with the game, we don't want to be howling at the referee and getting in his face. Maybe we do need to say a few more things to the ref. You have referees, assistants and fourth officials and you hope they'll do their jobs.'

So Norwich are a dirty physical team?

13 February 2012

Chris Wathan from Walesonline has analysed the Swansea/Norwich game and wondered what Paul Lambert's secret formula was for beating Swansea both home and away.

The simple answer from the Norwich Manager: 'There's no secret, we're just a good side.'

But it seems Wathan is of the same mind as Dyer, that Norwich are a physical team that littered the game 'with frustrating fouls, seemingly rotated by those in yellow shirts'.

I'm going to take that as bitterness because if you stop Swansea passing they have no plan B to fall back on. And if you've got no Plan B you could end up in trouble.

15 February 2012

On the 18 August 2008 someone on the *Pink'un* discussion board posted their thoughts on the hiring of Lambert:

'Can't say this appointment excites me to be honest. Think he will get us in the top 6, but that's only what's expected. Not achieved a lot and the history of Jock managers at NCFC aren't good. I will back him 100% but I'm not exactly overwhelmed by this.
Is anyone actually excited by Lambert being the new manager?'

What a thing hindsight is.

16 February 2012

Who'd have thought it, Norwich were responsible for 10 per cent of the transfer value in the January window. How often have you heard that said?

OK the amount of money changing hands was small compared to past years, but 10 per cent is still a considerable amount.

McNally said he'd heard that around £50 million was spent in January, Norwich bought in Leeds' captain Johnny Howson and Peterborough centre-back Ryan Bennett for reported fees of £2 million and £3 million respectively.

17 February 2012

It's a date. Next weekend I will be back in Norwich for a night out and a few beers with the boys. It'll be like a stag do without someone throwing their lives away at the end of it. First Saturday and fun and frolics, then Sunday and a corking football match against Manchester United. Perfect.

18 February 2012, Norwich 1–2 Leicester City

And that's the FA Cup over with for another year. I thought people were getting a little bit ahead of themselves by talking up the possibility of playing at Wembley. It doesn't matter who you play or if it's at home or away, it's a one off game when anything can happen.

Luckily for me I wasn't anywhere near either watching it or listening to it, as this Saturday was about taking George to ride on a steam train, and I'm so glad I did.

By all accounts Norwich did little to deserve a positive result and from the team that started – Steer, Russell Martin, Barnett, Ward, Drury, Fox, Bennett, Pilkington, Hoolahan, Morison and Jackson – few came away with much merit.

But when all's said and done it's next weekend's game that is the priority, we haven't hit the 40 point marker yet, so it's still all hands to the pumps.

19 February 2012

Chuckling to myself about the imposters trawling the Norwich discussion boards – most of whom I assume are Ipswich fans – trying to wind up the locals:

'Just got back. What a joke of a club we are. This pathetic performance just goes to show that we will never ever win a major trophy. What an embarrassing performance. Although it does prove my point that there is no difference between the standard of football in The Championship to the Premier League. In fact apart from the top 3 or 4 in the Prem, I think the Championship is actually a higher standard. As I said last week we should get Clark in now and get rid of Lambert, he has absolutely no desire to progress us as a club. Pathetic. I'm furious.'

20 February 2012

Ben has renewed his season ticket, all is right with the world again.

21 February 2012

Jonny has very kindly offered to let me crash at his house on Saturday night. It's a bit like going back to being a teenager when, on a cold winter's night back in 1996, all of us would head to Great Yarmouth for a night on the beers – The Brunswick, Bourbourn Street being the usual hotspots – returning back to a mates house to sleep off the night's excesses.

We were underage, but how many youngsters don't try and get into nightclubs during the spotty-skinned, testosterone-fuelled, self-loathing stage?

Cruso's mum made a mean cup of tea and bacon sandwich in the morning and there was always a trip to the 24 hour garage and a chocolate milkshake to recharge the system. I wonder if Jonny's breakfast refreshments will be up to that level.

22 February 2012

Jonny has bailed on the Fulham game, something about the London Marathon being the weekend after it and he should really be training for it. Seems like a feeble excuse to me but who am I to question, how many awful excuses have I come up with in the past?

It does now mean that I can trudge down to the game with a Fulham fan, Kana's friend's husband, Tristan, and perhaps have a relatively highbrow conversation on the match, the state of the game and perhaps garner some top tips on how to balance family life with football.

Tristan still amazes me. He followed Fulham around Europe even when his wife was on the verge of labour. He even manages to somehow work family holidays around matches so that he doesn't miss a second of the season. The guy's a genius.

23 February 2012

Must remember to actually apply for a Fulham ticket, the same for Tottenham Hotspur on 9 April.

24 February 2012

Gary Lineker's mum is a Norwich fan? Well according to the man himself she is, after he took the bait from a post on Twitter from David Head who said: 'Shame @GaryLineker_ doesn't give Norwich the credit they deserve on #motd.'

To which Mr Lineker replied: 'You kidding me? My mum's a big Norwich fan. How many times can we say how brilliantly they are doing?'

25 February 2012

Well that has to be the most disappointing night out in the history of night outs involving myself, Jonny, Twon, Button and Cruso. At home (well Jonny's), by midnight. I've never heard such a sad tale of inexperienced partying.

Having said that, now that the majority of us have reached the grand old age of 32, are tied down by the chains of marriage and children, the days of frolicking around dance floors in the coolest of clubs have long since gone.

And the ability to make an arse of ourselves to live music has been curtailed by the demise of the Blueberry pub. We turn up after having a few drinks in the Mischief to find absolutely no bugger inside and a for sale sign outside. The end of an era was made an even bigger reality as the only drink they had on tap was a cheap and nasty lager.

One thing the Blueberry did still manage to provide was pain. Jonny once again thought that he should start the play fighting by smacking Twon. Unfortunately, with his back turned he left himself open to an incursion from me, and a swift right hook to his arm. Contact was sweet and Jonny's scream of pain was a sign that contact was also powerful. Oh how Twon did laugh.

And it didn't stop there, no sooner had we left the pub than Twon and Jonny tried to put me in the wheelie bin outside. Luckily my skinny frame is also quite dense so they couldn't get the purchase to pick me up and tip me in.

From the Blueberry we went to the Glass House, a chain pub that does cheap drink. Jugs of cocktails for £10. And it was there that Jonny thought he should continue his quest to be named the most masculine of the group by swiping Twon on the forehead.

This wasn't any old swipe though. As Jonny stood up to buy the next round, Twon was casually talking to Button, no doubt about work related things – something they always do, an electricians life is all about the light fixtures. Jonny wound back his arm, hand flat, palm ready to strike.

Twon was unaware, but Jonny managed to wind his arm up to such an extent that when contact between Twon's forehead and Jonny's palm happened the noise bellowed out, overpowering even the noise from hundreds of drunken customers, both screaming girls and peacocking boys on the prowl. It was an almighty slap.

26 February 2012, Norwich 1–2 Manchester United

Unchuffing believable. We lost but how flipping brilliant are Norwich City? I tell you how brilliant. So brilliant we played United off the field, even Sir Alex Ferguson, the manager who gives credit to no one said that we deserved something from the game.

'I have to say we were lucky in the sense that although we made a host of chances – Danny Welbeck could have scored four – I thought Norwich were the better team. They kept at it and kept at it and deserved their goal, there's no question about it. They deserved a result actually. They had a lot of thrust about them, determined and kept crossing that ball into the box.' How many teams has he said that about?

It was just a shame that the gods were against us and it was Ryan Giggs' 900th appearance for United, which could only mean one thing: he was destined to score the winner, and score it he did in the 93rd minute.

But, barring the god awful first goal we conceded, we completely outclassed Fergie's team for the majority of the game. The statistics don't lie. We had 52 per cent of the possession and 16 shots on target to United's 11.

So close – Ryan Giggs spoiled the party with a late, late winner.

If it hadn't been for an in-form De Gea between the sticks we could have been out of sight.

First Kyle Knaughton chipped the ball over the United defense for Anthony Pilkington to bring under control with one touch and shoot (De Gea saved with his feet), then Holt sprinted into the box glancing his header straight at the 'keeper, but he made up for it in the 83rd minute.

Holt had been giving Rio Ferdinand and Jonny Evans a torrid time all afternoon, and a half cleared corner allowed Adam Drury to pump the ball back into the area and, when Zak Whitbread headed on, Holt showed great touch and strength to turn Ferdinand and thrash his left-footed shot into the top corner. Cue unbridled ecstasy.

Pandemonium as every Norwich fan went berserk. 'WHO ARE YA?' screamed and shouted by every man, woman and child, and directed at the 2,000 United fans who had spent the entire match goading us for being inbred, having six fingers, sleeping with our sisters and generally not being worthy of playing the mighty United. For 10 minutes we were their equals, if not their superiors, that was until Ryan Giggs popped up at the back post to push in the winner only seconds from time. It was heartbreaking because all the effort was for nothing, heartbreaking because we'd been the better team and heartbreaking because we deserved so much more than congratulations.

But we deserved the congratulations, and it didn't only come from Sir Alex Ferguson, but also the pundits on the BBC's *Match of the Day 2*. Both Lee Dixon and presenter Colin Murray were almost fornicating over how good Norwich were in this game and have been all season. It's good to be a Norwich fan.

27 February 2012

Even after a storming first season in the Premier League Grant Holt still can't get a call up to the England squad. Neither, for that matter, can John Ruddy – Scott Carson and Robert Green are ahead of him in the pecking order.

28 February 2012

A plan has been concocted for the Fulham game on 31 March, none of it has my stamp on it. Kana's friend has suggested that we all go to hers for lunch, and then her husband and I will catch the tube down to Craven Cottage. Perfect.

In a poll on the Telegraph website, Grant Holt has 33.01 per cent of the vote when readers were asked a simple question: With Wayne Rooney and Darren Bent out of action which strikers should England start Euro 2012 with?

He's the leading candidate, even with peers such as Peter Crouch, Danny WelBeck, Bobby Zamora and Jermaine Defoe.

29 February 2012

Application is soon to be posted for Fulham and Spurs tickets, which should make up for the fact that I'm not going to the Liverpool game on 28 April, instead I will be at a wedding party for one of Kana's friends. She doesn't realise what an utterly selfless husband she has. If only before agreeing to attend I'd checked the fixture list. Stupid brain.

1 March 2012

For all the to-ing and fro-ing over whether or not Ben would renew his season ticket, which he did making both Jonny and I very happy, it seems not everyone will be ticking the yes box.

There's a website, *Holtamania*, which is a very well written blog, but the owner has had enough and won't be going to Carrow Road anymore. Some of it is down to cost, season tickets never get any cheaper, but some of it is also down to the troglodyte nature of some fans:

'I'm not alone in gradually feeling priced out of football, but it's not something I hold any resentment for. Beyond that, I have a general, growing weariness with football & especially the fan culture that surrounds it. I'm not like some fans who like to go to Carrow Road as much for the atmosphere as the match itself. I love the sport because I love the sport, not the badly spun attempts at 'banter', the abuse dished out on a weekly basis or the undercurrent of tribalist nonsense that seems to get stronger each year. I go to Carrow Road because I understand the game better for seeing it in person than on a TV screen, but as time has gone on I've grown more and more disillusioned

with fellow fans, and I don't mean just at Carrow Road though there have been incidents.

So let me go into just two. Firstly, at a home game last year, a man who sits on the row behind me and several seats across spent the entire pre match warmup screaming 'faggot' at David Nugent. Over and over, he screamed and shouted and abused with homophobic taunts. Not five minutes after Nugent finished his warm-up, Stephen Fry was introduced onto the pitch and this fan, his tiny brain completely unaware, happily applauded the Norwich director onto the pitch. Secondly, at the home QPR game this year, the man who sits next to me was happy to shout 'there's only one John Terry' at Anton Ferdinand who was stood about 10 feet in front of us. This was followed not long after with a rendition of the same chant coming from the Snakepit.

Many grown men, and lets face it, it is almost entirely men, become entirely different people when they walk through a turnstile. And it's a large number. It isn't everyone. I've had the pleasure of meeting a great deal of pleasant, decent football fans at every stadium I've been to, but these aren't the fans who make me embarrassed to be a football supporter, and they belong to every club. The incidents with Terry and Fedinand, and Suarez and Evra, highlight the depressing amount of tribalism in terraces and the ridiculous reaction of LFC in particular legitimised a culture of victimisation, and gave voice to the disgusting taunts that were thrown at Tom Adeyemi. Football fans haven't been trusted for years to sit together, and it only feels like it's getting worse. There has always been abuse and vitriol from idiots, and twitter has given them an even bigger platform to act like the neanderthals they are. Just look at the abuse our own James Vaughan got. Look at the abuse Stan Collymore gets on an almost daily basis. And at a recent Fulham game, Danny Murphy's wife and one year old child were screamed at and called cunts while sat watching the game.

For some, it's easy to ignore. It's easy to say that this stuff has always gone on, and it's just passion. Just banter. But personally, I can't deal with it in that way. All I want to do is watch the game, and my enjoyment of the game is being limited by idiots. So it's made my decision easier. It's not that I'm not renewing because of these mindless tools, but when you add all these things up, the money, the time, and the tribalism, it blends into something that I don't feel happy with right now. There is more to life than sitting next to a bloke who looks like he's about to have an aneurysm because Morison keeps pulling out wide.'

It's a sad inditement of the game that some fans can turn into a ferrel bunch once they've walked through the turnstile and taken their seat. Not only that but it is seen as acceptable.

3 March 2012, Stoke City 1–0 Norwich

This game was simply described by a fellow automotive journalist and Norwich fan as atrocious; to paraphrase he simply asked, if you enjoy watching the ball in the air for 87 minutes get a season ticket to watch Stoke play. Effective? Yes they took home the three points today. Attractive? Not by any stretch of the imagination. And unlike us it's the only way they know how to play.

6 March 2012

Stupidly forgot to post my application for the Fulham game, but never fear as there are still tickets available in the neutral stand at Craven Cottage, so I will be purchasing one of those.

7 March 2012

I have decided to put the 'We're a League One/Champiosnhip side' argument to bed for once and all. According to the that website of quite brilliant knowledge, football-lineups.com the Norwich team of the 2009–10 season consisted of the following:

Goalkeepers: Theoklitos, Alnwick, Forster, Rudd, Steer

Defence: Askou, Doherty, Nelson, Whitbread, Stephens, Drury, Rose, Wiggins, Otsemobor, Spillane, Martin, Francomb

Midfield: Hoolahan, Russell, Smith, Adeyemi, Hughes, Tudur-Jones, Gill, McNamee, Lappin, Dawkin, Whaley

Attack: McVeigh, Cureton, Martin, Holt, McDonald, Daley, Johnson

Now if you look at last season in the Championship the squad changed a fair bit:

Goalkeepers: Ruddy, Rudd, Steer

Defence: Ward, Askou, Barnett, Nelson, Whitbread, Smith, Drury, Tierney, Martin, Francomb

Midfield: Hoolahan, Crofts, Lansbury, Smith, Hughes, Fox, Tudur-Jones, Gill, McNamee, Lappin, Surman, Dawkin

Attack: Martin, Vokes, Holt, Jackson, Wilbraham, Pacheco, Daley, Johnson

And now moving into the Premier League we have the following players:

Goalkeepers: Ruddy, Rudd, Steer

Defence: Ward, Barnett, Whitbread, Ayala, Bennett, Drury, Tierney, Naughton, Martin, Francomb, DeLaet

Midfield: Hoolahan, Crofts, Howson, Johnson, Smith, Adeyemi, Fox, Lappin, Surman, Dawkin, Bennett, Pilkington

Attack: Vaughan, Martin, Holt, Jackson, Wilbraham, Morison

So as is perfectly clear, a large proportion of the squad still remains from our campaigns in League One and the Championship. Bugger, that wasn't how it was meant to come out.

8 March 2012

I am going to be sitting in the Putney end in block P4, row XX, seat 85 for the Fulham match. God bless the club for having a neutral stand and for still having tickets available.

From the chatter on the discussion boards the whole of the neutral area should be taken up by Norwich fans, which means 6,000 of the yellow and green army descending on west London for the game.

9 March 2012

So the pressure is on Norwich to beat one of the big teams this season, all because someone from the Swansea camp thinks so.

In the words of PGFWhite on the Not606 discussion board: 'You have done the double over the Swans and QPR but the Swans have beaten Arsenal and Man City and QPR have beaten Chelsea and Liverpool.'

PGFWhite should watch his words, Norwich will have its day, we'll claim a 'big' scalp as well as stay in the League.

10 March 2012

Someone in Wales thinks that Paul Lambert deserves to be manager of the season. Not going to argue, nice to see a bit of enigmatic writing in the press for once. Who gives a stuff about Brendan Rogers and his achievements with Swansea.

> 'There is no disputing that Rodgers has done a wonderful job. However, despite being the Premier League's 'diet Barcelona', that still doesn't make him manager of the year. That honour belongs to Paul Lambert.
>
> Lambert has only had two and a half years at Carrow Road and took the helm of a side bottom of League One having conceded seven at home to Colchester on the opening day.
>
> He took them up that season, won automatic promotion from the Championship at the first attempt and now has the Canaries level on points with Swansea with an identical record of wins, losses and draws. The Swans have a better goal difference, but Norwich have scored more this season.'

I wonder how many people read the *South Wales Argus*, and so, come the end of the season will agree with these view?

11 March 2012, Norwich 1–1 Wigan Athletic

A good game to miss according to Jonny, too many chances for Wigan, no killer instinct or desire from Norwich.

12 March 2012

Apparently the reason for the poor performance yesterday was the warm weather training camp the lads were taken on by Lambert. Spain is no place to be seen:

> 'Maybe then they would actually have to run to keep warm. Thank God we may have enough points otherwise we would be right in it now!
>
> And maybe all these Lambert worshippers would now realise he is human after all

and as I predicted the Leicester game was the turning point in our season. A game we could have won with our true first team and instead "rested" players , those rested coinciding with a dip in their form, cannot remember doing it in lower leagues and far more matches!

I am really struggling with what Lambert is doing in team selection throws Howson in after lengthy injury and one reserves match then he disappears today and R Bennet from Peterborough who is match fit and rated as one of best center half's around not even on bench.

Please Lambert do NOT say the lads were terrific and cannot fault them etc , only in one of the last four matches have they put any real effort in, and it's becoming a habit!'

(Care of someone named CJ who is not a happy bunny).

13 March 2012

It seems not everyone is a fan of Norwich. Another business related trip, this time to Stuttgart and once again the small talk turns to football. The initial conversation went thus:

'So you're a football fan too then. Who do you support?'
'Norwich City.'
'Ah, so not a football fan then.'

What exactly does that mean? Have we been lumped in with the Stokes of this world and deemed to be a long ball team with no ability to play the game on the ground? And there was me wrongly thinking that we were able to adapt our game to suit the opposition, playing the attractive stuff whenever possible and the more direct style when so required.

It appears that to the outside world we, by that I of course mean Norwich, are nothing more than a bunch of hit and hopers.

That is surely a tad unfair, especially considering the praise we've had from the pundits thus far this season and even more so when the person making the unnecessary derogatory comment is a Preston North End fan. I despair sometimes.

14 March 2012

Damn my lack of patience. I booked the coach to Norwich for the game verses Everton during the Easter holiday thinking I was being economical and at least a little bit organised. In a way I was, bargain price of £6 from London to Norwich and only slightly more, £7.50, for the return journey.

Unfortunately, as I checked I had the email receipt for my travel plans I received an email from the press office at Kia saying that the hybrid Kia Optima was now on the fleet and ready to be booked out, and I had first dibs.

That's a car, for a week, with a full tank of petrol and a four day holiday to drive it.

What to do. I've paid my money and there are no chances of getting a refund from National Express coaches, which while I think is a con, doesn't help me.

Sitting on a coach for three hours each way seemed like a good idea when the other option was sitting on a train for many more hours (there are engineering works that weekend), and paying many more pounds for the privilege. But now a car, with a radio, cruise control and four wheels is available, and I don't have to pay for the petrol, which at 139.9p a litre is extortionate and makes driving in my own car highly uneconomical.

15 March 2012

I've booked the Kia Optima for the Easter holiday. I may change my mind but at the moment logic is telling me that I could then use the vehicle for other more family orientated adventures after the football has finished.

16 March 2012

Transportation for the Manchester City game has been arranged; Volkswagen's press department is lending me a Tiguan SUV, the more economical version, for a week. Sometimes being an automotive journalist has its advantages.

Of course it isn't the primary reason for borrowing the car, it will serve as a useful comparison to the Mazda CX-5, which I will be driving next month and will also be given pride of place on my new website, www.thecartweeter.com. My little piece of the world wide interweb, while also being twitterised by my good self and hopefully read about by my now humongous following (1,705 people).

17 March 2012

Football seems irrelevant. A young Bolton Wanderer's player had a cardiac arrest on the pitch as his team took on Tottenham in the FA Cup. It took 11 shocks from a defibrillator before Fabrice Muamba's heart began beating again, and the entire episode was played out on national television as the game was aired live on ESPN.

18 March 2012, Newcastle United 1–0 Norwich

A game I was never likely to go to and although I was slightly jealous of Jonny making the 293 mile journey to St James' Park (I'm not going to call it the Sports Direct Arena as Newcastle's owner wants), I'm glad I didn't have to make the biblically long journey home after a defeat.

But while I think 293 miles is too far to travel, Norwich's exertions are being watched far and wide. Take *The Times of India* for example, or perhaps the many other newspapers in South Korea, Japan and Thailand to name but a few, watching, commenting and reviewing our games.

19 March 2012

There really are some imbeciles in the world, some utterly heartless, ignorant, abhorrent so-called human beings. Some chap from Texas in the US has been using twitter to rant and tirade racist obscenities not only about black people but more specifically Muamba.

I won't mention the person's name as it will only encourage him, but really, in this day and age how people can still use such vile language is incomprehensible:

'Don't blame me for your soccer players' problems. Wouldn't be surprised at how many drugs he took to make his heart explode'
'Every time I seen a XXXXXX collapse it was cause it was high on drugs. Just one less criminal…Let him die and let it be'.

20 March 2012

Bugger shouldn't have read the *Pink'un* discussion board as we are now certainly doomed if we don't beat Wolves at the weekend, all because we have dropped to 14th in the League.

According to someone called First Wizard if we don't win on Saturday there will be no other game where we could possibly bag all three points, and in his words: 'The bottom five are showing signs of fighting, while we would be at the cusp of a Blackpoolening slump.'

And no matter what reasons his fellow fans give him he is so depressed with the prospect of dropping out of the League he ignores them all, happy (?) to be delirious with depression.

Just for the record our remaining games are; Fulham, Everton, Spurs, Man City, Blackburn, Liverpool, Arsenal and Aston Villa. While there are definitely some toughies in there, there are also some winnable games surely?

21 March 2012

Arsenal application forms are now available for download from the club's website. I was expecting it to be priced according to the rules of the so-called big clubs of the Premier League, £50-£60, but no. The Gunners have priced them very reasonably at £35, so it's now time to find out if Jonny and/or Ben are willing to go too.

There's bad news on the bottom front, I have a pile or as Button delightfully calls them, arse grapes. I don't like grapes anymore.

22 March 2012

Muamba update: he's talking freely to friends, family, doctors and associated others. It's a minor miracle considering that all the newspapers and other media were telling the world that the player had effectively been dead for 78 minutes – the time his heart had stopped for. He's a very lucky lad.

23 March 2012

Joy of endless joys, football is returning to the household of Scoltock. After nearly a month of nothing but seeing the scores come up on a computer screen I will be back in residence at Carrow Road. It couldn't have felt like more of a prison sentence – having your rights as a human being taken away – the past four weeks have felt slightly empty. (I am of course being melodramatic and have enjoyed some quality family time, taking the boy to St James' Park in central London, riding trains and chasing big red buses for his enjoyment and generally acting like a normal family.)

But from this evening, the car will be packed, the family shoe horned into the back seats and cruise control will be set at 70mph as we trundle up the A11 once more.

24 March 2012, Norwich 2–1 Wolverhampton Wanderers

You little ripper, you beautiful wonder of a human being, you unbelievable machine. You superstar, you miracle worker, you adorable little man. We f**king love Grant Holt.

Two goals and he wins us the game, takes us back up to 11th in the League, on the cusp of safety, while also sending Wolves to the bottom of the table, and sure to be saying hello to Ipswich next season.

I am choosing to ignore the fact that he was sent off in the 85th minute for an ill-judged tackle, which meant that my nerves were also frazzled as Wolves searched, in vane, for an equaliser.

Jonny was equally at the end of his tether, and unfortunately for my diminutive fellow fan, out of pocket – well kind of.

Before a ball had even been kicked, before the corner flags had been put in the ground, Jonny in truly clairvoyant fashion predicted the score would be 2–1, and that Grant Holt would score both our goals. Had the wee man not bothered with his second pint of CHB and put his money where his mouth was, he may have been able earn himself a pretty penny or two. Instead he had to make do with the glory of correctly predicting a match result for the first time. Ever.

The scoreline made the newspaper website match reports happy reading, especially *The Independent*. What better headline than; 'Wolves tamed by Holt power and precision'.

And my appreciation for the paper's journalist at Carrow Road, Jack Pitt-Brooke's only grew when I read the following:

'In truth, it did not take long for Norwich to settle into dominance. Their 3–4–1–2 system, gave the hosts a numerical advantage in defence and in midfield. David Fox and Jonny Howson were a well-balanced midfield base, and combined with Wes Hoolahan to pass their way through Wolves' rigid lines.'

And if that wasn't enough praise, how about:

'Norwich started to attack with more numbers and imagination. In the final minute of the half, they produced their best move to take the lead. A string of passes led to Holt's shot being blocked by Stephen Ward, and the ball moved back to Simon Lappin on the left. He set up Hoolahan, whose shot was intercepted by Eggert Jonsson's arm. Holt took the penalty with power and Norwich had a deserved half-time lead.'

And to show just how adaptable Norwich are as a team, Pitt-Brooke finished his piece with this final paragraph:

'Lambert replaced Lappin with Kyle Naughton at the break, dispensing his 3–4–1–2 for a more regular 4–3–1–2. Their forward movement was just as good, and they continued to pass and create chances throughout the second half. With four minutes left Holt was sent off for a second yellow card. But Norwich finished comfortably while Wolves struggled.'

And long may they struggle, because as the terrace chant says, we only hate Ipswich and Wolves.

25 March 2012

That man Jack Pitt-Brooke is at it again, ingratiating himself with the yellow and green army. This time he is talking Grant Holt up as an England possible – though Norwich fans have been saying the same thing for months.

I might have to start buying *The Independent* rather than just reading it for free online if the quality of the pieces is always this high.

'The talk is serious: Grant Holt is a genuine candidate to go to Euro 2012 with England. And if he is not, he ought to be. After scoring both in Norwich City's 2–1 defeat of Wolverhampton Wanderers on Saturday, Holt has 12 Premier League goals this season. Only six strikers have scored more, and of those, only one – Wayne Rooney – is English.

Holt's Norwich teammate David Fox hopes Holt makes the squad, even if it keeps him away from his wedding. "He is meant to be coming to Cyprus for my wedding," Fox said. "I don't know now. I have told him not to book his tickets yet. I don't know whether to put him on the table plans just yet. We'd miss him. His dance moves are very good."

It would be quite an achievement for a forward in his first top-flight season, who spent 2008–09 playing for League Two Shrewsbury. Holt has looked at ease in the Premier League, but Fox admits he is not like that every day. "He is ridiculous," Fox said. "Sometimes when you see him in training you wonder how he has ever scored a goal. But on a Saturday he is unbelievable. The fella has so much confidence in him. The boys look for him to do something and pretty much every Saturday, he produces for us."'

I would definitely have a far greater interest in England if one of our own were playing for them. And if Holt and John Ruddy were in the team, well I might even start buying tickets for England games at Wembley again.

Arse grapes are subsiding thanks to the bullet shaped giver of pain relief that are suppositories.

26 March 2012

There seems to be a lot of rumours being thrown around about how and why certain players aren't in the team, or aren't performing to the best of their abilities on the pitch.

One such rumour is that Marc Tierney, our long absent left-back, has had a tiff with Steve Morison – the reasons for the tiff aren't worth mentioning. The result is that Tierney is out of the squad and Morison's head isn't in the right place.

It's also been suggested that Holt and Morison aren't best of friends, and they've had a major bust up. The rumour mill was sent into overdrive when Holt ran out on the pitch with a black eye – due to a fracas with Morison supposedly.

Morison has unfortunately been at the blunt end of most of the rumours, I think mainly because he's had a slight dip in form.

Some fans feel a little aggrieved, and while some look to make up reasons for his poor form, others have decided to confront him directly.

I wasn't there, didn't see it and haven't heard any firsthand accounts, so again it's a rumour but apparently after the game on Saturday, Morison went up to the Gunn Club, I know not why.

It's the same place where the great and the good are wined and dined pre-game, Jonny and I had the pleasure for the Blackburn and Bolton games, and were allowed to have a few drinks and watch some presentations post-match.

Some well-oiled, middle-aged, attendee decided he should confront Morison for his current lack of ability, shouting blue bloody murder at him.

At first Morison was said to have ignored the drunken fool but as the language became more and more fruity, his temper got the better of him and he shouted back. Luckily before anything physical could happen security stepped in to eject the idiot 'fan'.

Well that's the rumour anyway. It was posted on the *Pink'un* message board but now seems to have disappeared. Perhaps I need to stop gossiping and do something more constructive.

On a more positive note, former loan defender Ritchie De Laet has been singing Norwich's praises.

'I could see in pre-season how well they were going to do this year in the Premier League because they've got some quality players there. The style of football they play down there is the right way to play when entering the top flight and the backroom team there are fantastic as well,' said the United youngster. 'They've shown everyone this season how good a team they are and they have proved very hard to beat at both home and away. I hope that they can continue to do the same for the rest of the season and then take it into next year and onwards because the fans there deserved to see top-flight football again.'

It's nice to be respected.

27 March 2012

As football fans we are merely zombies to the cause, as I try and affect each game by wearing a specific pair of socks, Jonny wears his lucky pants, others perform similar acts. To the individual they are nothing but a harmless act, although incredibly important when your team needs a win, to those who live outside of the football goldfish bowl they're illogical idiocy.

Perhaps viewing what other fan's foibles are makes you consider how you appear to the outside world. ILoveDelia's post on the Not606 discussion board certainly made me wonder how much of an insane degenerate Kana thinks I am. The loss to Leicester in the FA Cup seemed to have a severe effect on dear old ILoveDelia:

'Went to wardrobe to get replica shirt ready for the game, what going on? No shirt!!!

Shouted to wife, 'my f...ing shirts missing' Oh my god, we'll never win if I don't wear it. For god's sake came Mrs Delia's reply, calm down, I washed it and it's in the airing cupboard. You did WHAT? You washed my f...ing shirt, are you completely mental, you know the shirt never gets washed, someone will have to **** on it before that happens! It had got chocolate ice cream down the front, I tried to dab it off but you could still see it she says. I HOPE YOU REALISE THAT YOU'VE JUST BUGGERED UP A WINNING RUN, I just don't believe you've done that. My treasured shirt has had its entire winning streak washed away. I'm frantic, almost in tears, what the hell can I do to counteract this terrible situation, Holty and the boys stand no chance of winning today now. Going through my sock draw, I find 4 pairs of socks (Christmas presents) never worn, ummmm, 1 pair with Blue tops, disregarded, 1 pair with Red tops, disregarded, now I have a dilemma, for the next 2 pairs are 1 Yellow & 1 Green topped. Yellow, yes it has to be Yellow, which will help the boys! I put on the first Yellow sock (left foot), a bad feeling comes over me, it doesn't feel right (no pun intended), put the other one on my right foot, NO, it's no good, just doesn't feel right. Mrs Delia appears, as I seem to have been having a conversation with myself about these socks, whatever are you doing she asks? Trying put your mistake right I reply, I just can't get a positive vibe from these Yellow socks. Poor wife, shaking her head in disbelief she gets her scarf out, and announces, well I'm ready if your not. HOW can I be ready, I need a positive feeling, and it's not happening. I'm not going I announce, I can't, the shirts wrong, the socks are wrong, the whole f...ing situation's wrong. Mrs. Delia is now staring at me in disbelief, for god's sake grow up, I only washed your shirt, it won't make any difference. Huh, what does she know! Final attempt, Green socks, ummmm close but still not there. Now I'm into Green sock left foot, Yellow sock right foot syndrome, this is as good as it felt so far. Just one more thing to try, socks pulled up or left down. Mrs. Delia is ringing a solicitor now, I think a divorce may be in the offing. OK finally I feel ready, right sock (Yellow) pulled up, left sock (Green) left down, shirt still has that freshly washed smell, but I don't have a choice.

Off we go, I'm still not overly confident that the sock combination will counteract the shirt wash. Arrive at the ground, feeling a bit more positive now, go through the turnstile at the Barclay, it hits me, it's going to be a complete disaster, shall I change my socks round, maybe turn the shirt inside out, what the hell can I do to help. Wife *now threatening to call the police or an ambulance as I appear to be having some sort of fit. I need a sign, even* On the ball City, *doesn't allay my gloom.*

Game over, I knew it, we were rubbish, lost 1–2. I round on the wife, see what you've done!!! Don't you ever touch my shirt again!!! Drive home in complete silence.'

I'm surprised his other half puts up with him, especially as it has taken him so long to pen his thoughts on what turned out to be an unbelievably traumatic day (we played Leicester back in the middle of February), which must mean he's been a ball of unbridled anger for more than a month now.

Hopefully I deal with my anger issues with far greater effect, as Norwich return to perhaps one of the worst grounds the team has ever set foot on. Not the worst in terms of the seating, the location or any other element, but worst in terms of the final result.

On a sunny afternoon in May 2005, Norwich travelled to Fulham and Craven Cottage for their last game of the season. A win was needed to guarantee survival and another season in the Premier League. History shows it was an unmitigated disaster.

But rather than dwell on the past I'll be meeting Kana's friend's husband, Tristan, for a pre-match drink back in west London. I have to go somewhere called the Pear Tree on Margravine Road near Barons Court tube station.

I've no idea if it's a Fulham pub, an away pub or perhaps just a normal, run of the mill beer house with no interest in football. It begs the question: do I wear colours or keep them at home?

28 March 2012

Norwich is one former vice-chairman lighter today, as Jimmy Jones has passed away. The man that shared the stage with Robert Chase, was partly responsible for the successes and the failures that the club welcomed and endured.

The two businessmen each bought £25,000 worth of shares to join a board in 1983. Norwich hit new heights during their time in office, after becoming Division Two champions in 1986, they finished fifth in Division One in 1987, fourth in 1989 and third in 1993. That achievement by Mike Walker's team brought European football to Norwich for the first time.

The board survived an extraordinary general meeting in January 1988 that followed protests over the sacking of manager Ken Brown, and demonstrations followed relegation from the Premiership in 1995.

Arsenal ticket application is in the post.

29 March 2012

According to that most reliable of sources, *The Daily Mirror*, Brighton and Hove Albion are going to make an offer of £1.2 million for Chris Martin. The very limited story in the newspaper said, in its entirety:

'The former Luton forward, 23, who is on loan at Crystal Palace, is out of favour with the Canaries and Poyet wants to bolster his attacking options.'

Nice business if it happens. Although having a local lad in the team would be nice, since leaving League One he hasn't been in such a rich vein of goal scoring form, which strikers need if they are to succeed. Was League One his level?

Who knows, but at 23 he has time on his side to hit the heady heights should he put enough hard graft in.

30 March 2012

Stiliyan Petrov, the Aston Villa captain has acute leukaemia. He played against Arsenal, developed a fever and has now been diagnosed with the disease.

Makes it hit home that it doesn't matter who you are or what you do, some things can affect anyone at anytime.

31 March 2012, Fulham 2–1 Norwich

At what point do you decide that the football being played on the pitch isn't of a high enough standard that you think the £35 cost of a ticket and the time and expense of travelling all the way from Norwich is worth wasting, so you leave the stadium?

According to the chap two seats from me that time is after 45 minutes.

I know we were two-nil down, and the players hadn't necessarily been playing the brand of football we have come to expect from them, but even so, there was still another half of football to come and given our track record of scoring late goals every chance we could still get something from the game.

I wasn't the only one to be sat near Norwich 'fans' who were apparently quickly disillusioned. One poor fan had to write his frustrations out, glad I wasn't sat near him:

'A day out at Fulham

I made one of my occasional away trips on Saturday and arrived home tired but with some satisfaction from seeing the Canaries make a tirring come back and almost recover their disastrous start. There was much to appreciate about the day - the opportunity to visit a real football ground after my first visit many years ago, the good humoured (if subdued) attitude of the Fulham supporters, an encouraging debut from Ryan Bennett who exuded class, and a premiership goal for Wilbraham who also scored his 100th league goal in the process.
In addition the support from the vast majority of Away fans was nothing short of superb and a credit to the Club.

But why oh why do a small minority of "alleged" Norwich supporters,in front of whom I had the misfortune to stand, have to let forth a torrent of foul and abusive language from the moment they arrive (late) until the final whistle? Their ignorance of the English language(they only seemed to know one adjective and one noun) was only exceeded by their ignorance of the game of football.

Altogether now – Fulahm's neutral area view obscured, unfortunately it didn't hide the goals we conceded.

Every Norwich player was mercilessly assassinated by this bunch. Their language was awful and the comments made about players brought nothing but shame on a great Club that I have supported for many years. I dont know where they stand at Carrow Rd but pity anyone who has to endure it week in week out.

People can say what they like about the lack of noise from parts of the Jarrold but give me that any day over such a negative and vitriolic attitude. Why do they bother!'

But for all the problems we had in the first half, we were a different team after the half-time orange segment refreshments and team talk.

Simeon Jackson came on to play with Morison, and then Lambert's master stroke, Morison off and Wilbraham on.

The former Milton Keynes man scored his 100th League goal, and has now scored in all four divisions. And he also gave us hope that we could get something from the game.

It was sustained pressure, Fulham were on the back foot as we camped out in their half. We had 16 shots on target. So painfully close.

Lambert said it all after the game: 'We should have got something from the game. We were relentless in the second half. But you can't give teams two goals at the start. It's a mountain to climb from there. But the response was absolutely terrific. We went about it and tried to retrieve the game. In the second half I thought the lads were excellent.'

No hard feelings, it just means that now Fulham are level on points with us and Swansea. We've all achieved 39 points, putting Fulham 10th, Swansea 11th and us 12th, with only goal difference separating us.

I quite like Craven Cottage. Tidy little ground, lots of history, quaint buildings and stands – very little atmosphere unfortunately, but it's an old ground with old acoustics – and a pretty location next to the river Thames.

A neutral section filled with Norwich fans meant that the songs were constant and loud. Pre-game was good too.

A quiet drink in the Pear Tree with Kana's friend's husband Tristan. He's a Fulham fan but that shouldn't count against him, as he has a track record of being a general football nut. So much so that his trip to watch Fulham in the Final of the Europa League only three days after his son was born is legendary. How on Earth did he get away with that?

1 April 2012

A scan of the Sunday papers and it seems there isn't much interest in a mid-table battle between Fulham and Norwich. The best I could do was this:

The Sunday Telegraph: 'Texan Clint Dempsey the marauding midfielder, who ended up playing in attack due to a 35th-minute injury to Pavel Pogrebnyak, scored once and set up another to settle this mid-table clash against also-safe Norwich in west London.'

The Observer: 'Clint Dempsey's early goal set Fulham on course for a hard-fought but deserved victory over Norwich that ended a three-match losing streak.'

The Mail on Sunday: 'Dare to wear bright orange boots and you had better play well. Clint Dempsey did just that, for the first half at least, and ultimately steered his side to victory.'

The only real point of interest during the 90 minutes of football, according to the national media, is the fact that Fulham's Clint Dempsey is out of contract soon and if the Cottagers want to stay in the Premier League past the midfielders 2013 current deal, they need to get him to sign on the dotted line.

2 April 2012

There seems to be some mutterings that there is unrest in the Norwich camp. So much so that David McNally has felt the need to go on twitter and call for calm and for the fans to get behind the players.

I don't know what the rumours are specifically, I've heard a few, but they seem to have riled the powers that be. McNally has so far tweeted the following thus far:

'Can we just get back to supporting our players please. All this negative untrue stuff from faceless keyboard warriors is unhelpful.'

'The rumours circulating are unfounded and untrue, and yet they are very unhelpful. All NCFC deserve your support.'

'All NCFC players deserve your support.'

I really want to know what the rumours are, so I will now have to spend the next few minutes/hours/days finding out what has been said and by whom.

Thankfully I can rule out any serious food-based problems in the camp. As McNally helpfully replied to one concerned fan who asked: 'So you're saying Grant Holt didn't take two of Zak Whitbreads Jelly Babies?'

And although apparently two jelly babies are missing, it hasn't caused any arguments in the squad according to our chief executive.

3 April 2012

There is something on the market that could well be the savior of everyone who suffers from ulcerative colitis. It's called bog in a bag, and it is exactly as described, a bog in a bag.

So you never have to fear being caught short again, for a mere £15 you can keep a travel toilet in your car, or wherever else you may need it. And when you aren't bursting for the loo it can also be used as a seat.

That may sound like an advertisement, but if you suffer from dodgy guts, that niggling concern at the back of your mind can stop you from doing such activities as camping, long rambling walks and other outdoor activities, a bog in a bag could open up a host of new persuits.

I washed my yellow and green trainers today, were looking a little shabby. I did it in the washing machine but have put them on the radiator to dry so Kana doesn't realize I've done it. She still seems to think washing shoes in the washing machine will break it, but how else are you meant to get them all shiney and fresh?

Slightly more interesting than that is Adam Drury's testimonial match has been announced. He'll play in a Norwich team against Celtic at the end of May.

Shouldn't really be a surprise that it's Celtic given Lambert's connections and playing history.

I'm glad for Drury, how many players stay at a club for over 10 years nowadays? But Celtic, admittedly they are a big Scottish club, but they're also only a big Scottish club. If it were me I would have preferred an English top four side, one of the Spanish giants, an Italian name or perhaps, again given Lambert's contacts and playing history, a Bundesliga team.

4 April 2012

#GrantHoltforEngland is trending on Twitter. So it should be, I don't care what you say given the scoring ability of English forwards in the League this season, Holt needs a ticket to Poland and Ukraine. The table shows the man is holding his own:

1 Robin van Persie 26 Arsenal
2 Wayne Rooney 21 Man United
3 Sergio Agüero 17 Man City
4 Demba Ba 16 Newcastle United
5 Clint Dempsey 15 Fulham
6 Yakubu Aiyegbeni 14 Blackburn Rovers
7 Emmanuel Adebayor 13 Tottenham Hotspur
7 Grant Holt 13 Norwich City
7 Edin Dzeko 13 Man City
7 Mario Balotelli 13 Man City

5 April 2012

Much as we did before the start of this season, the boys down the road have released a video to advertise their 2012–13 kit. Yes, Ipswich are well and truly in our shadow and lifting their big ideas from the team in yellow and green.

The difference is that rather than sprinkle a little Italian style on the video, Ipswich have decided to stick to the biggest Suffolk cliches possible.

Players practicing their football skills on a farm, with a tractor among other things in the background.

But, whereas the Norwich video attracted over 240,000 views and national coverage in newspapers including *The Daily Telegraph*, Ipswich's attempt has managed just 70,000 hits.

It's childish I know, but tee hee, forever a smaller club than us.

6 April 2012

EDP journalist Michael Bailey's prediction for tomorrow's game: Norwich City 2 Everton 2. I wonder how close he'll be come the final whistle, personally I've given up predicting scores, mainly because I'm always wrong.

Should we grab three, Norwich could hit the 250 goal marker in the Premier League.

7 April 2012, Norwich 2–2 Everton

So that's another referee that won't be welcomed in Norfolk again. Andre Marriner you complete arse.

How could you not see that Steven Pienaar had obstructed the ball, and then to add insult to injury stand in the way of Wes Hoolahan as he attempted to track back to stop the danger from Marouane Fellaini. Marriner should have blown his whistle for at least a drop ball, instead Pienaar got up got hold of the ball from Fellaini and passed to Nikica Jelavic to score. 1–2 to Everton but a sense of injustice pervaded the entire ground. Stupid bloody match officials.

Thankfully Norwich didn't give up, and with Grant Holt back in the team we scored an equaliser. We fuckin' love Grant Holt.

When Tim Howard couldn't hold on to Aaron Wilbraham's shot it flew back into the striker's path who, cool as a cucumber, squared to Holt to score.

So after laughing at us for letting Jelavic score, Everton's fans were now serenaded with a short ditty to the tune of *You'll Never Walk Alone*:

'Sign on, sign on,
With a pen in your hand,
Because you'll never work again'

I had to go to the Irish media to get some sort of sense of the game, something called the *Enniscorthy Guardian*:

'Norwich manager Paul Lambert likened Jonny Howson to Barcelona maestro Andres Iniesta after watching the Canaries midfielder inspire his new team to a vital 2-2 draw with Everton at Carrow Road.

Howson signed for Norwich from npower Championship side Leeds in January and has had little trouble stepping up a division, easily slotting in to Lambert's starting XI. The 23-year-old opened his Canaries scoring account by slotting home a Wes Hoolahan cross.

Lambert, whose side reached the safety yardstick of 40 points with the point, said: "It was one of the best midfield performances I've ever seen. I couldn't pass it like him. At times he passed it like Iniesta. He's an all-rounder and I'm delighted with his contribution."

The game looked destined to be a drab affair in the opening quarter before it sprung to life when Nikica Jelavic poked Everton ahead with a majestic flick from close range. Both teams then embarked on some attacking play in an end-to-end encounter, with Jelavic cleverly turning home a second following Howson's equaliser.

Grant Holt continued to press his claims for an England call-up by converting Aaron Wilbraham's cross late on and Norwich were unlucky not to grab a winner in the dying minutes after throwing everything at the seventh-placed Toffees.

Lambert said: "It was a brilliant game, as good as I've seen in my time here. Considering the calibre of the team we were playing against, it was a brilliant display. It was relentless at times. We played with enthusiasm and hunger. We had a lot of the ball and we showed we have an end product to our game."

Jelavic's presence up front caused Norwich havoc throughout the game and his double will do much to boost confidence in the Merseysiders' ranks ahead of Saturday's FA Cup semi-final against Liverpool.

"Jelavic scored two really good goals," Everton boss David Moyes said.

"He's come in and made a big difference to us. We've been needing that type of centre-forward - somebody who can score, lead the line and threaten the opposition and he's certainly been doing that. He's a steely character with real presence and he sees scoring as part of his job.

"He also helps to link us up. He's given all the players a massive boost. That's what happens when you bring in a player who scores regularly. We couldn't score in the first half of the season but he makes us look as if we are going to do that more often."'

I may be biased but we could have quite easily won the game, but a draw was a reasonable result, especially as Ben thought we were going to lose (pessimist), but bugger me it was nerve-racking.

End-to-end games are good if you support neither team, not if you have a personal interest in the teams on the field. But who cares, the game might have had some truly atrocious refereeing decisions and one too many close calls for my liking, but a draw puts us on 40 points, the general point where teams are deemed safe for another season in the top flight.

Two hundred and forty-nine goals for Norwich in the Premier League, and Bailey predicted the score correctly.

8 April 2012

Who'd have thunk it, Amanda Holden, that woman who is a 'TV personality', TV talent show judge and former wife of comedian Les Dennis was at the football yesterday with her six-year-old daughter. I had no idea but she is an Everton fan. More than that, she spends quite a bit of time in Nelson's county as she has a pad in Burnham Market.

She tweeted: 'Great day at the footie! Fair score! Lexi's first match! Out having a pint!'

She has gone up in my estimations. If only I'd been invited to sit in the Director's Box by Lotus, I could have not gone up to her and got a snap like I've now done with Delia twice.

In other news Mark Lawrenson is embarrassing himself again, after I thought he'd redeemed himself.

When asked on *Match of the Day* if Grant Holt should get a call up to the England team he simply answered 'No'. What a, for the want of a better word, dick.

Seems Holt's fellow teammates agree.

Both Anthony Pilkington and Simeon Jackson tweeted their thoughts last night:

@Pilkington_11: *Wow #MOTD embarrassing how can Mark Lawrenson wag his chins and say NO just like that! 2nd highest English scorer #crazy! Who else is there?*
@JacksonSimeon: *MOTD is ruthless... If the 2nd highest goal scorer in the country can't get a call up wat chance you got*

9 April 2012, Tottenham Hotspur 1–2 Norwich

We.Are.Massive. We have scored against every team in the Premier League and now sit on 43 points – the same as Liverpool – and are in the top half of the table.

The BBC's star commentator, John Motson, loves us: 'If anyone likes unpredictable football then White Hart Lane was the place to be. Norwich have pulled off a shock result, which is a massive blow to Tottenham's Champions League hopes.'

And the players are buzzing. I know this because of the wonder that is Twitter, once again it is alive with the sound of elated Norwich players and fans. Makes you proud.

I had absolutely no expectations as it's Spurs, a team heading for the Champions League, but as Lambert said after the match, we were immense.

'It was the best performance in the three years I've been here, that is the magnitude of it. I thought we were brilliant, right from the off,' said the big man.

And because of how well we played, for once the Norwich faithful won't be worrying about the match report from the BBC – usually a point of contention for most fans after a big game – because its reporter, Mandeep Sanghera made a good fist of it.

'Tottenham's stuttering Premier League form continued as their challenge for a top-four spot suffered a damaging setback with defeat at home to Norwich.

Anthony Pilkington sidefooted the Canaries ahead before Grant Holt was denied a penalty for Norwich.

Jermain Defoe dinked in an equaliser and Gareth Bale hit the crossbar for the hosts before Elliott Bennett arrowed in Norwich's winner.

The loss leaves Spurs fourth, above Newcastle only on goal difference.

Newcastle beat Bolton to increase the pressure on the Londoners, while Chelsea are also hot on the heels of faltering Tottenham, who have one win from their last eight games.

After spending so much of the season looking upwards, the swashbuckling style and swagger of early season Spurs was replaced by uncertainty and frustration against a Norwich side who had the quality and verve to take advantage.

The Canaries went ahead when the home defence failed to clear their lines and Pilkington was on hand to slide in his eighth goal of the campaign.

Holt was furious referee Michael Oliver refused to then award him a penalty after Ledley King appeared to pull his shirt and his anger was compounded when Spurs immediately levelled.

Jake Livermore's piercing pass found Defoe and he coolly dinked the ball over the on-rushing John Ruddy.

It was only the outstretched hand of Ruddy which then stopped Spurs taking the lead.

Tottenham left-back Benoit Assou-Ekotto broke free after a clever one-two with Emmanuel Adebayor, only to see his shot brilliantly saved by the Norwich keeper.

Tottenham's desire for a win against a Norwich side playing with energy and exuberance made for an enthralling, end-to-end game.

Norwich's top-flight security has been all but assured and, in Holt and Ruddy, the Canaries had two players who enhanced their claims for an England place in front of Spurs boss Harry Redknapp, who is tipped to take over the national team.

Another penalty claim for the visitors was turned down when Adebayor thrust his shoulder into the back of Wilbraham, before Bale cut inside and shuddered a shot against the crossbar.

The buccaneering runs of Bale and promptings of Luka Modric for Spurs have diminished as the season has worn on, while substitute Rafael van der Vaart, introduced with 20 minutes left, has also started to have less of an impact for them.

A lack of assuredness in defence, with Spurs missing holding midfielder Scott Parker, also did not help the home side and Norwich took advantage to score the winner.

Bennett ran at a backtracking Spurs backline and drove in an angled shot from the edge of the box for his first goal for the club.'

I guess the only downside is that I wasn't there, but with Manchester City heading to Carrow Road on Saturday, where I will be in attendance, I'm hoping I can expect a much closer game, and a similar performance and result.

Spurs fans aren't so happy of course, intial reactions have included:

1) WTF?

2) OMG!

3) I never thought we'd win the League nor did I think 3rd was nailed on but in my worst nightmares I never imagined we'd go through a run of : L L L D D W D L and be struggling for 5th!

4) FFS!

5) No doubt certain players will already be getting excuses readys to why they need to leave i.e. to play champions League football (which they blew).

6) WTF?

7) Does this mean Bentley stays...?

8) Aaaaaarrrrrrgggggghhhhhhh!

9) Thank **** I never bragged to gooners and Chelsea mates when we were flying high.

10) Hope the players take a long look at themselves

11) And WTF again

10 April 2012

There is a programme called Talking Balls, which I can't decide whether it's just a YouTube phenomenon or on an actual real-life TV channel. But whichever it is they had John Ruddy as a special guest, and although his voice is quieter than a gnat farting, he comes across as a genuinely normal bloke.

Now I'm not sure about the show's presenters, Chris Cohen and Jim Smallman, but they did at least manage to make Ruddy say some genuinely funny things: When he saw Andre Villas-Boas the ex-Chelsea manager jumping up and down on the touchline he felt like kicking a ball at him, if Fernando Torres had been wearing red he probably would have scored against him and he likes singing boy band songs.

He's also 6ft 5in and doesn't like the single carriage way road going through Elveden, and at some point the Norwich squad did discuss the benefits of Michael Owen joining the team – apparently they said it would be useful as he has a helicopter and it'd be a free ride to the horse racing. Oh and he also managed to do 43 keepie uppies. It was a worthwhile use of 54 minutes of my life.

11 April 2012

There is a website dedicated to getting the nation thinking about Grant Holt playing for England at this year's European Championships. It's very simply called www.holtforengland.com and as I type this 7,551 people have 'liked' it on Facebook and 906 people have tweeted the website.

It has a nifty graphic with Grant Holt's football strip slowly changing from Norwich to England, but the idea of Mr Holt playing for the national team isn't to everyones taste.

Nick Howson on the givemefootball website wrote a tidy little article that I have no doubt many non-Norwich fans will agree with.

It's not worth parroting the entire thing but the nub of things was in one of the opening paragraphs:

'It's difficult to overlook Holt's 13-goal haul in England's top flight this season, however his agricultural style and lack of experience at the top level, means his season's goal record pales into insignificance.'

It doesn't get any better, in fact the closing paragraph is perhaps a little insulting:

'If England are travelling to Poland and Ukraine simply for a holiday, then maybe Holt deserves his time in the sun.'

I think this is the problem with not only our national team and those that run it but also the majority of fans.

We moan about the overpaid, egotistical overrated players that, every tournament without fail, make our lives miserable, but then as soon as someone mentions bringing in different players there's uproar.

God forbid that we don't take Peter Crouch, Emile Heskey or some other useless piece of wotsit. At least Holt's teammates think he should be given a chance.

Morison is sure he should go, he said: 'If he doesn't get called up to the Euros, it will be a travesty. Look at the scoring charts, you go by players who are playing well and scoring – and he is doing everything. If he doesn't at least get a chance it will be an absolute disgrace.'

The more I think about it the more it winds me up. I'm going to watch *Match of the Day* and calm down. Well spit at the pundits for their stupid analysis and worry about the game on Saturday – Manchester City won 4–0 this evening, I thought they were meant to be having a slump!!!

12 April 2012

I always thought that the NHS's computer system was a pile of the proverbial and that countless governments had spent many millions of pounds trying to turn it into something that was beneficial for both NHS workers and patients.

Well it turned out that although doctors may not be able to grab hold of your medical records to find out what history of illnesses you may have they can use their computers to find out the score of a football game that happened months ago.

It's something anyone with an internet connection can do, but not what I expected my GP to be looking up when I went in to complain about my loose bowels.

He swore that Arsenal beat Norwich 1–3, I knew it was 1–2.

He might be a well educated, highly knowledgable doctor, but he also has a memory like a sieve, and more to the point a far rosier recollection of the game at Carrow Road earlier in the season.

Still it makes the aforementioned GP far easier to talk with, and he has a definite advantage in his bedside manner (is it still a bedside manner when you're in the doctor's surgery?), if he can discuss football and ulcerative colitis.

And as an Arsenal season ticket holder I have a certain amount of respect for his dedication to the cause. Who knows may be I'll bump into him at the game.

Arsenal tickets have gone to a ballot for those in category three – season ticket holders without 10 away ticket stubs. Keeping my fingers, toes and eyes crossed that I'm successful.

13 April 2012

Sleep is the order of the day, tomorrow is the long drive to Norfolk for what could be one hell of a game. Manchester City may have turned us over when we played at the Etihad stadium, but this time we're at Carrow Road. What could possibly go wrong?

It seems Reading will be joining us in the Premier League next season as they beat Southampton 3–1 tonight. Both are vying to be champions of the second tier and Reading are now in the driving seat.

14 April 2012, Norwich 1–6 Manchester City

Well that wasn't the result that I wanted, nor was it the result that I was expecting but it was the result I had feared. Yesterday's gusto was perhaps a little premature and definitely a little optimistic.

The score is a bit harsh but it doesn't tell the whole story, the fact that for 70 minutes the score was so much closer and we, for all the tens of millions of pounds that the Citizens have spent, gave them a bloody good game.

If Pilkington had put his chance away in the forth minute who knows how the game would have turned out. Unfortunately, after making both Zabaleta and Nasri look stupid with some deft turns and touches his curling shot from 10 yards shaved the wrong side of the post.

If it had gone in, Manchester heads could well have dropped, but it didn't and the attacking threat of Tevez, Aguero and Silva was too much for our defence.

I don't know how it went in, but 14 minutes after Pilkington's effort Tevez dispatched a shot that sailed passed Ruddy. It came from nothing, it didn't look dangerous but somehow it went in.

The second goal was pure class. Aguero supplied Tevez in the inside-left channel and then picked up his fellow countryman's backheel to fire past Ruddy. Aguero is a class act.

Lambert tried to mix it up for the second half by bringing on Hoolahan and Surman. It nearly worked; Drury crossed, Hart weakly punched it away and Surman controlled it on his chest before firing the ball into the back of the net.

But then four goals in the last 17 minutes of the match put an unarguable shine on the Citizen's performance. Though they were gifted one goal from a horrific backpass from new defender Bennett and another just seemed to loop up and over Ruddy – from where I was sitting I could have sworn he should have caught it.

Better by far - Put to the sword by Manchester City

So that was that. The blue team from Manchester scored six. Disappointed with their fans, they wanted to take a picture of them doing the poznan, but their supposedly famous goal celebration never really got going.

More disappointed were some of our own fans though. How you can complain about the performance I don't know. The constant cries of *'shoot, shoot'* and *'turn and run, turn and run'* were annoying, but some of the swearing at the players was just uncalled for.

Perhaps people should remember that Man City have turned over quite a few teams this season: Smashed Swansea 4–0 and Tottenham 5–1 in August, beat Blackburn and Aston Villa 4–0 and 4–1 respectively in October and also beat Man United 6–1 the same month at Old Trafford. Liverpool lost 3–0 to them at Anfield in January, and a month later beat Porto 6–1 on aggregate in the Europa League. Oh and let's not forget that three days ago they beat West Brom 4–0. From that we can deduce that they are a reasonable team. I'm going to go and watch Match of the Day, we're first on the schedule.

15 April 2012

So if we constructed a League based on cleansheets Norwich would be bottom. This is the result of one *Pink'un* discussion board member's work on the Football365 website. I don't know why that's important.

	Team		
1	Manchester United	18	52.9%
2	Manchester City	14	41.1%
3	Newcastle United	13	39.3%
4	Swansea City	13	38.2%
5	Arsenal	12	36.3%
6	Tottenham Hotspur	12	36.3%
7	Liverpool	11	33.3%
8	Sunderland	11	32.3%
9	Everton	10	30.3%
10	Fulham	10	30.3%
11	Chelsea	9	27.2%
12	Stoke City	9	27.2%
13	West Bromwich Albion	8	23.5%
14	Aston Villa	7	21.2%
15	Wigan Athletic	6	18.1%
16	Queen's Park Rangers	5	14.7%
17	Bolton Wanderers	3	9.3%
18	Wolverhampton Wndrs	3	8.8%
19	Blackburn Rovers	2	5.8%
20	Norwich City	2	5.8%

I'm also confused by the table that plots every teams position in the Premier League based on the final result after keeping a clean sheet.

	Team	Pld	W	D	L	F	A	GD	GFA	GAA	PpG	Pts
1	Manchester United (1)	18	18	0	0	47	0	47	2.61	0.00	3.00	54
2	Everton (7)	10	10	0	0	17	0	17	1.70	0.00	3.00	30
3	Blackburn Rovers (19)	2	2	0	0	4	0	4	2.00	0.00	3.00	6
4	Manchester City (2)	14	13	1	0	34	0	34	2.42	0.00	2.85	40
5	Arsenal (3)	12	10	2	0	21	0	21	1.75	0.00	2.66	32
6	Queens Park Rangers (16)	5	4	1	0	8	0	8	1.60	0.00	2.60	13
7	Newcastle United (5)	13	10	3	0	17	0	17	1.30	0.00	2.53	33
8	Tottenham Hotspur (4)	12	9	3	0	22	0	22	1.83	0.00	2.50	30
9	West Bromwich Albion (13)	8	6	2	0	12	0	12	1.50	0.00	2.50	20
10	Fulham (10)	10	7	3	0	20	0	20	2.00	0.00	2.40	24
11	Chelsea (6)	9	6	3	0	12	0	12	1.33	0.00	2.33	21
12	Stoke City (14)	9	6	3	0	8	0	8	0.88	0.00	2.33	21
13	Bolton Wanderers (18)	3	2	1	0	9	0	9	3.00	0.00	2.33	7
14	Liverpool (8)	11	7	4	0	15	0	15	1.36	0.00	2.27	25
15	Sunderland (9)	11	7	4	0	14	0	14	1.27	0.00	2.27	25
16	Swansea City (12)	13	8	5	0	18	0	18	1.38	0.00	2.23	29
17	Wigan Athletic (17)	6	3	3	0	5	0	5	0.83	0.00	2.00	12
18	Norwich City (11)	2	1	1	0	2	0	2	1.00	0.00	2.00	4
19	Wolverhampton Wndrs (20)	3	1	2	0	2	0	2	0.66	0.00	1.66	5
20	Aston Villa (15)	7	2	5	0	3	0	3	0.42	0.00	1.57	11

As someone points out, thinking about all the ifs, buts and maybes is a waste of time; the only table that matters is the official League table, and at present we're 11th.

16 April 2012

Buggering hell, Wigan beat Arsenal at the Emirates stadium 1–2, there's hope for Norwich yet.

The grainy images on the internet stream I watched made everything a little hazy, but sitting in a hotel room, work has brought me to Vienna to drive the Mazda CX-5 (nice little motor, good engines, roomy and fairly cool looking), but it's nice to get away from the other journalists and watch a bit of football in the peace and quiet of your room.

17 April 2012

Norwich's new kit is being announced tomorrow, and it'll also include a viral video that I'm sure will receive countless hits on YouTube. I wonder how they'll beat the Italian video from last summer?

Now I just need to sign up to something called Global Canaries to receive the email newsletter, which will include exclusive pictures of the kit.

And it's all thanks to being in the highest division in English football. According to the Norwich website 58,000 people follow the club on Twitter, and they're from all over the world too: There are the Scandinavian Canaries, Botswana Canaries, German Canaries, Canaries Down Under, New York Canaries, Hong Kong Canaries, UAE Canaries, Bermuda Canaries, Irish Canaries, Scottish Canaries and God knows how many more (though I do know there's a growing branch in Japan).

18 April 2012

I am destined to cross sabres with Diane from the club's online shop again after the release of next season's kit. Damn and blast, why couldn't they have kept the current shirt for one more year?

Now it's back to the drawing board, deciding what number and lettering to have on the shirt, whether to go for Premier League badges on the arms and what the best size would be (having passed the age of 30 by some distance now my body disagrees that I am still a medium).

But considering my first shirt purchase via Diane couldn't be described as a complete success, and then the DVD I ordered wasn't the correct one: my hopes of getting my hands on the new shirt, with the correct numbering and lettering first time don't appear high. And at £45 plus postage and packaging, you expect everything to be right first time.

Still those concerns are ignored when there is a new video – which has now been viewed 313 times – starring Stephen Fry.

All the way from New Zealand as he films *The Hobbit* (I didn't realise he was in it, and will now have to find out which character he plays), the big Norfolk comedian and actor is doing his bit to spread the Canaries name.

It isn't the comedy advertisement that last year's video was, it's got the tag line, *Pass it on*, and wants people to take a video of themselves in the new shirt passing a ball.

Mr Fry said: 'You know how when you're travelling and you see someone in Canary colours and then you leap up to them only to discover it's a Brazilian kit? Well, in New Zealand I was amazed by how often it really was Norwich. I do hope as many fans as possible will join in with the "Pass It On" campaign and enjoy wearing their colours with pride. On the ball City and never mind the danger!'

I think the idea is to get NCFC fans passing the ball around the world, so will now have to do my part for the club.

There was a nice quip from New Zealand as Fry stood in front of a pond talking up the new kit and encouraging people to take part in the *Pass it on* thingy-me-wotsit. As well as saying that there are more Norwich fans around the world than you realise – the ducks in the pond behind him were Ipswich fans. But not to worry, he was going to eat them for dinner, and he finished with a cheeky smile. I love that man.

18 April 2012

We really do have teeth. Can not even a new kit release be done without some sort of trauma? A 17-year-old called Chris Brown has been arrested by the police for leaking an image of Grant Holt on the internet 24 hours before the official event by the club.

It seems that hasn't gone down well with the powers that be, and if reports and pointy fingers are to be believed, more specifically David McNally, aka McNasty. And while there will be discussions aplenty about whether it's a step too far to arrest a teenager over a picture of the kit, it has given the fans something to think about. The ideas for songs are now plentiful:

Chrissy Brown is one of us, one of us, one of us.
Chrissy Brown is one of us, he loves Twitter.

He stole some pictures of our kit. Chris Brown, Chris Brown.
He thought he'd got away with it. Chris Brown, Chris Brown.
When the club found out of what he'd done. They rang him up and told his mum.
Super Chris Brown. Remanded in custody.

(Tune of *Rock the Casbah*/Clash)
McNasty didn't like it..
Chris Hacked his website!
Hacked his website!

(Tune of *Happy and You Know It*)
If you saw the shirt too early clap your hands (clap clap)
If you saw the shirt too early clap your hands (clap clap)

If you saw the shirt too early, if you saw the shirt too early,
If you saw the shirt too early clap your hands (clap clap)

(Tune of *Go West*)
Chris Brown's, got the in-ter-net,
Chris Brown's, got the in-ter-net,
Chris Brown's, got the in-ter-net,
Chris Brown's – Got the in-ter-net!!

(Tune of *Baby Give it Up*)
Nah nah nah nah nah naaah, They couldn't hide it up!
Hide it up!
Couldn't hide it uuup!

Finally:
Kick it off, throw it in,
have a little scrimmage,
Keep it low, splendid rush,
*Oh we've just been hacked…*Slow the hacked down like tubes does (Soccer AM)**

Few seconds silence, maybe some 'Shhhhh's' and 'Arrrgghhs' to build the tension

Then back to:

ON THE BALL CITY!!

(To the tune of *Knees Up Mother Brown*.)
Chris Brown is not going down
Chris Brown is not going down
Thankyou David Mcnally
Chris Brown is not going down

(Sung to the tune of *Only Fools & Horses*)
No internet
security
No website hack
its bloody free
Our brand new kit
for all to see
but all our shirts have VAT
God bless Chrissy Brown, Viva Chrissy Brown

I think the last one is the best, would be funny to hear that sung by the Barclay.

19 April 2012

Chris Brown is a lucky boy, McNasty and the club have decided to back down over the palaver of the new kit. The club statement was a bit lengthy though:

'THE CLUB can confirm we have met with one of our fans to discuss the posting of images of our kit on to twitter prior to yesterday's scheduled 2pm official launch.

Following our meeting with Chris Brown, we are satisfied his decision to download the images was prompted by his enthusiasm and passion for the Club and not by any malicious intent.

We're pleased to confirm no further action will be taken by the Club or Police over the matter.

The Club also recognises and has listened to the very strong feedback from supporters criticising our initial handling of the matter and this is something we have acknowledged to Mr Brown and his family, and apologised for.

Mr Brown said he was sorry for any inconvenience to the Club caused by posting the images, which he obtained from a website hosted and maintained by an independent marketing company and not by Norwich City FC.

He commented: "I'm sorry if me posting the images earlier than the launch caused problems for the Club, that was not my intention - I was just excited about seeing the new kit. But I do understand this sort of thing is important for the Club.

"I'm glad we've had a meeting to sort things out with the Club and now I just want to move on and look forward to Saturday's game against Blackburn."

The pictures appeared on twitter shortly before 1am on Wednesday morning and fans alerted the Club to their presence. Mr Brown had also suggested he may later be posting the Club's full kit promotion video in advance of the scheduled launch later that day, which clearly had commercial implications for the Club.

The images and video were being hosted on an independent website which was not live at that time and was password protected. However, Mr Brown confirmed he was able to access the source code where links to the kit imagery were revealed and post the images on twitter.

He also posted instructions as to how to access the material on a popular online fans' forum, which was another concern for the Club.

Matt Emmerson of independent marketing company Emmerson Marketing, which was employed by the Club to provide a website to promote the kit launch and host the kit imagery, said: "We are all extremely disappointed and I feel especially so for letting down our client Norwich City.

"We knew security was very important to Norwich and although we believe we took appropriate security measures to secure the site we were devastated to learn that there was a way for images to be obtained earlier than the planned launch."'

I know most Norwich fans had become sick and tired of being labelled a family friendly club with no bite, but there is a time and place to bear your teeth and I don't think this was the time. Good on the club for apologising. Now footballing matters...

20 April 2012

I re-read a blog from the beginning of the season that said that Norwich were learning the harsh lessons of the Premier League, and now we have all but achieved mathematical survival the first comment on the piece is quite interesting:

> *'It's difficult to not compare Norwich with Blackpool from last season, they're very similar. I think they've came up too early, I think relegation will be the best thing for them. The £30M parachute payment will allow them the build upon their squad for another challenge. I think there won't be an exodus as, to be honest, they don't have any 'real' Premier League quality. And I think this season will give Lambert (who's excellent) good PL experience. I expect Norwich, Blackburn, and Swansea to go down.'*

It seems the poster, Stevesmith99, doesn't work in football in a professional capacity for a reason, he doesn't know his arse from his elbow.

Tomorrow, all things being equal, mathematical safety will be achieved and we can start looking forward to next season.

21 April 2012, Blackburn 2–0 Norwich

Bugger. Will have to wait until Liverpool on Saturday for mathematical safety and to start looking forward to next season.

But for one day during the season I don't really care, I didn't even think about the game as it was the boy's birthday and your young son having a good second birthday is more important than a football game.

If it wasn't for the fact that the snooker was on in the background, which just happened to finish and be swiftly followed by *Football Focus*, it wouldn't have crossed my mind.

You win some you lose some, and today we lost. Paddy Davitt over at the *Eastern Daily Press* summed it up well: 'Difficult as it is to digest, Blackburn wanted this Premier League win more than Norwich City.'

Not what most fans want to read, but as he goes on to say it isn't necessarily because our team was unprofessional and didn't try, though I'm sure some people would say that was the case. Rather it was the destinations of the two clubs and how far apart they are.

'Rovers' motivation was clear before kick-off; anything less than a win and a puncher's chance was their only remaining salvation. Norwich's, on the face of it, appeared less obvious. A point would have given them the mathematical comfort of safety the vast majority of their performances have warranted.'

And while we lost and there was some concerns about the defence, or lack of it, there were some positives, which I will have to take for granted as I'm only reading what Davitt wrote: 'Vaughan alongside Holt may well have been what Lambert had in mind when he first recruited the ex-Everton striker. A fusion of aerial strength and pace, muscle and guile. A union of predatory intent. The initial signs were encouraging.'

22 April 2012

Holt for England, *The Sun* are even talking about it now, and Stan Collymore. Britain's biggest tabloid said:

> **'GRANT HOLT is ready to impress the next England boss – and seize his chance if he gets picked this summer.'**

'The Norwich striker has banged in 15 goals this season and Wayne Rooney is the only Englishman with more in the Premier League.

Rooney is banned for the first two Euro 2012 matches and Holt, 31, has emerged as an option.

He said: "I've got to do it for Paul Lambert first and if the new boss wants to pick me I will take the opportunity on."

Holt has played in all four divisions and is confident about making the next step up.

He added: "If you put the ball in the area I will do my best to finish. I've got good players around me and I always said I would score goals at any level."

While Stan Collymore has penned the team he thinks should start against France in England's first game of the European Championships: Joe Hart in goal, Kyle Walker, John Terry, Gary Cahill and Ashley Cole in defence. Steven Gerrard, Scott Parker, Theo Walcott, Oxlaide-Chamberlain and Ashley young in midfield and none other than Grant Holt up front. I've always said I liked Collymore.

Like the big man says: "We need to start asking England players how much they want to play for the nation...Since when has Welbeck and Sturridge proven they can lead the England line better than having Grant Holt in the squad? Teams, not names."'

23 April 2012

It's time to act like a kid in a sweet shop, a dog with two tails and every other saying that indicates one is quite happy with their general outlook on life. I got an Arsenal

Luck of the dip – Emirates here I come.

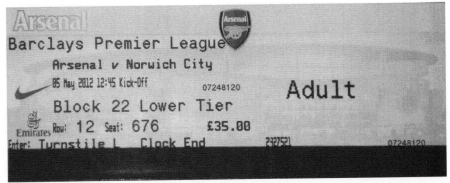

ticket in the ballot. Block 22, lower tier of the Emirates stadium on the 5 May is where I'll be. Haha, in your face Jonny (he is deservedly jealous after a season of freebies including two trips to Carrow Road courtesy of Lotus and a trip to Newcastle through his company!).

25 April 2012

There is a song, a song for Grant Holt, a song supporting Grant Holt and his inclusion in the England squad for the European Championships. And for once it isn't by a Norwich fan, it is by someone called JD, who lives in London.

I don't know anything about him, but both the man himself, Grant Holt and Stephen Fry have both heard the song and thought enough of it to tweet about it.

From JD's website, www.jdsfootballsongs.tumblr.com I have found out:

1. He has long, girly eyelashes.
2. He runs the Crystal Palace fanzine *Five Year Plan.*
3. He hosts the fortnightly *Five Year Plan* podcast.
4. He is afraid of dolls.
5. He has written about football for Goal.com, *The Guardian* and others.
6. He once drank a cup of tea with 21 sugars in it for a bet.
7. You can follow him on Twitter @jamesrmdaly
8. He writes about Crystal Palace FC for the *Croydon Advertiser.*
9. He writes jokes and performs stand up

So far it's been viewed 11,655 times on YouTube.

26 April 2012

Why are we called the Canaries? It's a fair enough question, but not one that seems many people can answer.

Now if you're a traditionalist you'll go with the historic link between East Anglia and Flemish weavers. The Flemish themselves imported canaries from the Dutch colonies in the Caribbean and then passed them over to us. Rearing canaries was a hobby.

Not what I'd been telling everyone. The in-laws currently think that Norwich are nicknamed the canaries because the little birds were used down the chalk mines to act as a warning system for dangerous gases. Miners knew if the bird dropped dead it was time to get out into the fresh air. Apparently that's a load of chuff.

According to www.footballbadgesguide.com: 'Norwich City's nickname, "The Canaries", has long influenced the team's colours and crest. Originally, the club was nicknamed the Citizens.'

The earliest known recorded link between the club and canaries, comes in an interview recorded in the *Eastern Daily Press* with newly appointed manager, John Bowman in April 1905. The paper quotes him saying 'Well I knew of the City's existence…I have…heard of the canaries.' This as far as we can tell is the first time that the popular pastime of the day, rearing canaries was linked with Norwich City FC. The club still played in blue and white, and would continue to do so for another two seasons, but the city of Norwich had long connections with canaries owing to its 15th and 16th century links to Flemish weavers who had imported the birds to the Low Countries from the Dutch colonies in the Caribbean. A simple canary badge was first adopted in 1922.

The current club badge consists of a canary resting on a football with a stylised version of the City of Norwich arms in the top left corner. A competition was held to select the badge, with the winning entry designed by local architect Andrew Anderson.'

Of course, our colours could be linked to something completely different to canaries should you chose to believe what was written by Steve Jones in his book, *The Language of the Genes* and his musings on falciparum malaria: 'The disease spread over the whole world…it was once common in East Anglia. Norwich City football team wear yellow jerseys because the local population were once called 'yellow-bellies' after the jaundice caused by chronic malaria.'

27 April 2012

The day before the big game means that Mark Lawrenson is predicting the weekend's results on the BBC website. For Norwich fans that usually means him ignoring our form and saying the opposing team will win. As we're at home to Liverpool I was expecting him to come out with some long winded garbage on why Liverpool would dominate and win by 100 goals, but the bloke's actually gone for a draw:

'*Liverpool's run will be sending their manager Kenny Dalglish crazy because he will know last week's defeat by West Brom was another example of the number of home games his side could and should have won this season. Instead, they lost 1–0.*

Again, the Reds played well against the Baggies and created loads of chances. But they just cannot score.

Their problem has been evident for a long time and it is that they need a regular goalscorer to play alongside Luis Suarez up front because nobody looks like scoring for them from midfield on a regular basis.

Norwich got a draw at Anfield in October because of Liverpool's wastefulness and, as in so many other games at Anfield this season, the Reds could quite easily have won.

Their results and their League position is not great but, if I were Dalglish, I would be pointing at those performances and saying to the club's owners "we are not far away".

The Canaries come into this game on the back of a couple of defeats, at Blackburn and before that a pasting at home to Manchester City, and you would expect a response from Paul Lambert's men, which is why I am going for a draw here.

As I have said before, it is important Norwich strengthen in the right way in the summer. It will be difficult but they have got it spectacularly right in the last couple of years. At the moment Lambert has got the right balance in the dressing room and nearly all the players he has got have a point to prove, whether it is to themselves, their manager or the club.

I think Lambert will try to continue that in the summer, and go domestic in almost all of his signings. He needs hungry players and, judging from what we have seen of him so far, that is exactly who he will go for.'

Perhaps 'Lawro' is starting to warm to the East Anglian football giants.

28 April 2012, Norwich 0–3 Liverpool

Buggering, arse-mongers. Bloody Luis Suarez and his stupid ability to score goals, make our defenders look like Sunday League players and generally cause a nuisance of himself all afternoon.

I didn't go and I'm glad I didn't, because watching the game from the comfort of my home at least I had the choice of sitting through the dross or getting up, making a cup of tea or using the little boys room. The latter two giving far greater relief and joy.

We weren't bad so to speak but we weren't good either, and with that bugger Suarez leading the attack for Liverpool, we weren't likely to get anything from the game.

His last goal, completing his hat-trick was a 45 yard shot, after dumbfounding Ward he saw Ruddy off his line and lobbed him. Had I been a neutral I would have enjoyed it; as a Norwich fan I hung my head in shame.

Why couldn't Lawrenson have done what he usually does every week and predict us to lose, that way, using reverse psychology we might have grabbed a point.

Unfortunately, the praise heaped on Suarez was justified, even though newspapers such as *The Independent* were getting very close to sycophancy:

'There are times, watching Luis Suarez play football, when the only option is admiration. For all the controversy, the unpleasantness and worse, he is capable of things that no one else in the Premier League can do. Last night, he produced a performance of bewitching imagination, craft and bravery, scoring two excellent first-half goals and one brilliant late 50-yard chip. There have not been many individual performances like it this season,' said Jack Pitt-Brooke.

Even Suarez's captain, Steven Gerrard was glowing, specifically about that annoyingly good last goal: 'I was about to give him a bollocking for not passing me the ball, but that soon turned into applause.'

Maybe things will seem better tomorrow.

29 April 2012

Things aren't better, Lambert is being linked with the job at Aston Villa as Alex McLeish continues to drag the club towards the relegation battle. Everything should be rosy given that QPR lost 6–1 to Chelsea today confirming, that we will be in the Premier League next season. But it's a rumour that just sinks the spirits and dampens the mood.

I think *The Sun* started the rumour but it has now been picked up by Goal.com, hopefully the fact that Lambert is quoted as saying that the idea of him taking over at Villa is unhelpful shows that he's not interested in the position:

'Speculation about players is something you can never do anything about. That happens. It happens with managers as well and you can't stop that. If my players get linked with other teams there is not a thing I can do about that. It is the same situation about myself. It is extremely unfair with me being linked with Aston Villa when they have got a really good manager up there who is doing everything he can to stay in the League. It is an unfair comment for me to say anything on that.'

I hope it doesn't turn into another Burnley when the not commenting turned the whole thing into a saga that just wouldn't go away.

Anyway as Villa have been dragged in to the relegation dogfight maybe they'll go down to the Championship meaning there'd be no logical reason for Lambert to want to leave Norwich.

Roy Hodgson has been approached by the FA to manage the England team. Should he get the job I'm not sure what Holt's chances are of getting into the team.

30 April 2012

'We look so out of our depth it's unreal. Elliot ward is a joke and Ryan Bennett looks a complete waste of money. Our defence is a shambles. We've got nothing going forward either, everytime a midfielder breaks forward they have to stop turnaround and pass backwards. Wrong team and tactics again. Not happy.'

Bit harsh on the boys and manager considering how well we've done this season, but according to Lincoln Canary the game against Liverpool was a disaster.

It also seems that if you disagree with his thoughts you are immediately labelled a 'happy clappy' supporter.

'We were awful for the third game in a row and well and truly beaten. Your happy clappy attitude will see us accept second best and ultimately result in relegation whether it be this season or next. We've been fantastic for the majority this season but I'll not let that get in the way of a terrible performance. The team takes plenty of credit usually but needs to know when they've been poor, that goes for Lambert too.'

Oh well, it seems I am merely a happy clappy supporter as I'm yet to see the bad in the squad and the management.

The last three results have not only wrangled some of the home fans, but also dragged out some opposing supporters from our time in League One.

The infamous, 'you'll be deducted numerous points and fined millions of pounds' Colu_mike7 is back on the discussion boards. He's happy because we've been losing. Among his gems of whit and banter are:

'Norwich 1–6 Man City, Blackburn 2–0 Norwich, Norwich 0–3 Liverpool:

This is what Norwich in the Premiership for me is all about, you budgerigars getting stuffed week in week out. Now that the other teams have well and truly sussed your team out, it's not looking too good for next season. Oh what a shame, I hope you choke on the drool in your beaks.

I cannot wait for the infamous second season syndrome to hand you Derby County's record for the least number of points on a platter. Don't worry my feathered little foes you'll be back in League One before you know it.'

And perhaps my favourite:

'The World needs to be reminded that everything you've built over the last three years is based upon a fraud.'

It was a close call though, his parting shot was this little gem:

'The overinflated budgerigar bubble has burst and I am going to LOVE watching your demise.'

You'd think after three seasons colu_mike7 would have got over the fact that Colchester may well have beaten us in the first game of the 2009–10 League One season, but thereafter we took Lambert and his backroom staff away from them and then ran away with the title – thumping Colchester 5–0 along the way. Bitterness thy name is colu_mike7.

1 May 2012

The build up has started and it's only Tuesday. Gotta love the work of the Arsenal fan who put this match preview together, I doff my cap to SuperJackWilshere19 on the not606 discussion board. How much time must this have taken him?

'Arsenal take on Norwich City at the Emirates this Saturday and the Gunners are within touching distance of clinching that third spot. It's in their hands and that is the position you want to be in come the end of the season. But, Arsenal have not won any of their last three League games and that is a worry. After the Wigan defeat, the Gunners have earned back to back draws against Chelsea and Stoke City. In both games, Arsenal had the chance to get all three points but a lack of cutting edge has thwarted them. Against Stoke, they went a goal behind after Peter Crouch put the Potters into the lead with a trademark header. Arsenal equalized through their main man, Robin Van Persie who got on the end of a Thomas Rosicky cross. Considering Arsenal's poor record at the Britannia Stadium and Stoke's ability to stop the big teams at home, it was decent point for the Gunners. But with Tottenham Hotspur and Chelsea winning on the following day, it did mean that their gap on the chasing pack was reduced. Norwich City have lost their last three League games but with nothing to play for it is somewhat understandable. Norwich's last League game was against Liverpool at Carrow Road, and they were on the wrong end of a Luis Suarez

master class. The Canaries lost 3–0 and they were never in the game from start to finish. The amazing thing is the fact that Norwich have nothing left to play for is because they have already made sure that they will remain in the Premier League for another season. Many tipped Norwich City for relegation so it's been an amazing achievement by Paul Lambert's men. Norwich have stayed well clear of the relegation scrap all season and it's mainly down to their amazing team ethic. Norwich really are a team in the true sense and despite their recent slips, they are not an easy team to beat because they never stop trying. Norwich pushed Arsenal close in the first meeting between the two sides in the League this season. Norwich took the lead through Steve Morrison, but Robin Van Persie got Arsenal back in it after converting a pinpoint cross from Theo Walcott. In the second half, Arsenal and Van Persie got their second goal with a lovely chip into the near post. It was very tight game and Arsenal should expect yet another tight game if Norwich turn up with the same intensity and drive.

Norwich City under Paul Lambert has been one of the most remarkable stories in English football. Before he took over the managerial reigns at Norwich, he was in charge of a Colchester side that trashed Norwich by six goals at Carrow Road in the 2009/10 season. That was Lambert's last game as manager of Colchester as he decided to join Norwich. Back then, Norwich languished in League One and despite being one of the bigger sides in that League there was no guarantee that they would bounce back into the Championship. But under the leadership of Lambert, they did work their way up and they went on to claim back to back promotions which was a truly astounding feat. Norwich have players in their squad that have played in League one and those players have helped them with this amazing rise. One of those players is Grant Holt, he in fact made his debut for Norwich in that disastrous game against Colchester. His rise has been as spectacular as that of Norwich. In his first season for Norwich in League One, Holt scored an impressive 24 goals, he then scored another 21 goals in the championship which helped Norwich into the Premier League. Grant Holt is Norwich's top scorer in the League with 13 goals. His goals have been absolutely vital for Norwich this season. From the players of the bottom ten sides, he has the most goals. Teams like Bolton, Wigan, Aston Villa and QPR have lacked such an efficient marksmen in front of goal. Steve Morison has also contributed with goals and he has eight to his name, so the Norwich forward line has an impressive 21 goals between them, and when you analyse the teams in the bottom half and where some of them go wrong, it explains why Norwich have done so well compared to those teams. Norwich Ctiy have scored 47 goals in the League and out of the bottom ten sides, only Blackburn amazingly can match that goal return.

Norwich have won five away games this season, and the most famous one was in North London against Tottenham Hotspur. A result that stunned many and it was probably Norwich's most impressive win of the season. Although they did also record another impressive win against one of the top six sides but that was at home. That win was their 4–2 victory over Newcastle United, Norwich have managed to get a possible seven points out of 33 against the top six sides this season. A win against Arsenal at the Emirates will be yet another highlight in a season of many for Norwich City. The game against Norwich City will be Arsenal's last home game of the season and the Gunners have had some undoubted highs at home this season but they have been a few lows. The defeat against Wigan was very unexpected and Arsenal could *yet look back at the result with dismay should Arsenal finish outside the top four. Arsenal currently have a four point lead over Tottenham Hotspur who sit in fourth place. But the three teams below Arsenal do have games in hand. Arsenal fans will no doubt be keeping an eye over some of the midweek games in the Premier League this week. The good thing for Arsenal is the fact that they have their own destiny in their hands. If Arsenal win their last two games, then they do not have to worry about anyone else because third will be secured. With Chelsea reaching the Champions League Final, third has become even more important and it's crucial that Arsenal end the season well. To do that, Arsenal will have to end a three game run without a win. Norwich at home might seem like a great chance to get a win but if Arsenal fail to match Norwich's work ethic, then like Spurs they could be in for a long afternoon.*

Robin Van Persie finally scored from open play and that was his first in eight games. Van Persie has started to look more and more tired as the season come to an end, and that is expected, Van Persie has had to lead from the front, on and off the pitch. Also, this is his first real season without an injury so it's been a new experience for him. The great pity has been the fact that Arsenal do not have other forwards who are good enough to share the work load upfront this season. But Wenger has already signed a player for next season who might lessen the burden on Van Persie. That player is German international Lukas Podolski who was signed from FC Koln just this week. The news was greeted well by Arsenal fans and they hope that it's a sign of things to come in the transfer window. So Arsenal have had some good news off the pitch this week, and a win against Norwich will great news on the pitch because it will take Arsenal one step closer to finishing in third. Norwich will not make it easy and the Arsenal players will have to match the drive and energy of the Norwich players if they are to impose their style of football on the game. It should be a great game and as it's Arsenal's last home game of the season, so the team will hope to end it on a winning note.'

Not too sure about some of the replies to this mammoth piece of pre-game writing though, far too much cockiness floating around the place. I know Arsenal play some magnificent stuff but are comments like, 'should win. Norwich have nothing to play for and have been dreadful recently,' and 'To be honest the form Norwich are in, if we can't beat them at home, then we don't really deserve 3rd,' really necessary?

2 May 2012

Roy Hodgson has been appointed England manager – something I'm happy about – but it seems that it could do Grant Holt and John Ruddy's chances of a call up more harm than good.

Hodgson for all his positive attributes – he speaks four languages, has managed both at club and international level, and is a very nice chap to boot – seems already set to pick players that he either has already worked with or the usual suspects that are forever and a day in the England team.

So come 11 June when England begin their European Championship campaign against France it could well be a team made up of the same names: Steven Gerrard, Ashley Cole, Frank Lampard et al and people like Scott Carson and Bobby Zamora from his time managing at Fulham and West Brom. So perhaps Holt and Ruddy should start booking their summer holiday because at this rate they won't be going to Poland and the Ukraine.

I guess it was only ever a long shot that any Norwich player would get into the squad, and there is still time to be proved wrong – though why Hodgson should change the habit of a lifetime, and chose different names to fill his squad, isn't immediately obvious. Past managers haven't bothered so should he?

But even with that in mind, my enthusiasm for the national team has found some renewed vigour. Hodgson managed to get Switzerland's world ranking up to third during his time there, and was even offered the job of taking charge of the German national team in 1998, though he refused because he was happy at Blackburn (they sacked him two months later). So maybe he can pull off a miracle and get the England team, with the same players, to work as a team where others have failed. I had wanted to find out more as the sports radio shows would have been a thrum of debate and discussion about his selection, but my driver – I had to catch a flight from Heathrow airport to go to Germany for an Audi technology day tomorrow, so the kind people in the press office arranged for an Audi A8 limousine to collect me and whisk me down the M25 to terminal five – kept talking to me even after I asked him to put Talksport on the radio.

Audi do a lot of limousine driving, all the red carpet events and whisking football players to and from different appearances; mainly Manchester United players as Audi sponsors them. Unfortunately, he didn't have any revealing stories to tell. Not like the staff on the charter planes we occasionally catch for vehicle launches.

Audi, which seems to have a fairly sizeable budget for its new vehicle launches, tends to use the same airport – the private terminal at Stansted – and plane company. But the plane operator also flies various football teams around the country for games, one of which is Manchester United. And apparently Wayne Rooney doesn't like sleeping in the chairs, so rather than getting some shut eye sitting down like a normal person, he beds down on the floor of the plane. Admittedly the plane in question does appear to have shag-pile carpet so it would be comfortable.

Thinking about it, I might have to send him a message on twitter and ask him if that's true or just a load of tosh.

(Talking about luxury aeroplanes makes it difficult to get anyone to believe the life of an automotive journalist is hard when you're swanking about in brand new cars, sleeping in five star hotels and flying on the same private jets that footballers use).

3 May 2012

No reply from Rooney, rude bugger. My voice must have been drowned out by the cacophony of his 4,021,953 followers.

4 May 2012

Tomorrow's the day, the day I can tick off another ground from my list. Stamford Bridge and Anfield done, the Emirates not far off. And now that we're safe for another season, next year I'll be trying again to get to Old Trafford, the Etihad and St James' Park – I'm not going to call it the Sports Direct Arena.

No idea how I'm going to get there though. Have checked the football grounds guide website, www.footballgroundguide.com, but I am just going to wing it. What could possibly go wrong?

If you believe Mark Lawrenson the result could go wrong. He's got us down for a 2–0 loss.

'This is a massive game for Arsenal in the race for third place in the Premier League and the good news for the Gunners is that Norwich look like they have hit the wall in recent weeks,' he said on the BBC website.

I think Lawrenson should give up, I've tallied up his predictions since the beginning of the year, if he'd got every score right we'd currently be on 22 points, having lost 24 games, drawn seven and won only five (which if he'd made that prediction for Wolves he wouldn't be that far off, they've lost 22 and are on 24 points at the foot of the table).

5 May 2012, Arsenal 3–3 Norwich

Best game ever!!!

What a match, we really showed that we can compete with the best teams in the country, and on our day are able to give them one hell of a fright.

The cynics might say that, as with Spurs not so long ago, Arsenal weren't at their best, but as clichéd as it is, you can only beat what's put in front you. In this case we drew but, with my yellow and green tinted spectacles, we could have won today.

How different it could have been. The omens weren't great. I forgot my glasses so had to use the pair I keep in the car, taped together as the screws on both arms have popped out. When I got to the Emirates – and for a modern ground with little

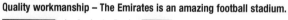

Quality workmanship – The Emirates is an amazing football stadium.

character it isn't a bad little stadium – I bought the Arsenal fanzine, *The Gooner,* instead of a match programme, inside, the old boy next to me had drunk one too many sherbets and within 30 seconds of the kick-off he was swearing at the team. And of course the biggest sign that things could go against us was the goal by Yossi Benayoun after 65 seconds. At that point I feared a slapping.

But thanks to Hoolahan and Holt in the 12th and 27th minute respectively the day got a lot better.

The goals weren't classics but they all count. Hoolahan equalised with a simple shot that Wojciech Szczesny allowed to squirm through his hands and Holt's shot hit the boot of Kieran Gibbs before looping over the 'keeper and into the net.

I hadn't spoken to the bloke next to me, but when those goals went in the old boy and I jumped around like a couple of head bangers at a heavy metal gig. After the jumping stopped we shook hands and carried on watching the game.

The final away game of the season – no matter who it was against – should have been cause for a party, and this was. People were throwing inflatable toys around long before the whistle blew to get the game started. Even after the Arsenal goal and two quick strikes everyone was in full voice.

The usual 'On the ball city' and 'We fucking love Grant Holt' was accompanied by 'Let's all do a Wenger' (2,000 Norwich fans mockingly waving their hands in the air in incandescent rage), 'We'd rather have Holt than fucking van Persie' and a bit of banter between the Norwich fans with 'We're the left side, we're the left side, we're the left side over here' followed by a similar chant by those fans on the right of the away section.

In the second half Arsenal came out all guns blazing, and the inevitable equaliser came in the 72nd minute, and then, eight minutes later the goal that gave the Gunner's the lead.

But they hadn't reckoned on Morison linking up with Howson to grab our own equaliser in the 85th minute.

Howson flicked the ball over the Arsenal defence and Morison shot into the far corner of Szczesny's goal. The old guy and I hugged again, and in our explosion of

Who dares wins – Morsion scores, silencing the Arsenal crowd.

joyous exuberance ended up punching the lady in front of us on the back of the head. Thankfully she was just as happy to see Norwich score that she didn't complain and the spurt of adrenaline everyone was feeling dulled the pain. (She did keep rubbing her head after things calmed down until we were all walking out of the ground.)

And post match even Arsene Wenger said that we played well – his usual choice of blaming the referee, the negative tactics of the opposing team were all dropped and he gave an honest appraisal of the game, though he did manage to slip in some sly negative comments:

'It is more than frustrating because we were very poor in the first half, not switched on. The quality of our first half was absolutely not at the level we wanted in a decisive game like that. In the second half we did very well. We created at least 10 chances but again not only did we not take our chances, but on top of that we gave them a third goal in a situation that was absolutely unbelievable. In the end we got punished for our mistakes,' said Wenger on Arsenal's official website.

'We have to analyse the reasons why we were not sharp enough in the first half. There is no obvious reason because we prepared normally as we always do, but maybe subconsciously [we thought] we would win it. Norwich played well, you have to give them credit. We were [too frail], of course. We lost too many challenges and it is surprising because recently we were quite good, but today I feel that defensively the whole team was very poor.'

And the newspaper match reviews were equally honest; *The Telegraph* said: 'Robin van Persie capped a remarkable week by equalling one of Thierry Henry's records with two late goals – but they were not enough give Arsenal a victory they desired but did not deserve against Norwich City.'

The Guardian on the other hand said: 'In keeping with this season of the sublime and the ridiculous, Arsenal and Norwich served up a see-sawing draw that dripped with drama. When it was finally over, Arsenal's players were crestfallen. In Norwich, they came up against the most gutsy of opponents, who delivered a performance that delighted Paul Lambert.'

And while Lambert was delighted, Piers Morgan, the chap who used to edit newspapers and is now a supposed big-shot TV personality in the UK and US, is now a pissed off Gooner.

Poor bloke was having an aneurism on Twitter: 'Pathetic defending AGAIN. Worst I've seen since the 8–2 drubbing at United.'

I did try and wind him up some more by tweeting him 'Thursday nights, Channel 5' but unfortunately, like my question to Wayne Rooney, it went unanswered.

But dear old Morgan does seem like a fair reflection of the other Arsenal fans, who I have got to say are the biggest bunch of moaners I've ever heard.

Reading some of the discussion boards and all you can see is comments such as 'I will sound like a sore loser, but **** me! Norwich are a snidey bunch of cheating twats' and 'Yes norwich are a bunch of mugs. But we knew that beforehand.'

But possibly my favourite was this: 'I don't mind them kicking lumps out of each other as that's honest thuggery (a la Stoke), but I detest snidey players like 90% of Norwich today.'

There's nothing like a good helping of bitterness to make fans sound like complete idiots. It was 3–3 and we were brilliant, get over it. Onwards to the final game of the season next weekend against Aston Villa.

6 May 2012

Grant Holt really was a tyre fitter back in the day. He tweeted his City & Guilds certificate. And it seems while he was good at the practical stuff – useful when changing tyres – he wasn't so crash hot at the written tests.

For everything from jacking the vehicle up, removing the tyres and of course fixing them he received a distinction, but when it came to the written test and his final assessment he only managed a pass. Good job he was relatively useful with a football and was determined enough to press on until he reached the top of the footballing tree.

And that determination could still see him get a seat on the plane to Poland and the Ukraine. Even journalists from such accomplished and respected newspapers as the *Daily Mail* and *Daily Express* are in agreement.

Martin Keown, former Arsenal defender turned *Daily Mail* columnist said Holt should be on the plane: 'Wayne Rooney is the only Englishman to score more Premier League goals than Grant Holt's 14 this season and the Norwich striker showed again against Arsenal why he needs to be taken seriously.

It is an unfair misconception that he is just a target man – he offers much more – and if I were Roy Hodgson, I would take a look at him in the two friendlies ahead of Euro 2012. He has really good imagination in his finishing. At Everton, he backheeled his way out of a tight situation and Lionel Messi would have been proud of his chipped finish against Wolves.'

While Matt Law over at the *Express* has had to eat some humble pie since we were promoted to the big time.

'FIRST, an admission. On bumping into Grant Holt a fortnight ago my first thought was that he was disappointingly slim. Where was the slightly overweight former tyre fitter, who looked like he finished every Norwich game with a pie and a pint?' he said.

It's that perception and the fact that Holt plays for Norwich and not one of the top six teams that could be the stumbling block to him going to the European Championships. But at least our star striker is proving people wrong and getting the likes of Law to change their views.

'If Hodgson picked his strikers on statistics alone for next month's Euros, Holt would be the second name on his list behind Wayne Rooney. Manchester United star Rooney is the only Englishman to have scored more goals than Holt, who took his Premier League tally to 14 against Arsenal,' wrote Law.

Now I know we're supposedly at opposite ends of the international spectrum, but if the Welsh national team can put Steve Morison into the squad why can't Holt be given a go.

Speaking of Morison, he sounds fairly happy to have shut some of the more negative fans up with his goal yesterday.

'It was great, we will see how many people now ring up on Canary Call and say I'm the worst player to ever wear the Norwich shirt. It's fantastic. It shuts a few people up and we move on to the last game of the season and see how we go there,' Morison told Michael Bailey at the *Pink'un*.

I wondered why he made the 'shhh-ing' gesture at the away supporters after he'd stuck the ball in the back of the net.

7 May 2012

Arsenal fans aren't happy. Norwich are a dirty team, the referee was against them and the entire universe is swinging in favour of the opposing teams they come up against. But some fans have taken the idea of Arsenal not getting the rub of the green to the next level and have suggested match fixing is the cause of the team's problems.

Tony Attwood writing on the emiratesstadium.info blog has been the centre of this drivel.

Attwood said: 'If the match was in some way 'influenced' who would be doing that influencing? Surely not Norwich, who are too small a club to be involved in such things. Indeed if we suggest that a club like Norwich would be involved in match fixing then we suggest any club could be – and that every match is open to match fixing. Norwich have no chance of a finish in the Euro places, and no chance of relegation, so it all seems too unlikely.

So who then?

Presumably clubs that wanted to ensure Arsenal were hampered in their attempt to secure third position in the League. That would suggest Tottenham, Newcastle, and Chelsea. It doesn't suggest that any of them have been attempting to fix referees all season but it does suggest that one of them might have thought it worth enhancing their chances now.

If you think that is all too unlikely then fine – but I do suggest you might consider: was it a fairly refereed match, or was it a badly refereed match – and if the latter, why?'

What???

Have Arsenal fans really got such a complex that they think the teams around them would go to the lengths of bribery and corruption to stop them gaining a place in the Champions League. Delusional.

And the comments under the main article are no better, the best of which by someone named zdzis. Whoever they are they went to a lot of trouble to describe how badly Arsenal were treated and how lucky Norwich were:

'1) Norwich penalties? The first one wasn't there, Coquelin got the ball and gave only the slightest touch to the guy. The second is more tricky. Yes, Koscielny tugged the guy's shirt, but you can clearly see the guy holding his arm somewhere near Koscielny's tummy. My bet is both held one another. A penalty there would have been a disgrace. It wouldn't even be 'soft.'

2) Benayoun red? My problem with this is the comparison commentators made to the Beckham/Simeone situation. Did anything like this ever happen in the EPL? Did any ref hand out a red card for a slight trip out of play? You couldn't even call it a kick. Still, the ref was right to whistle it out.

3) Vermaelen yellow? Very debatable. He definitely got the ball, the other guy tripped over his leg. It's not Kompany on Nani, it's Johnson on Lescott. Shouldn't have been booked, no foul.

4) Sagna stamp? I think it might have been deliberate. Didn't see a close-up replay, but it's strange to get a stamp in this kind of a situation. I'm almost sure it was deliberate. Yellow card, if so.

5) Norwich players throwing the ball away? In each case, the player should have been booked or told not to that again.

6) Holt red? He kept Koscielny on ground by clearly pushing him down (penalty?). Clear-cut situation, but it would've been a 'soft' one. He was on top of Norwich's physical game – pushes, shoves, trips, etc. His play up until that point warranted at least a yellow. Could anyone explain to me why the ref gave Holt two free kicks after supposed Koscielny fouls, one around 35th(?) minute mark, the second at 52nd minute? Both looked like Holt fouls to me.

6) Ramsey red? No, sir. Yes, the second foul was ugly and should've earned him a booking. But the first was purely accidental. I was shocked by the commentary, which suggested the two situations looked more or less the same. No, they didn't. In the first case, Ramsey caught the guy with his trailing back leg, which he couldn't control in any way. In the second, he caught the guy advancing, studs to the foot. Completely different case. Perhaps the ref knew the first yellow was too much.

7) 54th minute, Naughton holding off Benayoun. Should've been a free kick to Arsenal. He used his hands to push Benayoun away.

Howson yellow? 62nd minute, pulled Benayoun (?) back. Right after that, Howson fell after an apparent push from Song. Can't say much about that. Was the push so much? Hard to judge.

9) Hoolahan, 64th minute – clear yellow for a foul on Benayoun, would've been red.

10) Morison yellow for tugging Vermaelen when he was about to bring the ball back into play. Holt was involved there, and a couple of minutes before he also fouled Song in the Arsenal box. Again, why wasn't he booked?

11) 73rd, penalty for Arsenal? Handball by Howson, could've been booked as well. The only reason why this might not have been called was that he was raising his arm level with his face, so the ball would have supposedly hit his face otherwise. Not sure about that, but I think it would've been a whiff too soft.

12) 76th minute, Holt definitely should've seen red by now. A clear foul on Song, kicked in the Achilles (nasty stuff), then kept him away from the ball with his body. Clear yellow, so it would've been red by that point.

13) Morison yellow for putting the ball away. Another red by that point.

14) Arsenal penalty, 88th minute? It could only happen if we assumed some ref mistakes are ok. They missed Gervinho offside before RVP was pushed. But I'm mighty curious about how Taylor explained his decision after the game. However, even if it wasn't a penalty, and no offside was given, it should've been a corner. Even Naughton claimed to have gone for the ball, and it changed direction. What else do you need to rule for a corner? A prize, or what?

15) 91st minute, just before Song's failed flick at the goal: handball in the penalty area. This time, it did affect the way the ball went.

16) 92nd minute, Morison could've gotten red-carded twice in one game knocking about violently, tugging at the shirts, pushing about.

So, in sum: if a penalty for Norwich, two penalties for Arsenal. If a red card against Arsenal, two (or three) red cards against Norwich (Holt, Morison, Hoolahan). The ref's performance obviously affected the outcome, and it did it against Arsenal. Again, I wouldn't go as far as to say it's a conspiracy, that's too far-fetched. But, despite appearances, this was a one-sided performance from the ref, who obviously went against Arsenal far too often. It was worse than usual.

As for the players, I'd say the whole team played poorly in the 1st half, and I think Ramsey was one of the poorer players then. But they rallied in the 2nd, and then he started to shine, even. Hell, did you see Chamakh? He was also better than usual. I think what did us in was lack of communication at the back and stupid errors amassed. Song and Vermaelen also had a poor game IMHO. I'm waiting impatiently for RefReview coverage.'

8 May 2012

Jonny is a complete plonker, he thought the final game of the season was on Saturday and he calls himself a fan. Although so does Ben but as he's missing the final game against Aston Villa then I am starting to question his priorities too.

I am of course just trying to make myself feel better for all the games that I have missed, and while Jonny is just a bit dim, Ben's other half is doing something worthwhile for charity meaning he can't make the match. Still going to wind them up when I see them though.

9 May 2012

Success in the current world order can be defined by how many famous – minor or major – people you can get to reply to your tweets. So far I haven't fared very well, with only a small spat with Robert Llewellyn (he played Cryton, the robot in the *Red Dwarf* comedy), to my name. It's a worthy entry though as I retweeted him and tagged 'arse' on the end. He didn't like that very much.

But today my number of responses has doubled as Darren Huckerby answered one of my questions during his Twitter Q&A session. Mine was but a simple question, Holt or Crouch for England? But it was answered: 'Tough one, think @holty30 deserves a crack, but Crouchy already proven'. Not too shabby for a nobody such as myself.

Not that it matters what either of our opinions are, as it seems the fact Liverpool's misfiring striker Andy Carroll has now found some sort of form, the media pendulum has swung in his £35 million favour rather than our nearest and dearest Holt.

It's amazing to see the fickleness of fans equalled by that of the sports journalist. Carroll has done nothing since his move to Liverpool in January 2011, but just because he has a decent half of football in the FA Cup Final, and then an OK game against Chelsea in the League a few days later every football pundit under the sun seems to think he deserves to be in the England squad this summer.

Well all will be revealed as the England squad is due to be announced this time next week, so fingers crossed.

10 May 2012

Two explosive stories published in the press today. Firstly in *The Daily Telegraph* it divulges the finances of the teams that were in the Premier League last season; secondly in the local press, Steve Morison keeps chickens.

Of course, the bigger of those two has to be Morison's chickens: he had four according to the article, but lost one recently – the family is still getting over the loss. How and why do we know this? Because he was telling Micheal Bailey at the *Pink'un* how and why he is still happy to be playing for Norwich and living in Norfolk, even after all the grief he has receieved.

The striker said: 'I'm playing in the Premier League, scoring goals, of course it's easy to keep a smile on my face. I've got a lovely family at home. I've got my animals. What's not to be happy about in life? I've got my dogs, got my chickens…I did have four chickens but I had a bereavement in the family this week. I lost a chicken. I don't name them – just brown one, black one…He drowned, fell in some water. I never had them before I came up here. I'm enjoying the country life!'

It's not as big a story, but according to *The Daily Telegraph's* report on football finances, Fulham have a debt of over £190 million. How is that possible?

The club only makes £77 million a year, but over £57 million is used to pay the wages of players and other staff. That's a huge amount for a club that is smaller than Norwich. They're lucky to have a rich benefactor in West London otherwise they could be in deep doo doo.

The leagues as it finished last season makes an interesting debt related read:

1   Manchester United, -£308.3 million
2   Chelsea, -£91.7 million
3   Manchester City, -£42.9 million

4   Arsenal, -£97.8 million

5   Tottenham Hotspurs, -£56.8 million

6   Liverpool, -£65.4 million

7   Everton, -£44.9 million

8   Fulham, -£192.9 million

9   Aston Villa, -£113.7 million

10   Sunderland, -£76.8 million

11   West Bromwich Albion, -£1.9 million

12   Newcastle United, -£130.5 million

13   Stoke City, -£0.3 million

14   Bolton Wanderers, -£110.6 million

15   Blackburn Rovers, -£26.3 million

16   Wigan Athletic, -£20.5 million

17   Wolverhampton Wanderers, £25.5 million

18   Birmingham City (didn't file accounts and are currently under a transfer embargo)

19   Blackpool, £7.9 million

20   West Ham United, -£41.6 million

So only Blackpool and Wolves managed to be debt-free, makes what Norwich owe to creditors look like small change. If any of the teams with wealthy benefactors decide to walk away and call in their debts the team could be in big trouble. Not as much trouble as Jonny though.

Jonny is an imbecile, he needs a rod hot poker taken to him. At precisely 11am he calls me leaving a voicemail. In the voicemail he tells me he has lost his wallet. This isn't something that I would usually worry about, come to think of it had circumstances been any different I probably would have laughed at his misfortune, as any good friend would. But this time is different. This time his wallet not only contained all of his bank cards, money and cherished photos of his wife and child but it also contained my season ticket.

My season ticket is possibly the most valuable component of my wallet – I rarely have cash on me and my bank cards are worth next to nothing due to the lack of funds in my bank account – and is treated as such. Now Jonny has lost it and that demands repercussions.

11 May 2012

Jonny's skin is saved, he found his wallet. His little girl decided to hide it as a joke. If it wasn't for the fact that she is as cute as a button – I think that's the phrase they use in Hollywood films – and can sing *On the Ball City* I would be demanding she be punished.

She also has the fact that she made her dad look stupid in her favour. In his panic he called the club and arranged tickets for us to collect on Sunday so we could still see the game. So the short arse at least has his priorities in the right order as he called the club before calling his bank to cancel his debit and credit cards.

Even with all the trauma of lost wallets, going to the football is still easier than arranging a night out with the boys. Jonny can't make it out on Saturday, Cruso can't make it out on Saturday – I swear I suggested meeting up a long time ago giving everyone huge amounts of time to organise and make arrangements. You just can't get the staff nowadays.

Oh well it will be down to Button, Twon and I to go to the supermarket for provisions, and get the kendo sticks and lighter fluid ready for one more shindig. I hope no pornographic video watching is involved.

12 May 2012

How difficult is it to get five blokes together for a bit of a beer, a chance to talk utter rubbish and set the world to rights? It turns out quite difficult.

Jonny, Twon and I managed to get together but Cruso and Button were left by the wayside.

The older you get the more difficult it becomes: marriage, children, responsibilities, all seem to get in the way.

Which is weird, because once you do get together all of those mature things go out of the window. Jonny continued with his mum jokes, Twon continued to fart the most obnoxious gases out of his rear end, and once the computer games were fired up a smidgen of competitiveness entered the proceedings.

Twon was better at golf, Jonny was better at…nothing…and I was better at bowling. And Twon's going to be at the game tomorrow, I don't think I've ever been to a game with him. I hope it's a cracking end to the season rather than a damp squib, CanariesSoccer is doing his usual best to get things going with his pre-match build up on the Not606 message board:

Hey Sports Fans! It's The CanariesSoccer Match Center for the ballgame featuring: Villains @ Canaries

Live from The DeliaDome™.
This season finale matchup ends a great year for Canaries in their inaugural EPL series. With safety guaranteed, Coach Lambert has used his last few ballgames to experiment with formations and developing new pass-plays, so it is fair to expect a fresh line-up with new tactics.
Coach Lambert: 'I thought we were brilliant. I thought the performance at Spurs wouldn't be bettered, but it has, that was better. To come here against a team that is flying and vying for Champions League football, and play the way we did, I can't praise of thank the lads enough for what they've given me.'
Canaries will be looking to build their performance in their Three versus Three tiegame @ Gunners, which saw Canaries fight back to secure one ballgame-point and dent Gunners hopes of a UEFA Champions Series qualification slot. In that matchup the (fairly or unfairly) discredited S. Morison converted an excellent semi-no-bouncer late on, which saw Canaries earn a well deserved tiegame.

Villains currently sit P16 in the EPL Divisional Standings, a position which has angered many Franchise fans who have been calling for the rejection of Coach McLeish. Traditionally a well-performing Franchise, Villains have struggled following the takeover by US investors, and until last week looked possible candidates for relegation.

Coach McLeish: 'Listen, I have taken a lot of weight on my shoulders this season. I was happy to take pressure off the players. I am not going to again next season though. They had better get their finger out. We've had to be in a bit of a dogfight all season. Our early-season form wasn't too bad but, since the New Year, we've had problems to contend with injury-wise. To lose two of your most experienced players (Darren Bent and Richard Dunne) for such a long time will hurt any team.'

Villains will have a point to prove against Canaries, however this matchup will be fierier than usual with the added prospect of the Team-UK selections to be announced by Coach Hodgeson next week. Canaries S-A-C G. Holt and S-A-P J. Ruddy have both been touted to be included in his European Soccer Championship squad, and will be sure to go all-out to prove they have what it takes

This sure is going to be a great Soccer matchup, so fill up your Coca-Cola tankards, get your hot-dogs and grab a seat for this smash-and-grab matchup, brought to you exclusively on Not606!

Also, may I add as a side note, it has been a real privilege and honour to host the match threads for this year. I've really enjoyed it and we've had some cracking banter with opposition fans, particularly the Liverpool and Geordie lot. Hopefully you will let me carry them on next year, and with the possible reintroduction of cross-board threads, we should have another cracking season!

13 May 2012, Norwich 2–0 Aston Villa

'We're shit and we know we are' was the chant from the terraces.

Not from the Norwich fans, but from the huge contingent of Villa fans who had to watch what was possibly the worst team I have seen at Carrow Road all season.

Talk about a disjointed, couldn't be arsed, manager is getting sacked in the morning, bunch of uselessness. As for Norwich, simply sublime.

The passing was crisp, the movement was brilliant and if it wasn't for some good saves from Shay Given it could have been five or six.

As it was Holt scored his 70th goal for the club in his 130th appearance, in the 9th minute of the first half, and after some good work Simeon Jackson doubled the lead in the 22nd minute.

Given how shocking Villa were the banter between the fans was far superior to their team's ability (they even let off a purple flare which was colourful); 'There's only one Paul Lambert' sung by both, 'Staying with a big club, he's going to stay with a big club' belted out the Norwich faithful.

But my personal favourite was when the Barclay started singing: 'You should've gone down, you should've gone down, you lucky bastards, you should've gone down.'

And so they should have, as Alex McLeish said Villa were rotten, and only managed to win seven games all season.

Flare team – Aston Villa's fans showed more guile and poise than their team.

The BBC Sport website summed it up quite nicely: 'Norwich capped a superb season with an easy win over Aston Villa that heaps more pressure on manager Alex McLeish.'

The Guardian focused on how rubbish Villa were: 'Alex McLeish remained defiant after a dire Premier League campaign ended in another defeat for his Aston Villa side. First-half goals from Norwich City's leading scorer Grant Holt and Simeon Jackson led to several thousand travelling Villa fans sending a loud and clear message that they expect much better next season.'

I think my favourite line was in *The Daily Telegraph*: 'Norwich were dominant and eased to victory.'

Until next season – See you again soon Carrow Road.

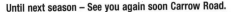

In it together – Jonny (left), Ben (right), and I (taking the picture) have witnessed the highs and the lows from the Barclay.

A dominance that Holt had a lot to do with, he's turned himself into not only a bull of a centre-forward but also a subtle link up man. And should he be picked for the Euro's in the summer he'll be a force to match any other team. And so to song:

'He'll score three goals against the French, Grant Holt, Grant Holt.

He'll score three goals against the French, Grant Holt, Grant Holt.

He'll score three goals against the French and keep Wayne Rooney on the Bench, super Grant Holt Norwich's number nine'.

14 May 2012

The morning after the night before. So that's it, the season is over, the table is set and Norwich finished 12th in the Premier League. Level on points with Swansea and West Bromwich Albion, but with a worse goal difference.

Who'd have thunk it hey? In August Norwich were favourites to go down, but in the end it was Wolves, Blackburn and Bolton who couldn't go the distance.

Holt's goal yesterday took him to 17 for the season in all competitions, but all in all Norwich have scored 52 times, conceding 66, winning 12, drawing 11 and losing 15.

I've been to Anfield, Stamford Bridge, the Emirates, Craven Cottage and Loftus Road, jumped with joy, held my head in my hands in despair but by god it's been fun.

But now things start again and the rumour mill is already spinning out of control. Alex McLeish has been sacked, and Paul Lambert has been installed as the bookies favourite to take over at the club.

I'd like to know where these rumours start, and whoever it is needs to be gagged and locked away so they can stop fans having palpitations.

But listening to *Talksport* didn't do me any good. Stan Collymore, the pundit who has been one of the most vocal of Grant Holt supporters, as an ex-Villa player has given his musings on the now vacant manager's position.

In his words the man who takes the reins needs to be capable of working on a shoe string budget, a strong man manager who can get the best from supposedly average players, and is ready, willing and able to find unpolished diamonds from the lower leagues – isn't that just a description of Lambert or am I being overly sensitive?

I am determined to find a positive though, and it comes from Norwich's chairman, someone that we don't often hear from, but who, through the power of Twitter and the club's official account has told the fans that come this time next year we'll be free from debt and ready to start investing heavily in making the team a force to be reckoned with in the Premier League. OK, I may have made that last bit up but we will be free from debt.

I am still worrying like a bonkers fan though. Please stay Lambert. I hope the new Audi A3 launch will take my mind off what could be a disaster for the club (is that overly dramatic?).

15 May 2012

I must be a soothsayer, I must have a sixth sense, I must be blessed with a gift that few others have. What did I say the other day about Stan Collymore more or less describing Paul Lambert as the man who should take over at Aston Villa. Well now he has come out and openly said it:

'My personal choice, and I have really enjoyed Norwich City this season and I am on good terms with their fans on Twitter so I don't want to offend them, but Paul Lambert is the most Martin O'Neill-like manager around for me. He has a proven track record of recruiting good players from lower leagues and getting the best out of them. He is organised and has a Plan A and a Plan B in games, whether it is getting the ball down and passing it or playing it into two front men so he would be my personal choice' said the former Villa striker, and chap who is now well and truly off my Christmas card list.

Thankfully while I'm being so depressed, some humour remains among the Norwich faithful, particularly Thurnby Canary on the Not606 message board.

'A very good contact of mine is high up at Villa Park and at 7 p.m. last night this happened...

Knock on the door, Mr.Lerner walks across the office and welcomes in Mr.Lambert

Hey good to meet you I've heard good things, come in sit down Phil and make yourself feel comfortable right and hey people round here call me Randy right, non of this Mr. Lerner crap. You don't mind if I take off my jacket do you? and yeah please take off your tracky top that's cool. That lettering right, PL is your initials, hey that's great, you English huh!

So here's the thing right. I put my ass on the line last time and I'll be upfront with you, made a big mistake OK. You see I picked a guy McLean and no-one told me but the guy is f**king scotch and jeez the guys here are Englanders for Christ's sake, bad call, it won't happen again.

Now we had a bad year here Phil last year, but this time with the right guy and I'll be frank with you here, I will give you a bunch o' money and you can go out and buy wingbackers, shooters whoever you want OK and I won't say a thing. Hey we could go on and win the prem, the Europe, hey even the World Cup right, this Aston is a great franchise and we could be bigger than Manchester, you know what I'm saying.

At this point my contact taps Mr. Lerner on the shoulder and says that PL has in fact left the room and Randy had been talking to himself for as while.

Where'd he go? what happened? jeez, whadda we do now? Hey hang on who was that wop outside?

My contact explains that this was Mr. Martinez the second candidate

Oh OK show him in, at least he'd got a f**king suit!.'

16 May 2012

Halfway between happy and sad. John Ruddy is in the England squad for the Euro's, Grant Holt isn't. There's uproar all over the internet and the Roy Hodgson out brigade have already started. Oh and the jokes have too. Well known and respected (?) TV critic at the *Mail on Sunday,* Ian Hyland jovially said: 'England squad update. Double blow for John Ruddy. 1. He'll have to postpone his wedding 2. John Terry will probably get to meet his fiancee.'

And the *Daily Mirror*'s James Nursey has chimed in too: 'Sorry for Grant Holt missing out but a brand new England boss was never going to risk ridicule by naming an ex-tyre fitter aged 30-odd!'

I don't think the Norwich faithful saw that as a little cheeky, sarcastic comment and have now called him every word under the sun, and terms that only the toughest of troopers use.

I did enjoy a Tweet from Granty Holt on Stewart Downing getting a call up (he hasn't scored all season and has no assists to his name), 'Stewart Downing. Or Pilkington. Or Sinclair. Or Jarvis. Or...John Fucking Barnes!!!! Least he can knock out a decent tournament song!!!'

The full team is made up of the same old names, plus Ruddy and Arsenal's Alex Oxlade-Chamberlain. So in full here it is:

Goalkeepers: Joe Hart (Man City), Rob Green (West Ham), John Ruddy (Norwich)
Defenders: Glen Johnson (Liverpool), Phil Jones (Man United), John Terry (Chelsea), Joleon Lescott (Man City), Gary Cahill (Chelsea), Ashley Cole (Chelsea), Leighton Baines (Everton)
Midfielders: Theo Walcott (Arsenal), Stewart Downing (Liverpool), Alex Oxlade-Chamberlain (Arsenal), Steven Gerrard (Liverpool), Gareth Barry (Man City),

Frank Lampard (Chelsea), Scott Parker (Tottenham), Ashley Young (Man United), James Milner (Man City)
Forwards: Wayne Rooney (Man United), Danny Welbeck (Man United), Andy Carroll (Liverpool), Jermain Defoe (Tottenham)
Standby players: Jack Butland (Birmingham City), Phil Jagielka (Everton), Jordan Henderson (Liverpool), Adam Johnson (Manchester City), Daniel Sturridge (Chelsea)

Well at least Holt can go on holiday now and get himself fresh for the new season – he's been injured at the beginning of the last two campaigns, so a good bit of time in the sun and he can come back firing on all cylinders in August. Anyone care to make a bet on him scoring 20 goals?

So that's it. The season is done, the England squad has been announced. A small greyish cloud still hangs over Paul Lambert as we wait to see if he'll stay or go. I reckon he'll stay.

But once that little niggle of a situation has been put to bed it'll be back to searching the rumour sites, listening to sports radio and thumbing through the press to see who we're going to buy, who's going to leave the squad and how many pundits think we're doomed and favourites to be relegated yet again.

All I know is, I now have to get back in touch with those lovely people at BDA Creative to make sure I am the star of the ESPN ads next season.